10-15-68

*Empirical Studies*

O F

*Indiana Politics*

# Empirical Studies

## OF

# Indiana Politics

---

## STUDIES OF
## LEGISLATIVE BEHAVIOR

### EDITED BY
# JAMES B. KESSLER

## INDIANA UNIVERSITY PRESS

*Bloomington and London*

Published in Canada by Fitzhenry & Whiteside Limited,
Don Mills, Ontario

Library of Congress catalog card number: 79–85089

Standard Book Number: 253–31950–1

Manufactured in the United States of America

# Contents

1528626

PART III  /  *Theory Building About Legislative Behavior*

PART IV  /  *Recruitment of Political Leadership*

TECHNICAL APPENDICES

# Tables and Figures

CHAPTER 6

CHAPTER 7

CHAPTER 8

CHAPTER 9

CHAPTER 10

### CHAPTER 11

# Foreword

A NUMBER OF POLITICAL SCIENTISTS HAVE WRITTEN EXTENSIVELY ABOUT
selected aspects of Indiana's political system. There are articles describing the legal and institutional framework of Indiana politics.
A recent publication of this type is a pamphlet commissioned by
the Indiana Sesquicentennial Commission written by Dr. Philip S.
Wilder, Jr., of California State College at Bakersfield, and
Dr. Karl O'Lessker, legislative assistant to Sen. Vance Hartke, entitled *Introduction to Indiana Government and Politics*. But studies
do not yet exist to provide a comprehensive and dynamic analysis of
political behavior in this state over time. Although this book does not
pretend to accomplish such a task, it does present a series of data-
based articles concerned with political behavior in Indiana which can
be refined and replicated over time. The book also includes two articles
suggesting methods for a fairly sophisticated analysis of legislative behavior. The substantive articles deal principally with aspects of legislative behavior, interactions and patterns of influence in the legislature,
political career building and the recruitment of political leadership.
The articles themselves do not by any means describe all aspects of a
political system; they do, however, constitute a respectable base on
which to build a scientific analysis of Indiana's state political system.
These articles show what can be done with limited resources to establish the base for empirical studies over time. The concept "over
time" is stressed for the following reason: although some of the articles
are several years old, nevertheless they are relevant to anyone interested
in current political analysis, because they serve as a standard in the
future for measuring changes in the operation of the political system.
Without the replication of such studies over time, all we really have is
a static description of the operation of the political system at a fleeting
point in time under very specialized circumstances. Such a description
does not provide an accurate picture of political behavior, since time

is one of the dimensions of any political system. For example, any study of power relations between the Governor of Indiana and the Indiana General Assembly at a given point in time tells us little about the range of possible relationships under varying conditions and the impact of numerous variables on legislative output.

The executive power in Indiana is plural—that is, it is divided among several elective officers, each of whom is elected independently of the other executive officers. These executive officers include a Governor, who serves a four-year term and cannot succeed himself; a Lieutenant Governor, whose term is concurrent with that of the Governor; and an Attorney General, an Auditor of State, a Treasurer of State, and a Superintendent of Public Instruction, whose terms are two years and who may succeed themselves. Obviously, the Governor may be a member of one party, and one or more of the other officers members of another party. The Lieutenant Governor presides over the Senate whether or not his party controls the Senate, and, among other things, is head of such important executive agencies as the Department of Commerce and Industry and the Division of Planning. If the Lieutenant Governor is not a member of the Governor's party, but is in fact the head of the opposition party which controls the Senate, the Governor's relationships with the legislature and a significant part of the executive establishment could be very different from the situation in which the Governor, the Lieutenant Governor, and a majority of the members of the Senate and House are members of the same party.

At the state level, Indiana is a two-party competitive state by any professional standard of measurement. This fact, plus the fact that several of the heavily populated counties constitute multi-member legislative districts which are two-party competitive, means that frequent substantial changes in the party composition of the two houses of the legislature are possible. Since 1960, the following situations have occurred which may alter significantly the relationships between the two branches of the legislature and between the legislature and the executive officers: In 1961, the Governor was a Democrat, the Lieutenant Governor a Republican presiding over a Senate organized by Democrats, and the House was Republican. In 1963 the variables were the same, except that the Democrats lost control of the Senate, but the Republicans did not have a constitutional majority in the Senate. In Indiana, a constitutional majority is an absolute majority of the authorized membership. Such a majority was impossible in 1963 because of the death of one Republican Senator after the general election, leaving only twenty-five instead of twenty-six seats occupied by Republicans in the fifty-member Senate. In 1965, the Democrats controlled the governorship, the other elected executive officers, the House, and the Senate. In 1967, the Republicans elected several executive officers and regained control of the House. It is a fair hypothesis that power relationships and policy output were affected by the intervention of these variables, and that a description of the political system which did not take into account variations in behavior under these varying conditions would be incomplete and would be inaccurate if it conveyed the impression, however unintentionally, that the static description was in fact unchanging over time.

The principal purposes of this book, then, are to present a series of data-based studies which can be replicated by students with limited resources over time, and used as a foundation for comparative studies involving other state political systems. The book includes two technical appendices: Appendix A explains in lay language those statistical methods used in the studies which are not explained in the studies themselves, and Appendix B consists of the questionnaire used by the authors in their study of legislative behavior in Indiana. Appendix B is included so that students who wish to replicate the studies of legislative behavior published in this collection may start from the same base as the authors of the original studies. The resulting analyses are more likely to be truly comparative. This fact does not mean that the questionnaire cannot be changed, but that when it is, it is done consciously and with some specific valid purpose in mind. It is suggested that students who are not familiar with the use of elementary statistical methods begin by reading the technical appendix and that they refer to it extensively while they are reading the articles.

The authors of the articles themselves would agree that the articles are not without fault and that there are different ways of examining the phenomena which are analyzed in this book. It is to be hoped that the students will become conscious of the research designs used to collect and analyze data and that they will subject these designs and the resulting analyses to critical examination. For those students who have yet to be introduced to empirical studies, some of these articles may seem to describe the obvious. These students will soon discover that the scientific investigation of the obvious often discloses that the "obvious" is a gross oversimplification of fact and may even be a myth.

The introductory essay by Dr. Charles McCall of Indiana University is designed to serve as a factual setting for the studies of legislative behavior which follow.

As editor, I wish to express the thanks of the authors for permission of the publishers to publish those articles included in this collection which have been published previously. The articles and their original publishers are as follows: *Legislative Politics in Indiana: A Preliminary Report to the 1961 General Assembly* (Bloomington: Indiana Univer-

sity Bureau of Government Research, 1961) ; Wayne L. Francis, "Influence and Interaction in a State Legislative Body," *American Political
Science Review,* LVI, No. 4 (December, 1962) ; Henry Teune, "Legislative Attitudes Toward Interest Groups," *Midwest Journal of Political
Science,* XI, No. 4 (November, 1967) ; and Kan Ori, "The Politicized
Nature of the County Prosecutor's Office, Fact or Fancy?—The Case
in Indiana," *Notre Dame Lawyer,* 40 (April, 1965) .

We also thank Professor James G. Coke, who, as Director of Kent
State University's Regional American Assembly on State Legislatures
in American Politics, commissioned the introductory chapter by Dr.
Charles McCall, for granting us permission to use his essay.

Special mention must be made of the detailed editing done by Mrs.
Robert McClure. We thank her for her time, her patience, and the
manner in which she executed her task. Valuable assistance in pre-
paring the manuscript for publication was also rendered by Mr. Gary
Salit, Mr. Alfred R. Nucci, and Mr. Jay S. Sanders, graduate students
at Indiana University's Department of Government. My thanks to
Mrs. Neal McNeill, who typed the manuscript, and to Mrs. James L.
Haynes, Secretary of Indiana University's Institute of Public Administration, whose patient assistance is appreciated.

The source of inspiration of all those who contributed to this book
is Dr. Charles S. Hyneman, Distinguished Service Professor of Government at Indiana University, to whom this book is dedicated. We thank
him for inspiring us and wish to express in public a sentiment we have
long held in common privately. We respect and love him for his dedi-
cation to the profession of political science, for his selfless service to his
many students, and because he is what he is.

The editor and authors accept full responsibility for any and all
errors repeated here.

JAMES B. KESSLER

*Bloomington, Indiana*

*Empirical Studies*

O F

*Indiana Politics*

# PART I

## Introduction

# 1 / The Indiana Legislature and Politics

*Charles H. McCall*

THOSE WHO EXAMINE THE INDIANA LEGISLATURE, THE MEN WHO COM-
pose it, and its product may do so out of a native concern with things
Hoosier. They may be in search of those characteristics which make it
unique. What they will first discover, however, is that it is in most respects typical of America's state legislatures. It is surely in the main-
stream of legislative structure and behavior. This typicality suggests
that an examination of Indiana's legislative system may bear fruit of a
more general nature. To study Indiana's legislature is to learn about
her neighbors.

## Formal Organization and Procedure

Like those of forty-eight other states, Indiana's legislature is divided into two chambers. Its one-hundred-member House of Representatives is of fairly average size. In all but four of the bicameral states,
the lower house is at least twice as large as the upper one. Here again
Indiana is not unusual. However a fifty-member Senate is rather large.
Thirty-eight states have smaller Senates while only seven have larger
ones.

Members of the lower house in Indiana, like those in forty-four
other states, serve two-year terms. Hoosier Senators and those in
thirty-seven other states serve four years; and, as in the majority of
states, the members of Indiana's upper house serve staggered terms.

The Indiana General Assembly meets officially every two years. The
length of the session is limited to sixty-one calendar days by the state
constitution. Some have suggested that this severe time limit on the Assembly accounts for the fact that the state has had three special sessions
since 1962. In 1963 the regular sitting ended with the state budget not
yet enacted so a forty-day special session was called by the Governor

5

immediately following the regular adjournment. The specific restriction on session length accounts for the practice of stopping the clock before midnight on the final day. Only three times since 1935 has the legislature been able to avoid this maneuver. However, here again Indiana's practice is hardly unique.[1]

In addition to the regular sessions, some legislators get together officially between sessions in most of the states in order to consider legislative matters. Indiana is among the forty-four states which now have Legislative Councils or similar institutions which undertake research about issues confronting the states and draft recommendations to the legislatures based upon such study. The sixteen members of the Indiana Legislative Advisory Commission represent both houses and both major parties as is the case in most other states. However, the appropriation for the commission and for related activities is smaller than most.

Hoosier legislators are also paid less than those of most of her sister states. In terms of compensation California ranks at the top with salaries of $16,000 per year. Indiana is one of the twenty-one states which pay their legislators less than $5,000 during a two-year period. However, Indiana's $4,820 appears generous when compared with New Hampshire's biennial compensation of $200.

The foregoing statistical report and comparison demonstrates, I hope, that in terms of formal organization, the Indiana legislature is well within the boundaries of conventional practice. The formal procedure, too, is typical of that of other states. Bills can be introduced in either chamber with the exception that revenue bills must originate in the House in conformity with the state constitution. Bills may normally be introduced only during the first half of the session in Indiana. This procedure attempts to insure that adequate time will be available for the serious consideration of the proposed piece of legislation. More than half of the states have some type of similar deadline for the introduction of legislation in at least one house.[2] Introduction constitutes first reading and is followed by referral to one of the standing committees—twenty-five in the Senate and twenty-seven in the House. After a committee returns a bill to the chamber, it is ordered printed. Twenty-four hours after printed bills are delivered in the House and forty-eight hours after they are delivered in the Senate they are eligible for floor discussion, debate, and amendment. After this second reading the bills are engrossed and advanced to third reading and the recorded vote on final passage, which must be by a constitutional majority. The bill then repeats its journey in the other house. Should the second chamber amend the bill, it will be returned to the house of origin for a vote there on whether or not to accept the change. If the amendment is rejected, a conference committee will be appointed to resolve the dispute. After the same bill has passed both houses in the same form, it is printed as an enrolled act, certified as passed by the Clerk of the originating house, examined by that house's Committee on Legislative Procedures, and signed by the Speaker of the House and the President of the Senate. It is then sent to the Governor for his signature. The procedure is a familiar one closely resembling that of every other state and congressional procedure as well.

## Influence and the Legislature

Students of government today are not likely to be exclusively concerned about formal structure and procedure in an institution. More often we are interested in discovering the sources of influence or the locus of leadership to which those in the institution respond. Generally we identify three leadership bases within the United States Congress: There are members who are influential because of their position in the party structure in Congress, those who are leaders because of their seniority, and those who are listened to because they are experts on particular subjects. These three categories are not exclusive. Senator Russell Long was Majority Whip in the party leadership hierarchy and at the same time senior enough to be chairman of the Finance Committee. Although they are even less distinct in the Indiana General Assembly, these three bases for leadership are the principal ones found there.

According to a study made over ten years ago, Indiana is one of thirteen states with a strong majority party caucus in the legislature.[3] Although the caucus is not uniformly potent,[4] it meets frequently and the leaders it chooses have considerable authority. The election of Speaker of the House and president pro tempore of the Senate at the beginning of each session merely ratifies the decisions made by the majority caucus. The caucus also selects the House floor leader and the chairman of the caucus. The Speaker is particularly powerful. He appoints the members of the standing committees in the House, recognizes members to speak, assigns bills to particular committees, hands down bills for second and third readings, and controls the calendar. Few bills emerge from the House over his serious opposition. This, coupled with the fact that the budget bill originates in the House, gives him some leverage in attempting to get his way with the Senate.

In the Senate, the presiding officer is not as strong. The Lieutenant Governor appoints the members of the standing committees unless he happens to be of the minority party. In that case, the appointments are made by the president pro tempore. The presiding officer in the upper chamber also recognizes members to speak. However, Senate members generally pick the committees to which the legislation they sponsor will be assigned, sponsors call down their own bills for second and third readings, and the presiding officer has less control over the calendar.

The importance of the party as a source of leadership is also illustrated by the impact of the majority caucus on the standing committees. The rules of the lower house allow the number of members on most standing committees to vary, but they prescribe that "insofar as feasible and practical, the membership of the committees shall be made proportionately to representation of the parties in the House." [5] In the Senate, the size of the committees is fixed, but no recommendation is made about the division of the committee seats between the parties. Where they are free to do so, the majority caucuses fix the size of committees and the apportionment of the memberships between the parties. The division of seats follows no uniform rule in the Senate. In 1961 the party balance in that chamber was twenty-six Democrats to twenty-four Republicans. Yet the majority party members averaged six committee assignments each to only three for the minority party. In 1965, when they controlled the Senate thirty-five votes to fifteen, the Democrats held on the average slightly fewer seats than the Republicans.

In Congress, the seniority leaders are powerful chiefly because they chair the committees, and from those positions they exert great control over the flow of legislation. In the Indiana legislature, committee chairmen are important because they can sometimes kill legislation by not releasing it from committee, and because the chamber usually accepts their word as informed on particular pieces of legislation which have been before their committee. The power of chairmen to stop legislation is weakened by the so-called blast rule in each house, which allows the sponsor of a bill with the support of a majority vote to call back to the chamber a bill which a committee has had under consideration for at least six days. While this rule is used rather frequently in the House, it is seldom used in the Senate because of an informal understanding among the members.

In the Indiana General Assembly there is no seniority system in the common sense. Freshmen legislators may hold chairmanships of standing committees, and frequently do. However, an anaylsis of both committee chairmen and chamber officers in the 1957, 1959, and 1961 sessions demonstrates that the more sessions in which a legislator has served the more likely he is to hold formal positions of authority.[6] While seniority is not as important in Indiana as in the nation's capital, nevertheless it is still salient.

When we discuss expertise as a resource which can be converted to influence in Congress, we cannot point to any institutional arrangements as clearly defined as the party and seniority hierarchies. The same difficulty exists in examining the Indiana General Assembly. Nevertheless, I believe that all careful observers would agree that knowledge about particular problems confers on the legislator who possesses it influence beyond that of other members whenever legislation touches his area of competence. I have already indicated that information about the substance of bills is a resource which the committee chairmen use in their attempts to guide their chambers. Another evidence of the importance of expertise can be seen in the legislative treatment of bills drafted by the Legislative Council, the Commission on State Tax and Financing Policy, and other agencies charged with investigating problems facing the state and then reporting to the General Assembly. Both houses clearly begin with the assumption that bills produced by these commissions are good ones. Finally there are particular members of the legislature who are, by reason of their background, experts on some technical subject area and whose word is taken as conclusive on those matters.

If seniority, party position, and knowledge about public policy areas and legislative problems mark the leaders inside the Indiana state legislature, what sources of influence outside the institution are important in terms of their impact on the policies adopted by the State Representatives and State Senators? At the national level, we identify the administration, the interest groups, and to a lesser extent, the constituency party. Again these sources of influence seem important when we focus on legislative politics in Indiana.

In his pioneering study of party and legislature, Burton Y. Berry discovered that during the period from 1901 through 1921 about 3 percent of the legislation enacted by the Indiana General Assembly could be traced to the state party platforms.[7] In 1963, 13 percent of the laws enacted in Indiana could be directly traced to the preceding Republican state platform, and the party succeeded in putting into effect approximately sixty percent of its platform support measures.[8] These figures suggest that party is important in the legislature, but they tell us little about the impact of local party officials on legislatures. The study of the 1963 legislature indicated that while the state party organizations were active and were consulted, they had little control over the introduction, development, and support of specific bills in the assembly. At the constituency level, most county chairmen made little attempt to influence the votes of members of the legislature. The exceptions to this rule were some county chairmen from large counties which composed or dominated multi-member districts.[9] Slating practices in those counties allow county chairmen to control the nomination process; and since straight ticket voting is common, all legislators are usually from the same party. Such chairmen have considerable influence on legislators—particularly on those who are politically ambitious.

The administration has an important influence on the actions of the legislature. Many of the bills before any regular session will relate to the existing government agencies. They will create clearer statements of administrative responsibility, change administrative structure, remove burdensome features of existing legislation or institute technical changes to make administration easier. Most such bills will be initiated within the agencies, and the legislators have come to depend upon the administration for such support. In addition, the agencies, perhaps because of close ties to the groups of citizens who are their clients, will often act as interest groups in attempting to influence the course of particular pieces of general legislation.

The Governor must be singled out for special treatment when we discuss the influence of the administration. The state's chief executive would probably be more powerful in relation to the assembly if he were the only elected executive official, if a number of agencies directed by other executive officials were answerable to him, if he had an item veto, if his veto could not be overridden by only a majority in the legislature, and so forth. Nevertheless, the Governor has resources which enable him to influence the legislators. First, in his messages, he helps set the agenda for the session. Second, his veto power, particularly his ability to pocket veto bills which come to him in the last two days gives him additional leverage, for most of the bills which pass do so at the very end of the session. For example, in the 1965 regular session, more than 170 bills came to the Governor in the pocket veto period as compared to 444 bills which were enacted during the session. Most important is the Governor's control of patronage. This gives him influence with individual legislators and with his party's county chairmen in the populous counties. The Indiana Governor is constitutionally prevented from running to succeed himself. This, coupled with the fact that most of his patronage is exhausted in his first two years in office, leads to the commonplace assertion around the assembly chambers that "the Governor's first session belongs to him while the second belongs to the legislature."

Interest groups are notoriously influential in America's state legislatures. Just as many bills are initiated within the administration, so many are conceived and drafted within the offices of private organizations. The host of services which such groups have performed for legislators in the hope of winning assembly support need not be arrayed here. There are interest groups operative in Indiana and they are sometimes successful in influencing the General Assembly. A study of all candidates for the 1961 State Legislature and of the twenty-five holdover Senators indicated that Hoosier legislators ranked eight interest groups in terms of legislative effectiveness in the following order:

1. State Teachers Association
2. Chamber of Commerce
3. Farm Bureau
4. AFL-CIO
5. Municipal League
6. American Legion
7. League of Women Voters
8. Chiropractors

Furthermore, the rankings did not differ substantially when the candidates were divided along party lines. The Democrats felt that the AFL-CIO was slightly more effective than the Farm Bureau, and the Republicans felt that the Municipal League and the American Legion were tied for effectiveness. Of the eight, seven were felt to be at least somewhat effective "in influencing public policy and especially . . . in making their case before the legislature." Only the chiropractors were seen as ineffective.[10]

Republican and Democratic candidates for the legislature were also in agreement about the qualities and resources which are necessary to "an effective lobbyist in the legislature." Seventy percent of those interviewed emphasized honesty and personal integrity as the principal quality required. Over half stressed the importance of a thorough knowledge of the subject. Thirty-eight percent pointed to the lobbyist's need of a pleasant personality. Sixteen percent wanted the interest group's representative to prove his helpfulness by providing information and conducting research. Twelve percent stressed the value of previous legislative experience. Formal education and persuasiveness were each mentioned by 5 percent of the candidates. In explaining the power of the various interest groups, the legislative candidates also indicated that the size of the groups and their electoral influence, the strength of the leadership in the organizations, and the financial resources available are of major importance.[11] The agreement about the effectiveness of various groups and about tools and techniques which produce effectiveness suggests that interest politics is important in Indiana. The fact that those who have served longer in the legislature are those most favorably disposed toward interest groups[12] suggests that those organizations may in fact perform services valuable to the state as well as to individual members of the assembly.

## The Legislators

The formal organization and procedure and the informal rules of an institution fix the boundaries within which the members must normally act, but the individual members are still the actors. The characteristics which they bring to the institution are partial indicators of the experiences which they have undergone. These experiences will influence their behavior even inside a highly formal and rather ritualistic body like the Indiana General Assembly.

The delegates to the 1850 constitutional convention understood clearly that by influencing the characteristics which men brought to the legislature, they would influence the legislative product. They intended that the House and Senate differ in their approach to legislation. Formally they differentiated the two bodies by making the Senate smaller, requiring that its youngest members be somewhat older, and allowing its members to serve terms twice as long as the legislators in the other house. They expected these few formal differences to have major consequences. One remark made by William M. Dunn in support of a smaller Senate demonstrates, I believe, the nature of the expectations.

> Reduce the Senate, and your Senators will be selected for their age, their experience, and their general information. They will have time to consider deliberately those propositions which large bodies are apt to act upon hastily and inconsiderately. Every Senator will act under high responsibility; he will have to regard the interests of a larger section of country, and a more numerous constituency than any member in the House of Representatives.[13]

I shall not attempt to compare the responsibility of Senators and Representatives. We do know that members of the upper house generally face wider electorates, and we can examine some important background characteristics of the legislators.

One apportionment in Indiana governed the selection of members of the assembly beginning with the 1923 session and continuing through the 1963 session. During that period, 1,443 individuals served in the legislature. Sometime during each session a form was distributed asking them to indicate their age, education, occupation, and religion. Not all members responded to all questions. In addition to these four characteristics, we can also determine the legislator's party from the official records. Table I summarizes this information for all who served as well as for the Senate and the House.

Mr. Dunn and his colleagues expected Senators to be older, better educated, and probably wealthier and more conservative than members of the House of Representatives. Senators do appear somewhat older upon entry into the legislature and somewhat better educated. The occupational distribution suggests that they may make higher incomes; and if party is used as an indicator of liberalism, then Senators appear a bit more conservative. The differences between the two cham-

## TABLE I

### COMPARISON OF BACKGROUND CHARACTERISTICS OF LEGISLATORS, 1923–1963, BY CHAMBER

|  | ALL MEMBERS | SENATE | HOUSE |
|---|---|---|---|
| *Age at First Session* | N = 1329 | N = 345 | N = 984 |
| under 30 | 8% | 4% | 9% |
| 30–39 | 26 | 23 | 27 |
| 40–59 | 51 | 58 | 48 |
| 60 or over | 15 | 15 | 16 |
| *Occupation* | N = 1437 | N = 365 | N = 1072 |
| Lawyers | 25% | 32% | 22% |
| Farmers | 21 | 16 | 23 |
| Businessmen | 25 | 21 | 27 |
| Other Professions | 10 | 11 | 9 |
| Labor & W. Collar | 10 | 7 | 11 |
| Other | 9 | 13 | 8 |
| *Party* | N = 1443 | N = 368 | N = 1075 |
| Democrat | 47% | 46% | 48% |
| Republican | 53 | 54 | 52 |
| *Education* | N = 1376 | N = 354 | N = 1022 |
| Attended High School | 97% | 99% | 97% |
| Attended College | 61 | 66 | 58 |
| Graduated from College | 33 | 36 | 31 |
| *Religion* | N = 1314 | N = 333 | N = 981 |
| Catholics | 11% | 13% | 11% |
| Methodists | 27 | 25 | 28 |
| Christian | 16 | 16 | 15 |
| Baptists | 6 | 6 | 6 |
| Presbyterians | 14 | 18 | 13 |
| Lutherans | 5 | 4 | 6 |
| Anabaptists & Brethren | 5 | 4 | 5 |
| Episcopalians | 4 | 4 | 3 |
| Other | 12 | 10 | 13 |

bers are of the kind the framers of Indiana's constitution envisioned, but they might be surprised that the differences are so small.

Religion is reported not because I expect it to have much to do with legislative behavior. Very few issues examined by the Hoosier legislature are likely to divide men of one faith from those of another. Religion may, however, have much to do with winning office. Louis Harris indicated its importance in Indiana in his survey for the Democrats in 1958 when he reported that Senator Vance Hartke would gain ground once it became known among Protestants that he was a Lutheran.[14] Religion does not clearly differentiate Senators from Representatives. However, Table II shows an important difference between Republicans and Democrats. A much higher percentage of Democrats are Catholic. Most of these have come from the cities, where the concentrations of Catholics are found. The other differences between the charac-

TABLE II

COMPARISON OF BACKGROUND CHARACTERISTICS OF LEGISLATORS,
1923–1963, BY PARTY

|  | DEMOCRATS | REPUBLICANS |
|---|---|---|
| *Age* | N=616 | N=713 |
| under 30 | 9% | 6% |
| 30–39 | 26 | 26 |
| 40–59 | 48 | 53 |
| 60 & over | 17 | 15 |
| *Occupation* | N=679 | N=758 |
| Lawyers | 25% | 25% |
| Farmers | 19 | 23 |
| Businessmen | 22 | 28 |
| Other Professions | 12 | 8 |
| Labor & W. Collar | 14 | 7 |
| Other | 8 | 9 |
| *Education* | N=644 | N=732 |
| Attended High School | 97% | 98% |
| Attended College | 55 | 65 |
| Graduated College | 30 | 35 |
| *Religion* | N=608 | N=706 |
| Catholics | 21% | 3% |
| Methodists | 21 | 32 |
| Christian | 13 | 17 |
| Baptists | 7 | 5 |
| Presbyterians | 13 | 15 |
| Lutherans | 6 | 5 |
| Anabaptists & Brethren | 4 | 5 |
| Episcopalians | 4 | 3 |
| Other | 1 | 14 |

teristics of Republicans and Democrats are again of the sort we would expect but also rather small.

Some of the most notable differences in background characteristics appear when freshmen legislators are contrasted for the last four sessions. These comparisons are shown in Table III. It is obvious that the profile of the legislature is shifting. More young men are entering the assembly as are more nonprofessionals. To what extent these changes result from shifts in party success in elections or from reapportionment remains unclear.

As Table III indicates, sixty-nine members were new to the legislature in the 1967 session. Turnover of members in the Indiana House of Representatives is constantly high. Duane Lockard classifies any session as a high turnover one when 40 percent or more of the members of its lower house are new men.[15] Using that criterion, nineteen of the twenty-three sessions of the Indiana House of Representatives from 1923 through 1967 were high turnover sessions.

## TABLE III

COMPARISON OF BACKGROUND CHARACTERISTICS OF NEW LEGISLATORS,
1961–1967, BY SESSION

| | NEW MEMBERS 1961 | NEW MEMBERS 1963 | NEW MEMBERS 1965 | NEW MEMBERS 1967 |
|---|---|---|---|---|
| *Age* | N=48 | N=39 | N=61 | N=65 |
| under 30 | 0% | 15% | 11% | 12% |
| 30–39 | 40 | 31 | 28 | 35 |
| 40–59 | 46 | 51 | 52 | 48 |
| 60 or over | 15 | 3 | 8 | 4 |
| *Occupation* | N=54 | N=46 | N=78 | N=69 |
| Lawyers | 24% | 22% | 18% | 22% |
| Farmers | 17 | 2 | 10 | 10 |
| Businessmen | 37 | 39 | 33 | 35 |
| Other Professions | 11 | 22 | 15 | 17 |
| Labor & W. Collar | 6 | 11 | 18 | 12 |
| Other | 6 | 4 | 5 | 4 |
| *Party* | N=57 | N=46 | N=79 | N=69 |
| Democrat | 25% | 63% | 84% | 16% |
| Republican | 75 | 37 | 16 | 84 |
| *Education* | N=50 | N=40 | N=71 | N=69 |
| Attended High School | 98% | 100% | 100% | 100% |
| Attended College | 86 | 78 | 76 | 87 |
| College Graduate | 56 | 62 | 51 | 58 |
| *Religion* | N=48 | N=39 | N=75 | N=67 |
| Roman Catholics | 15% | 18% | 24% | 15% |
| Methodists | 31 | 28 | 27 | 21 |
| Christian | 8 | 10 | 7 | 19 |
| Baptists | 10 | 3 | 13 | 1 |
| Presbyterians | 19 | 13 | 7 | 18 |
| Lutherans | 6 | 8 | 1 | 1 |
| Anabaptists & Brethren | 2 | 8 | 3 | 1 |
| Episcopalians | 0 | 5 | 4 | 3 |
| Other | 8 | 8 | 13 | 19 |

Political scientists and legislators share some apprehension about high turnover. One veteran State Senator regretted the fact that new legislators were less likely to accept the recommendations of the Legislative Advisory Commission as conclusive. He accounted for this in two ways. First, the new men are unlikely to understand the effort and study which lie behind such proposals. Second, they recognize that some of the men on the commission which reports to the General Assembly were defeated for re-election; and the freshmen argue that, if they are in turn to be rejected at the polls, they would rather it be for their own mistakes. Political scientists have argued that this high turnover is likely to lead to policy which is inconsistent for unintentional reasons and to hinder the development of expertise.[16]

I have already indicated that length of service is important to formal leadership in Indiana and that it is positively related to a favorable orientation toward interest groups. Some other evidence comparing the new men and the old hands is worth reporting. Freshmen in the Indiana state legislature tend to get together with other legislators less than experienced members do, both before and during the session.[17] The new men vote on roll calls considerably more frequently, but they sponsor fewer bills.[18] In their voting and other legislative service, they are more likely to think of themselves as delegates who must reflect the wishes of their constituencies regardless of their own views rather than as trustees who are free to act in whatever way they feel best serves their constituency.[19] Finally, the freshman legislator is not noted for being influential in the General Assembly, while those who have served longer are more likely to be thought of as influential in specific areas of public policymaking, and those who have served in at least three previous sessions are thought of by their colleagues as being generally influential.[20] I can do little better in summary here than to quote Charles S. Hyneman's remark in his early study of turnover in the Indiana legislature. He advised that "a wise public will temper its impatience by realization that it sacrifices something when it exchanges experienced lawmaker for novice."[21] Indiana seems continually willing to make the sacrifice. Whether it realizes the consequences of its actions is uncertain.

One of the major characteristics of the Indiana legislator still to be discussed is his partisan experience. By almost any standard, Indiana would have to be classed as a two-party state. The Republican and Democratic parties contest for office throughout the state, and both have considerable success. Table I indicates that the balance in the legislature during the long apportionment was only slightly Republican. Nonetheless, while the Governorship in Indiana has been controlled first by one party and then by the other, the legislature has usually been under Republican direction. This means that Hoosier legislators have had experience in operating within divided governments, and it may help to account for the importance of party organization within the legislature.

The pattern of party competition also affects the background of legislators. States with competitive parties produce legislators with greater prior partisan and governmental experience.[22] Indiana is not an exception. About a quarter of the legislators, in the 1959 session at least, served on party committees, and more than half of them participated in the state party conventions. In addition, 60 percent of them had either held public office or campaigned for election to one before they first ran for the legislature. Further, about 45 percent of those who retired from the legislature between 1945 and 1958 attempted again to win elective office.[23] These findings suggest that many legislators find personal rewards in partisan politics. Such men are likely to make valuable contributions to the institutions which they find so attractive.

## Apportionment and Reapportionment

With politics so competitive in Indiana, the normal control of the General Assembly by the Republican party suggests that the apportionment may be a contributing factor. That is undoubtedly the case. The Indiana Constitution requires that the legislature be reapportioned every six years. Had the document been complied with, the state would have been reapportioned ten or eleven times in this century. The Indiana legislature has adopted nine reapportionment plans since 1900, but six of those plans were adopted since 1963 in response to the entry of the courts into this field.

One apportionment governed the selection of legislators for forty years. While it may have accurately reflected the population distribution in the 1920's, it was clearly unrepresentative in the 1960's. In the House, Vermillion County had one representative for its 1960 population of 17,683 while St. Joseph County with three representatives had 79,538 citizens per representative. In terms of the "one man, one vote" criterion, a Vermillion County vote was worth approximately four and one-half times as much as a St. Joseph County vote. The situation in the Senate was similar. There, for example, one vote in Parke and Clay counties weighed four times more than a vote in Lake County. The long apportionment obviously overrepresented rural areas at the expense of the cities and aided the Republicans in controlling both chambers.

The reapportionment plan approved by the court in 1965 corrects the rural overbalance in Indiana. Its other social and political effects are more difficult to determine. An examination of turnover in the legislature, session by session over the long apportionment suggests that the proportion of new men has decreased fairly steadily over the forty years. From 1923 through 1931, the average turnover per session in the Senate amounted to 23 percent. During the last five years, turnover had fallen to only 16 percent. The change in the House was even more drastic. During the first period, turnover averaged 62 percent. In the period from 1955 through 1963, it had dropped to 43 percent. These comparisons, coupled with the 1967 turnover figures of 26 percent in the Senate and 50 percent in the House under a different apportionment, give some support to the notion that continuing reapportionment may reinforce the high turnover tendencies in Indiana.

The obvious short-run political effect of reapportionment in Indiana is to aid the Democratic party, but other consequences also deserve attention. The new districts are larger and that will increase both the personal and financial costs of campaigning. The fact that the urban centers will have increased representation means that the large multimember districts will gain additional seats. As I have already indicated, these are the districts in which the local party organization leaders are most able and most likely to control the behavior of their legislators.

Incumbents may find that the complexion of their district in interest terms changes from session to session. One experienced lawmaker reported that as he became acquainted with his new district he found himself becoming more and more conservative. For this reason, and because uncertainty about re-election is likely to increase, it may be that reapportionment of the House and Senate will also reapportion the unofficial third house by giving neglected interests access to the system and by changing the access points of those which have already achieved entrée. Finally, our concern with institutional memory and policy continuity in the legislature suggests that we should also concern ourselves with these factors when we look at party organization. The necessity to regroup, as electoral districts are redrawn every ten years, is likely to injure both party organizations in those areas where population shifts and the accompanying policy problems are most pronounced.

What kind of impact will reapportionment have on legislative policy? It seems too early to answer this question with anything approaching certainty. The 1965 session was influenced by urban-oriented Democrats, but the advantages which the rural areas in Indiana have enjoyed were not swept away in the political tide. As an example consider the distribution of the gasoline tax, which is earmarked for highway development and maintenance. While city streets carry 30 percent of the traffic in the state as compared with 9 percent of the traffic carried on county roads, the cities receive only 15 percent of the gasoline tax collected by the state while the counties are given 32 percent of the funds. A bill to change the formula for distributing the money in favor of the cities was allowed to die in committee. Rural interests may have something to fear from the legislature in the future, but they are not likely to be completely ignored.

The Indiana legislature is a typical one. It moves to meet problems as they emerge, and it does not consider them in isolation. It is not notably innovative, imaginative, or creative. Those who highly prize those values in an institution will be disappointed as they observe

Hoosier legislative politics. However, those who feel that political issues mark difficulties which must be met rather than problems which must be solved and who value political institutions most when they merge interests, avoid clashes, and reach compromises will be generally pleased when they turn their attention to the Indiana General Assembly.

# PART II

---

*Legislative Behavior*

## 2 / Legislative Politics in Indiana

*Kenneth Janda, Henry Teune, Melvin Kahn, and Wayne Francis*

DURING THE SUMMER OF 1960 WE INTERVIEWED ALL CANDIDATES FOR the 1961 Indiana legislature and all holdover Senators from the 1959 session. An attempt was made to inform each candidate and holdover Senator of this project by mail and at the same time to request an appointment for the interview at a specified time and date. A letter of explanation was mailed to each prospective respondent weeks in advance of the proposed interview date. Each letter also included a short summary of previous findings on the Indiana legislator prepared by David R. Derge of Indiana University and a return postcard which the candidate could use to confirm the interview appointment.

The success of the project can be judged by the results: Interviews were obtained from 238 individuals, or 86 percent of the total universe of 277. Interviews were secured from 93 of the 100 elected to seats in the House of Representatives and 44 of the 50 Senators. Matthew E. Welsh and Richard O. Ristine, Governor and Lieutenant Governor respectively in 1960, were also interviewed. Although a few schedules were filled in by the individuals themselves and returned to us by mail, 211 responses were obtained by personal interview in the homes, offices, farms, factories, and places of business of these prospective legislators and holdover Senators. The interview schedule used to collect data for this chapter is given in Appendix B.

With rare exceptions, the people interviewed gave us warm welcomes and their sincere cooperation, and we found them to be deeply interested in encouraging research of the type being conducted. They seemed to feel much as we do—that an improved understanding of the state legislature is not only important for today's citizens but will be of assistance to the legislators of the future.

## Comparison of House and Senate Members

In the Constitutional Convention of 1850, considerable debate was devoted to the institutional arrangements providing for the two chambers of Indiana's General Assembly. As did the makers of the United States Constitution, the founders of Indiana's present form of government thought it desirable to have different types of people serving in the two houses. The official *Debates* of 1850 report that delegates to the convention urged that the Senate be "composed of the older men of the country" who were "more stable in character." On the other hand, they wished the House members to reflect the characteristics of the "popular" segment of society. To achieve this end, they constructed institutional arrangements which established a higher age of entry for the Senate, allowed the Senators to serve a full session without threat of removal at the polls, and offered Senators the advantages of belonging to a less numerous, and therefore more select, social organization. If these then were their intentions, did the 1961 legislature demonstrate the differences intended by the constitution-makers?

The interviews produced data which allow some rough comparisons to be made between House and Senate members on the basis of selected social characteristics. A reading of Figure 1 reveals some small but discernible differences between the members of the two chambers on the basis of occupation, education, place of birth, and income. Moreover, these differences conform in a general way to the apparent intentions of the framers of Indiana's Constitution. Regarding occupation, the 1961 Senate had almost twice the proportion of lawyers as the 1961 House, and the practice of law claimed more than twice as many members of the Senate as any other occupation. Furthermore, these data are not peculiar to the 1961 session but are amazingly consistent over a long period of time. Of the 928 men who served in the Indiana House from 1925 through 1959, there were 211 lawyers and 211 farmers—each group comprising 23 percent of the chamber's membership. However, of the 330 men who served in the Indiana Senate over the same period of time, 33 percent were lawyers as opposed to only 17 percent farmers. If the premise is granted that lawyers as a group reflect the virtues of legislator–statesmen as conceived by the founding fathers while farmers voice the sentiments of the common people, then it follows that the founders' wishes were at least approximated in the occupational composition of the Indiana legislature.

Owing in part to the preponderance of lawyers in the chamber, Senators also show a slight edge in formal education. Not only are Sena-

## Comparison of Social Characteristics of Legislators by Chamber

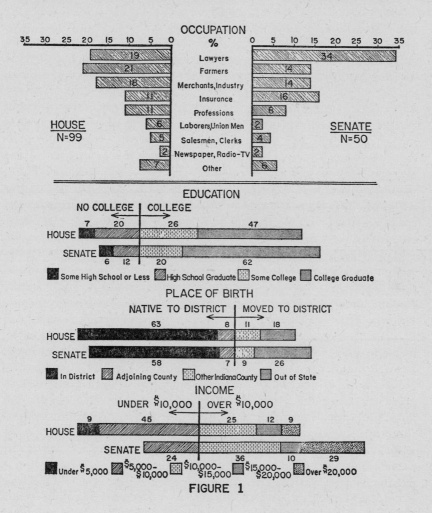

FIGURE 1

tors more likely to have attended college, but they are also more likely
to have received four year college degrees. As with the data on occupation, these differences are well established over time. Of the 1,258 men
who served in the legislature between 1925 and 1959, 65 percent of the
Senators had the benefit of a college education against 52 percent of
the Representatives. In passing, it is noted that the 1961 General Assembly appeared to be the best educated legislature in Indiana's history up to that time, with about 75 percent of its members having had
the road to knowledge made smoother by formal schooling past high
school, thus requiring only one-fourth of the membership to learn the
hard way from experience, where the test comes first and the lesson
afterwards.

Place of birth offers a somewhat crude test of "cosmopolitanism"—a
sense of having interests and experiences extending past the confines of
the locality in which the person was born. Measured against this standard, House members are slightly more likely to have been born in the
area which they represent than are Senators, one-fourth of whom are
not native Hoosiers. But for both groups, by far the largest proportions of members have been born and raised on Indiana soil. Nevertheless, the data show that the Senate is more apt to reflect views of men
who have lived in localities other than those they represent.

If the founding fathers intended to have the Senate reflect the sentiments of the wealthier members of the community, they were clearly
successful on this score. As in education, where both House and Senate
members were far above the average of the population in number of
years of schooling completed, members of the 1961 legislature were
also significantly above the median income for Indiana residents, but
there is a striking difference between the incomes received by Representatives and Senators. Whereas 46 percent of the House members reported making over $10,000 per year, 76 percent of the Senators dis-
closed incomes above that figure.

On the basis of these selected social characteristics, it is possible to
detect some consistent differences between the members of Indiana's
"upper" and "lower" houses, and these differences, in general, seem to
conform to the intentions of those who made the constitution 111
years ago.

## The Two-Party System in Indiana

A Harvard Ph.D. dissertation on Indiana politics described Indiana's two major parties as "strong, virile, well-disciplined and evenly
matched." That statement receives support in the findings of Professor

Derge of Indiana University who reports that during the eighteen-session period from 1925 to 1959 Republicans held 52 percent of the House seats to the Democrats' 48 percent and that Senate seats divided 54 percent–46 percent between the Republicans and Democrats. However, Professor Derge notes that, despite the overall division in seats held, Republicans controlled twelve of the eighteen House sessions and fourteen of the eighteen Senate sessions. These findings fit in with a common-sense evaluation which awards the edge to the Republicans over the years, although the Democrats could always boast of a frequently successful, healthy organization. If that evaluation is true for the parties over the years, the question then arises, how did the parties stack up in 1961 and what are the forecasts for the future?

Our interview schedule included a battery of questions concerning the strength of political parties in the legislative districts throughout the state. Responses to some of these questions are portrayed in Figure 2. Comparing the answers of all Republican candidates with all Democratic candidates, we found that Republicans and Democrats alike report "over the years" about 25 percent of the districts have been Democratic, 25 percent competitive, and 50 percent Republican. Considering that the greatest proportion of the Republican districts were designated simply as "mostly" Republican, these state-wide data verify and add precision to the judgment that, in the past, Indiana has been a two-party state with Republican leanings. But what about the future?

We can perhaps get some idea of things to come by examining the responses of only the candidates who won in 1960. Comparing Republican winners against Democratic winners, it becomes obvious that the 1960 election saw more Democrats win in districts they thought to be previously Republican than did Republicans in districts seen as previously Democratic. These responses seemed to indicate a considerable shifting of party sentiment toward the Democratic party in many districts across the state. This was confirmed by the candidates who gave answers to the question of whether or not they thought the political nature of their district was changing. As Figure 2 shows, exactly half of the Republicans and almost two-thirds of the Democrats saw their districts as shifting Democratic. Roughly one-third of both parties replied that there was no change in party strength in their districts, and less than one-tenth of all candidates saw the Republican party on the increase.

It is somewhat interesting to note the reasons given by members of the two parties for the changing political nature of their district. Turning once again to Figure 2, we can see that the Democrats were more likely to attribute this change in voting behavior either to the increased independence (and presumably, wisdom) of the voters or they

## Party Strength in Indiana

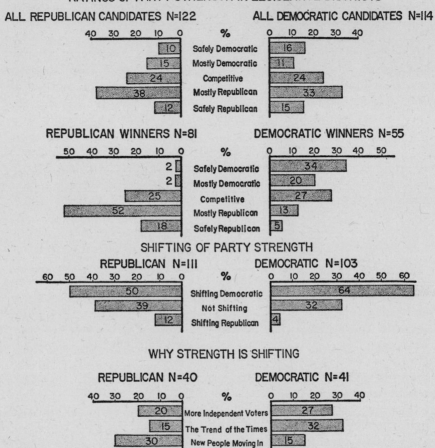

RATINGS OF PARTY STRENGTH IN LEGISLATIVE DISTRICTS

ALL REPUBLICAN CANDIDATES N=122     ALL DEMOCRATIC CANDIDATES N=114

40 30 20 10 0    %    0 10 20 30 40

| | Safely Democratic | |
|---|---|---|
| 10 | | 16 |
| 15 | Mostly Democratic | 11 |
| 24 | Competitive | 24 |
| 38 | Mostly Republican | 33 |
| 12 | Safely Republican | 15 |

REPUBLICAN WINNERS N=81     DEMOCRATIC WINNERS N=55

50 40 30 20 10 0    %    0 10 20 30 40 50

| | Safely Democratic | |
|---|---|---|
| 2 | | 34 |
| 2 | Mostly Democratic | 20 |
| 25 | Competitive | 27 |
| 52 | Mostly Republican | 13 |
| 18 | Safely Republican | 5 |

SHIFTING OF PARTY STRENGTH

REPUBLICAN N=111     DEMOCRATIC N=103

60 50 40 30 20 10 0    %    0 10 20 30 40 50 60

| | Shifting Democratic | |
|---|---|---|
| 50 | | 64 |
| 39 | Not Shifting | 32 |
| 12 | Shifting Republican | 4 |

WHY STRENGTH IS SHIFTING

REPUBLICAN N=40     DEMOCRATIC N=41

40 30 20 10 0    %    0 10 20 30 40

| | More Independent Voters | |
|---|---|---|
| 20 | | 27 |
| 15 | The Trend of the Times | 32 |
| 30 | New People Moving In | 15 |
| 18 | More Industrialization | 10 |
| 18 | Other | 17 |

FIGURE 2

were more apt to account for the change as part of a broad but vaguely defined swing to the Democratic party; it is the "trend" of the times, was the most frequently encountered response. The Republicans were not as prone to ascribe the increase in Democratic strength to either the intelligence of the voter or to fate, but they were far more likely to explain it all away with the simpler reasons that more new people (mainly Southerners) with Democratic attachments were moving into the district or that the district was becoming more industrialized, which means more laborers, unions, and thus more Democratic votes. But regardless of the accuracy of the reasons advanced to explain the increase in Democratic strength and mindful of the cautions to be observed in interpreting these data, it seemed justifiable at the time to conclude that the Democratic party was enjoying a period of prosperity which pointed toward the elimination of the slight Republican predominancy of the past and toward the emergence of Indiana as a state with a highly competitive two-party system of the first order.[1]

## Comparison of Party Members on Social Characteristics

Figure 3 depicts the same comparisons made between Republicans and Democrats, irrespective of chamber, as were made between House and Senate members without separation according to party. The same characteristics which distinguished Senators from Representatives also serve, in a lesser degree, to distinguish Republicans from Democrats. However, it was somewhat surprising to note that less differences existed when legislators were compared on the basis of party than when examined according to their chamber membership.

The 1961 General Assembly contained slightly more Republican than Democratic lawyers, but the ratio was not as large as the nearly 2 to 1 proportion which held between the chambers, in spite of the fact that Republicans were predominant in the House. Next to the lawyers, the largest occupational grouping in the session was the farmers, as they were throughout the previous 18-session period. Here, the spread between parties was greater than for lawyers; farmers tended to enter the legislature via the Republican party. Republican-Democratic differences were nearly identical with the Senate-House distribution of farmers, fitting with the fact that Republicans predominated in the House. In addition to the tendency of farmer-legislators to be Republicans, three other variations in occupational groupings deserve to be mentioned: (1) Republicans were twice as likely as Democrats to be merchants or officials in industry. (2) Democratic laborers were the rule; Republican laborers the exception. (3) The Democratic party contributed a disproportionate share of professional men, most of

Comparison of the Social Characteristics of Legislators by Party

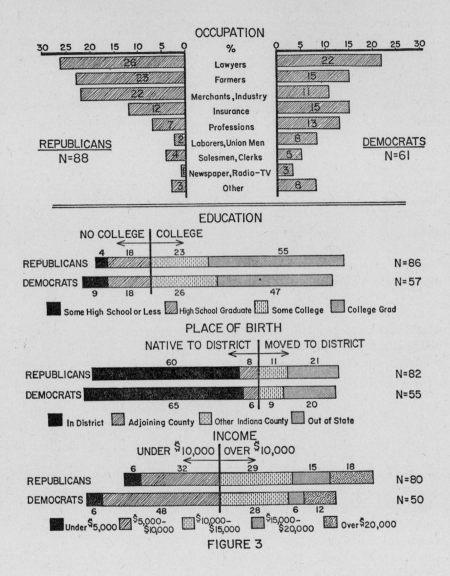

FIGURE 3

whom were teachers. It should also be noted that the 1961 session is not unique in this occupational distribution between parties. Comparable data exist for the thirty-six years prior to 1961.

Although the data reveal some differences between Republicans and Democrats in occupational groupings, none of these is as striking as the House-Senate variation in lawyer composition. House-Senate differences were also greater than party differences in education, place of birth, and income. Figure 3 reveals that the Republican edge in formal schooling was slight and that there was just a little difference between the parties on place of birth. Although the separation in income was more definite, it was not quite so strong as the disparity in the incomes of Senators and Representatives. Of the Republicans, 62 percent reported an income of $10,000 or more compared to 46 percent of the Democrats.

The House-Senate differences are even more striking because these differences in every case, are antithetical to differences associated with the two parties, whose members are represented in reversed proportions in the two chambers. Thus, although the Republicans tended to receive higher incomes than the Democrats, members of the slightly Democratic Senate ranked higher on income than did members of the strongly Republican House. The consistency of this pattern on each of these characteristics only points more strongly to the general conclusion indicated by comparing Figure 1 with Figure 3: considering social characteristics alone, greater differences existed between Senators and Representatives, irrespective of party, than between Republicans and Democrats.

## Comparison of Party Members on Political Attitudes

It was previously shown that social differences between House and Senate members seemed to conform in a general way with the intentions of the framers of Indiana's Constitution. However, it is somewhat ironic to note that these intended differences did not have the same consequences for the formation of public policy that the founding fathers expected. According to the official *Debates,* delegates to the 1850 convention hoped that their structural arrangements would "give to the Senate a more conservative character," and delegates viewed the Senate as a "conservative body, calculated to act as a wholesome check upon the more popular branch of the legislature." In fact, in 1961 the founders would have observed two political groupings which represented opposing political attitudes along the lines they anticipated, but they were wrong in thinking that these groupings would coincide with House and Senate membership. Instead, the really significant dif-

## Differences in the Political Attitudes of Republicans and Democrats

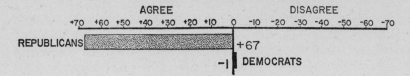

▶ BUSINESS ENTERPRISE CAN CONTINUE TO GIVE US
OUR HIGH STANDARD OF LIVING ONLY IF IT REMAINS
FREE FROM GOVERNMENT REGULATION.

AGREE                          DISAGREE
+70 +60 +50 +40 +30 +20 +10  0  -10 -20 -30 -40 -50 -60 -70

REPUBLICANS     +67

−1   DEMOCRATS

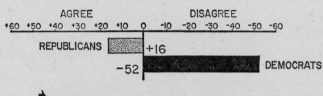

▶ ORGANIZED LABOR HAS FAR TOO MUCH INFLUENCE
IN THE INDIANA LEGISLATURE.

AGREE                          DISAGREE
+60 +50 +40 +30 +20 +10  0  -10 -20 -30 -40 -50 -60

REPUBLICANS    +16

−52    DEMOCRATS

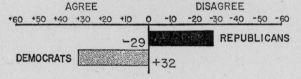

▶ THE GOVERNMENT HAS THE RESPONSIBILITY TO SEE
TO IT THAT ALL PEOPLE, POOR OR RICH, HAVE
ADEQUATE HOUSING, EDUCATION, MEDICAL CARE, AND
PROTECTION AGAINST UNEMPLOYMENT.

AGREE                          DISAGREE
+60 +50 +40 +30 +20 +10  0  -10 -20 -30 -40 -50 -60

−29    REPUBLICANS

DEMOCRATS    +32

INDEX OF AGREEMENT : +100 -- EVERY RESPONDENT AGREED WITH THE
STATEMENT
−100 -- EVERY RESPONDENT DISAGREED WITH
THE STATEMENT

REPUBLICANS  N=81     DEMOCRATS  N=54

FIGURE 4

ferences in political attitudes among members of the 1961 legislature are attributed to party alignment.

This involves an interesting paradox, and it might help to spell it out in more detail. The facts are that Representatives and Senators differed more on social characteristics than did Republicans and Democrats, but Representatives and Senators of the same party displayed very little difference in political attitudes while Republicans and Democrats stood poles apart. The small differences between Republicans and Democrats relating to social characteristics might have led some people to conclude that, after all, there really wasn't much separating the two parties. Our 1960 interview data revealed exactly the opposite: members of the two political parties held sharply differing attitudes on a whole complex of political questions conforming to the common distinctions between conservative and liberal orientations.

In the course of the interview, each respondent was handed a sheet of statements on political matters and asked to check whether or not they would "agree," or "tend to agree," be "undecided," "tend to disagree," or "disagree" with each statement.[2] Included in the series of statements were three items designed to disclose political attitudes. Figure 4 shows the outstanding differences between the average Republican and the average Democratic responses to these three items. Republicans overwhelmingly agreed that business enterprise ought to remain free from government regulation, while the Democrats were almost evenly divided on their opinions but tended ever so slightly to disagree. Republicans tended to agree that organized labor had far too much influence in the Indiana legislature, while Democrats strongly disagreed. Finally, the Democrats placed greater responsibility with the government in guaranteeing adequate housing, education, medical care, and protection against unemployment than the Republicans, who took the opposite stand.

For these three statements, all Democrats differed from all Republicans on an average of 66 index points per item. When comparisons are made between party members of the two houses, it is found that merely 6 index points separated Senate from House Republicans while only 10 index points measured the separation between Senate and House Democrats. The pattern is clear: the variable associated with liberal and conservative political attitudes is party and not chamber.

## Comparison of Party Members on Agreement with Group Policies

Having found that members of the two parties group in distinctly different places on the liberal-conservative continuum, we also expected to find them reveal the same difference in their agreement or disagreement with the policies and activities of various interest groups which operated before the legislature. The interview project provided data to test that proposition. The candidates were handed a list of eight of the more or less well-known interest groups in Indiana and were asked to check the extent of their agreement with the groups' policies and activities concerning public issues. There was no special significance in the groups listed; we simply wanted to have available a range of groups with different interests. The index of agreement was again computed for different groupings of legislators. Figure 5 depicts the patterns of Republican-Democratic scores for each of the eight groups, ranked according to the net difference in size of the two scores.

It can be seen that Democrats and Republicans were most clearly at odds with each other concerning the policies of the state AFL-CIO. The Indiana State Chamber of Commerce offered the next largest source of disagreement. Both of these follow as expected, but the pattern of the Indiana State Teachers Association may raise some eyebrows. Although both Republicans and Democrats placed themselves on the agreement side of the chart, the Republicans appeared to hold more reservations about the ISTA's policies than the Democrats. A partial explanation for this may be that more Democratic lawmakers were teachers, but the attitudes of these individuals toward the ISTA were not checked.

In order to make further comparisons between the parties' rankings of their agreement with group policies, it is helpful to introduce a simple measure of comparison called the rank-order correlation coefficient.[3] This is simply a statistic which ranges from +1.00 to −1.00 and expresses the degree of similarity between two independent rankings of any set of things judged on a common criterion. A score of +1.00 represents perfect similarity between the rankings, a score of 0.00 indicates no relationship whatsoever, and a score of −1.00 measures a complete inverse relationship between the rankings. For example, if the AP and UPI rankings of the top ten Indiana high school basketball teams were identical, the rank-order correlation coefficient would be +1.00. But if these press services disagreed completely so that the AP's top team was tenth in the UPI listing, and the AP's second team rated ninth by the UPI, and so forth, then the correlation would be −1.00. As a matter of fact, the rankings are usually quite similar and frequently result in a correlation of +.90 or better.

When the Republicans' index of agreement scores for these groups are ranked in order from the group with which they agree the most to the one they disagree with the most and when this ranking is compared with the Democrats' ranking for these same groups, the correla-

Republican-Democratic Agreement with the Policies of Selected Interest Groups:

INDEX OF AGREEMENT: +100 -- EVERY RESPONDENT AGREED WITH THE GROUP'S POLICIES
-100 -- EVERY RESPONDENT DISAGREED WITH THE GROUP'S POLICIES

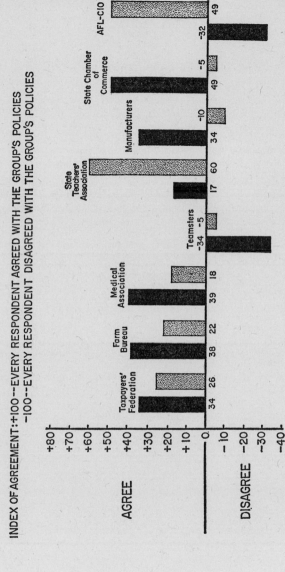

REPUBLICANS N=79    DEMOCRATS N=51

FIGURE 5

tion coefficient is —.36, indicating a substantial amount of difference between Republicans and Democrats on the extent of their agreement with the policies of these eight interest groups. That this phenomenon is attributable to inter-party differences and not to chamber variations can be seen by noting that Senate and House Democrats differed very little in their agreement with the policies of these groups, for their correlation coefficient is +.83. Similarly, Republican Senators and Representatives substantially agreed in their rankings and demonstrated a correlation coefficient of +.76.

It needs to be remembered that Republicans and Democrats were not opposed to each other on the policies of every group. Moreover, there were individual Republicans who frequently aligned themselves with the attitudes and opinions of the opposition just as there were some Democrats with more conservative leanings than their fellow party members. However, the data are clear: Republicans and Democrats in general displayed undeniable differences in their tendencies to agree and disagree with the policies of various groups which operated before the Indiana legislature.

It is a common charge of interested and intelligent citizens that there really isn't much difference between the parties. As long as one considers only social characteristics, this is not too far wrong. Although Democrats examined in this study differ from Republicans in established patterns on occupation, education, place of birth, and income, these differences are not as great as those demonstrated between House and Senate members. However, when one considers attitudinal differences as well, the parallel breaks down completely. The fact is that Democrats and Republicans differed on these items, and they differed in significant respects.

## Effective Organizations at the Indiana Legislature

One of the special purposes of interviewing was to provide data on the function of interest groups as participants in the legislative process. Modern legislators are burdened with the task of deciding public policy for a complex society. Many of the laws which need to be enacted are of a technical nature and affect only certain segments of the society. As a result, the legislator must frequently turn to the authorized spokesmen of established organizations to see how proposed legislation might affect members of the group. Often the legislator seeks information from opposing organizations to get both sides of the issue. In this respect, interest groups form an important part of the legislative process and play a significant role in influencing public policy.

In order to be able to study the attitudes of legislators toward these social organizations which have interests in the laws enacted by the 1961
General Assembly, we prepared a list of nine organizations and asked
the legislators to rate these organizations according to their effectiveness in influencing public policy. As a result of these ratings, we were
able to make some statements about the relative effectiveness of selected organizations in the Indiana legislature.

Figure 6 sets forth the Republican-Democratic ratings of the legislative effectiveness of nine organizations. The organizations are arranged
according to their effectiveness when both parties' scores are averaged
together. An index of effectiveness was calculated in the same manner
as was the index of agreement, except that here, the legislators were
asked to rate the organization as "very effective," "somewhat effective,"
"undecided," "relatively ineffective," or "completely ineffective." It
also warrants mention that only candidates who had previous legislative experience were asked to rate these organizations for their effectiveness.

There are several striking features about Figure 6. First, it is easily
seen that Democrats and Republicans demonstrated a high level of
agreement in their ratings of legislative effectiveness. The correlation
coefficient on this ranking is a very high +.98. When this statistic is
compared with the −.36 correlation between Democratic and Republican attitudes toward the policies of different interest groups, it at
once becomes clear that legislators seem to perform the very difficult
task of preventing their feelings about a group's policies from contami-
nating their judgment about the effectiveness of the group in the legislature.

In order to examine more closely the relationship between agreement with group policy and rating of group effectiveness, we studied
the rankings given to the four organizations included in each listing.
The organizations purposely included in both were the State Teachers
Association, the State Chamber of Commerce, the Farm Bureau, and
the State AFL-CIO. When only these four organizations are considered, the Republicans and Democrats demonstrated almost complete
disagreement in their attitudes toward group policies. The correlation
is −.80. However, the coefficient of correlation between Republican
and Democrat rankings of these same four groups' legislative effectiveness is a high +.80. Thus, although the Republicans and Democrats
were at opposite poles concerning their attitudes toward the policies of
these groups, party members did not allow their sentiments to over-
power their judgments of the groups' legislative effectiveness.

Ignoring the rankings of the groups and considering only the scores
alone, we found some systematic differences between the ratings of

Selected Interest Groups Ranked According to Legislators'
Opinions, by Party, of their Legislative Effectiveness

INDEX OF EFFECTIVENESS: +100 -- EVERY RESPONDENT RATED THE ORGANIZATION "VERY EFFECTIVE"
-100 -- EVERY RESPONDENT RATED THE ORGANIZATION "COMPLETELY INEFFECTIVE"

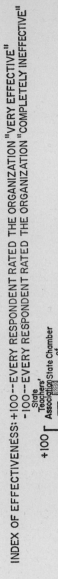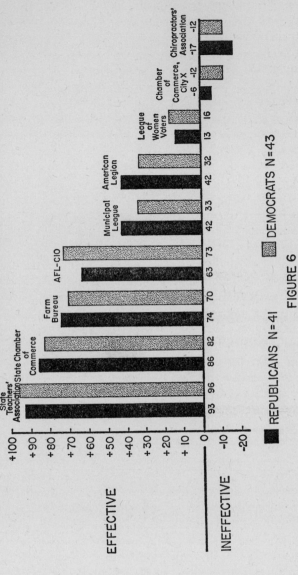

REPUBLICANS N=41    DEMOCRATS N=43

FIGURE 6

group effectiveness and attitudes toward group policies. In each of the four cases of overlapping groups, there was a definite tendency for party members who agree with the group's policies to score that group slightly higher in legislative effectiveness. Thus, Republicans scored the State Chamber and the Farm Bureau a little higher than the Democrats, who countered by assessing the State Teachers and the AFL-CIO higher than the Republicans. Apparently, this is in contradiction to the previous statement that attitudes toward policies do not influence ratings of effectiveness. However, these differences in scores are small and perhaps can be accounted for by the wording of the question. As was said, the question was designed for purposes other than a rating of groups according to effectiveness. Therefore, the question in the schedule was worded: "Could you give me your estimate of how effective these organizations are in influencing public policy and *especially of how effective they are in making their case before the legislature?*" (Italics added.) It is probable that a small percentage of legislators allowed the italicized portion of the question to affect their judgment, so that, if they tended to agree with the organization's policies, they tended to be more favorable to the presentation of the organization's case before the legislature. Pending further examination and other study, this explanation is advanced to account for these apparent exceptions to the general rule.

One other thing to be noted from Figure 6 is that not all organizations were rated on the effective side. Undoubtedly, there would be other interest groups which would have been rated ineffective, but we wished to include more or less well-known organizations which, almost by definition, are the effective ones.[4]

## The Most Powerful Groups in Indiana State Politics

During the course of our interviews with the legislative candidates, but before asking them to rate organizations for their effectiveness, we asked each legislator this question: "You hear a lot these days about the power of interest groups and lobbies in state politics. What would you say are the most powerful organizations of this kind here in Indiana?" We then recorded the groups named by the legislator. Figure 7 portrays the results of a Republican-Democratic analysis of the survey data on that question. Several important facts arise out of these data. First, labor, which is fourth in legislative effectiveness, was viewed as the most powerful organization in state politics, above the State Teachers Association, which ranked first on legislative effectiveness. It needs to be emphasized that these were two entirely different questions

## Selected Interest Groups Ranked According to Legislators' Opinions, by Party, of their Powerfulness

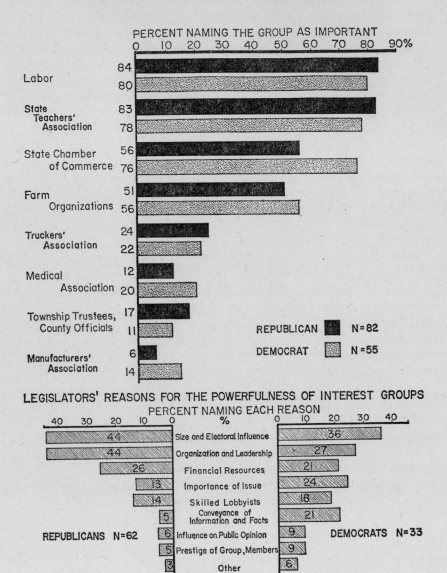

PERCENT NAMING THE GROUP AS IMPORTANT

| | Republican | Democrat |
|---|---|---|
| Labor | 84 | 80 |
| State Teachers' Association | 83 | 78 |
| State Chamber of Commerce | 56 | 76 |
| Farm Organizations | 51 | 56 |
| Truckers' Association | 24 | 22 |
| Medical Association | 12 | 20 |
| Township Trustees, County Officials | 17 | 11 |
| Manufacturers' Association | 6 | 14 |

REPUBLICAN   N=82
DEMOCRAT   N=55

### LEGISLATORS' REASONS FOR THE POWERFULNESS OF INTEREST GROUPS

PERCENT NAMING EACH REASON

| REPUBLICANS N=62 | | DEMOCRATS N=33 |
|---|---|---|
| 44 | Size and Electoral Influence | 36 |
| 44 | Organization and Leadership | 27 |
| 26 | Financial Resources | 21 |
| 13 | Importance of Issue | 24 |
| 14 | Skilled Lobbyists | 18 |
| 5 | Conveyance of Information and Facts | 21 |
| 6 | Influence on Public Opinion | 9 |
| 5 | Prestige of Group Members | 9 |
| 3 | Other | 6 |

FIGURE 7

designed to get at different information. When the whole complex of state politics is considered, both Republicans and Democrats named labor as powerful more frequently than they named any other organization. Of those who gave specific reasons for labor's power in state politics, about one-half of the Republicans and Democrats alike cited the size of the membership and the potential electoral influence—a factor which is somewhat removed from the legislative arena. The bulk of the other reasons given for labor's power could be labeled organizational factors.

For those who volunteered specific reasons for the power of the State Teachers Association in state politics, the prestige of the group and its members was named about 30 percent of the time, followed closely by credit given to organizational factors and also to its lobbyists.

About 40 percent of those who gave reasons for the power of the State Chamber of Commerce listed the information-providing function of the Chamber as its main asset. Another 30 percent emphasized the Chamber's financial resources, which frequently were mentioned for their contribution to the information-providing service in that finances enable the Chamber to maintain the staff necessary for the job.

In the eyes of the legislative candidates, the farm organizations owed their influence mainly to the size of membership (30%), to the prestige of its members (25%), and to organizational factors (15%). Included under the title "farm organizations" were some scattered mentions of the Farmers Union, but the bulk of the references were to the Farm Bureau.

Returning to Figure 7 and examining the reasons given for the power of interest groups in general, it is clear that both parties named size and electoral influence as the most important source of power for organizations which are influential in Indiana state politics. Organization and leadership emerge as the next most important reason for the power of interest groups in state politics. The only outstanding difference between the two parties and the reasons given for the influence of interest groups appears in the fact that Democrats seemed to attribute more importance to the information provided by these organizations. No satisfactory explanation of this occurrence was advanced, but one of the authors is pursuing additional research on personality factors and group-orientations which may provide the answer.

One additional remark about the data is in order here. It will be remembered that Republican-Democratic rankings of group effectiveness in the legislative process were substantially independent of agreement with the group policy. However, this independence does not exist when party members rate groups for their power in state politics. In most of the cases, party members who tended to disagree with the policies of specific interest groups were more likely to name that group as powerful in Indiana state politics. These relationships can be seen in the party ratings on agreement and power for the State Teachers Association, the State Chamber of Commerce, the farm organizations, the Medical Association, and the Manufacturers Association. A tentative explanation for this relationship, but one which requires further research, is that the phrase "most powerful" organizations has some unfavorable connotations, and that some respondents were likely to impute "power" to groups with which they disagree.

To conclude this treatment of interest groups in the legislative process, it may be well to report on the legislators' replies to the question: "What personal qualities and factors in his background make for an effective lobbyist in the legislature?" There were no significant Republican-Democratic differences in the responses to this question. About 70 percent of the legislators stressed, above all other factors, the honesty and personal integrity of the lobbyist. This was followed by a high regard for a thorough knowledge of the subject matter (53%), the importance of an agreeable personality (38%), a demonstration of helpfulness in conducting research and providing information (16%), and the benefit of previous legislative experience (12%). Only 5 percent of our sample of Indiana state legislators responding to this question thought formal education to be of special value to a lobbyist and the same percentage rated persuasiveness as important. The data indicate that legislators seek in lobbyists mainly those factors which promise to aid them in their difficult task of ascertaining facts and opinions involved in legislative issues so that they can be better informed when attempting to formulate public policy in unfamiliar subject-matter areas.

## Political Career Patterns of the Members of the 1961 Session

The summer interviews concluded by asking the candidates some general questions about personal aspects of their political careers. When asked how they would rate their legislative service as a personal experience, about 80 percent of the candidates who had served in previous sessions replied that their personal experience in the legislature was most enjoyable. Only 20 percent of the men rated the experience as simply "satisfactory," and none rated it "unsatisfactory." These data conform to previous findings by David Derge, who questioned a group of legislators who had retired between 1945 and 1955.

When asked whether or not they intended to continue their political careers if they won in the 1960 election, nine out of ten of the candidates answered yes. This indicated that the voters of Indiana would have an opportunity to pass judgment on 90 percent of the legislators for their jobs done in the 1961 session. About three-fourths of the 1961 legislators stated that they were content to continue their political careers by remaining in the Indiana General Assembly. However, the other quarter thought they might try their hands at running for other offices, with at least three individuals having congressional aspirations.

The public seems to have some feeling that legislative service can be of benefit to the earning power of a legislator in his own business or occupation. The argument runs that the legislator acquires new business contacts from different parts of the state or that he benefits from increased stature in his home community because of his high political office. The data show that this generalization cannot apply to all occupational groups. While it is true that about half of the lawyers reported that legislative service helps their law practice, about 30 percent of the lawyers claimed that they could not make up in two years what they had lost by closing down their practice for more than two months. Half of the nonlawyers believed that legislative service makes no difference in their personal earning power, while one-third claimed that their finances suffer from legislative service. The remaining 20 percent stated that their incomes are given a boost. At least until additional research is conducted on this question, it seems most accurate to conclude simply that no clear pattern emerges from the data and that legislative service appears to have different effects on personal earning power in accordance with particular situations.

## 3 / Influence and Interaction in a State Legislative Body

*Wayne L. Francis*

THE PURPOSE OF THIS CHAPTER IS TO INVESTIGATE DISTRIBUTIONS OF influence in a legislative body, to spell out the resulting hypotheses, to introduce a method for estimating the degree of interaction between legislators, and to demonstrate the relevance of specific indicators to the study of legislative behavior. The methodological task falls somewhere between the small-group laboratory situation and the more complex arena of community decision-making. Intense observation, control, and precision are sacrificed in favor of a real and vital situation. The analysis of a relatively self-sufficient political entity is lost in favor of maintaining some of the advantages of laboratory research. The universe selected for this study consists of fifty people who must directly or indirectly, but not remotely, rely upon each other in order to satisfy their official purposes.

### Distribution of Influence

Data classified here under the term "influence" are accumulated from responses to nine items included in a structured interview form. The items were administered to forty-seven of fifty members of the 1961 Indiana Senate while the 1961 session was in progress. The responses represent "attributed" influence; that is, each response is treated as a reflection of the degree of influence one senator attributes to another.

*Influence Data.* The reliability of attribution data is a function of experimental conditions. The writer judged that the conditions of this experiment were favorable. The respondents were members of a face-to-face group where knowledge about other members is likely to be relatively great, especially in view of the fact that the continuity of membership from session to session has been high. The respondents were encouraged to make only those choices about which they had information. The sample approached the total universe about which conclusions are drawn. And finally, pre-session interviewing contacts and the usual assurance of anonymity aided in establishing the proper rapport. For reasons of convenience the term "attributed" will not be reiterated in the presentation of data. It should suffice to keep in mind that interview responses are classified under "influence" because the key word in the questions asked of legislators is the word "influential."

The first question asked was as follows: Generally speaking and regardless of the legislator's formal position, who would you say are the most influential members of your chamber when it comes to determining policy?

The second question was stated in the following way: Regardless of the legislator's formal position, who would you say are the most influential members of your chamber in each of the following areas when it comes to determining policy?

Eight areas were then considered:

1. Local Government
2. Agriculture
3. Education
4. Appropriations
5. Labor
6. Business
7. Taxation
8. Benevolent Institutions

Legislators were invited to supply as many names as they wished for each item. Of the twenty-five Democrats and twenty-two Republicans interviewed for these items, no respondent named only his own party associates.[1] Approximately five names per respondent were obtained from the general influence question; the substantive area question elicited approximately two names per respondent for each item. Some respondents made no choice for certain items. Four of the substantive areas utilized reflect the names of senate committees (Agriculture, Education, Labor, Benevolent Institutions); the others do not. The distinction in design was made in order to avoid a group of responses that might adhere strictly to the formal structure of the legislature.

Senators were grouped and ranked according to the following distinctions:

1. General Influence—the number of times they were named in response to the question on general influence.
2. Specific Area Influence—the total number of times they were named in all substantive areas taken together.
3. The number of times they were named in each substantive area.
4. The number of substantive areas in which they were mentioned.

The distribution of responses for (1), (2), and (3) consistently characterizes a large majority of Senators as having relatively little or no influence. The number of mentions tends to accelerate when moving from the least to the most frequently mentioned Senator, in a graphic approximation of the "J" curve. In the substantive areas with designations that do not coincide with the names of Senate committees, the responses tend to be spread among more members. The data reveal the same distributions for each political party, when political party is held constant.

*General Influence and Specific Area Influence.* The ten Senators most frequently mentioned in the responses to the general influence question are named in a large number of substantive areas as well (Table I). Eight of the Senators ranking highest in general influence make up eight of the top nine ranked by the number of areas in which Senators were mentioned. Four of the top ten in general influence—numbers one, four, five, and ten—held Senate offices (excluding committee positions), and five of the ten were members of the minority party. Only two of the top ten general influencers were mentioned in relatively few substantive areas. Both exceptions held the office of Conference Chairman, but in opposite parties.

TABLE I

RELATIONSHIP BETWEEN GENERAL INFLUENCE AND THE
NUMBER OF SUBSTANTIVE AREAS IN WHICH GENERAL
INFLUENCERS ARE MENTIONED

| (QUESTION #1) RANK OF SENATORS BY GENERAL INFLUENCE | (QUESTION #2, ITEMS 1–8) NUMBER OF AREAS MENTIONED | | | | | | | | |
|---|---|---|---|---|---|---|---|---|---|
| | 8 | 7 | 6 | 5 | 4 | 3 | 2 | 1 | 0 |
| 1 | I | | | | | | | | |
| 2 | | | I | | | | | | |
| 3 | | I | | | | | | | |
| 4 | | I | | | | | | | |
| 5 | | | | | | I | | | |
| 6 | | I | | | | | | | |
| 7 | | I | | | | | | | |
| 8 | | | I | | | | | | |
| 9 | | | I | | | | | | |
| 10 | | | | | | I | | | |
| 11–50 | | | I | 3 | 7 | 9 | II | 6 | 3 |
| Totals | I | 4 | 4 | 3 | 7 | II | II | 6 | 3 |

## TABLE II

RELATIONSHIP BETWEEN GENERAL INFLUENCE
AND SPECIFIC AREA INFLUENCE

|  | HIGH SPECIFIC AREA INFLUENCERS | LOW SPECIFIC AREA INFLUENCERS |
|---|---|---|
| High general influencers | 21 | 4 |
| Low general influencers | 4 | 21 |

$x^2 = 23.12$, p $<$ .001.

The number of substantive areas in which legislators were named as influential, however, does not reveal the degree of influence they had in each substantive area. A handy way to gauge roughly the amount and scope of a legislator's influence is to total the number of times he is named in a variety of policy-making areas. The resulting total is described as the legislator's specific area influence score. In the Indiana Senate, Senators who scored high in specific area influence tended also to score high in general influence. To illustrate, in Table II the median serves to distinguish between high influencers and low influencers. High general influencers tend to be high specific area influencers. General influence appears to be related to several substructures of influence which are based upon policy determination within certain substantive areas.

## *Emergence of Influence*

If influence or power relationships are vital to an understanding of political phenomena, then the emergence of influence or power is of special significance. Insight into the emergence of influence can be acquired by examining attribution data. While the data and categories are derived from responses to interview questions, the resulting generalizations need not be untenable if they are otherwise consistent with our present knowledge of human behavior.

Observers of legislative activity do not need to be told there is a direct relationship between length of service and degree of influence (other things being equal). The Indiana Senate conforms to that expectation. Both general influence and specific area influence are strongly associated with length of service. In the full spread of the data for general influence rankings, there is a clear break between Senators serving in at least their fourth session and those still in their first, second, or third session. The former tend to be high general influencers, and the latter low.[2]

Specific area influence and length of service present a slightly different relationship. Of the six Senators in their third session of service
five rank high and one low in specific area influence; yet only two of
these Senators rank high in general influence. Senators in their first or
second session of service tend to be low specific area influencers.[3] Although the number of Senators involved in these correlations is fairly
small, the evidence does suggest that specific area influence tends to
precede general influence.

One cannot simply assume, however, that legislators always will first
become influential in rather specific substantive areas and then
broaden their scope of influence with time. Recall that the Conference

TABLE III

SENATORS IDENTIFIED WITH ONE SUBSTANTIVE AREA

|  | TOTAL NO. OF MENTIONS | NO. OF MENTIONS IN ONE AREA | NAME OF AREA | NO. OF AREAS MENTIONED | SPECIFIC AREA INFLUENCE RANKING |
| --- | --- | --- | --- | --- | --- |
| 1 | 44 | 41 | Benevolent Institutions | 3 | 5 |
| 2 | 39 | 36 | Labor | 3 | 6 |
| 3 | 30 | 28 | Education | 3 | 8 |
| 4 | 30 | 17 | Appropriations | 5 | 9 |

Chairmen were named a large number of times in response to the
question on general influence; yet they were named relatively few
times for the more specific influence items. It is possible that their policy specialties were not included among the influence items; however,
it was the writer's observation that they seldom attempted to argue the
specific content of important legislation. Their roles were more at-
tuned to the maintenance of party organization and discipline. One
would need to search their earlier records to see if they once possessed
an influence now lost in specific areas.

The evidence also indicates that some legislators become highly specialized without the reward of becoming generally influential in the
legislature. Of the top ten specific area influencers, four do not fall
among the top ten general influencers. The four exceptions have a
fairly similar influence description (Table III). Their recognized influence fell primarily into one substantive area. They received respectively 93, 92, 93, and 57 percent of their mentions in that single area.
Among the top ten general influencers, only the minority party Conference Chairman received more than 60 percent of his mentions in
one substantive area, and only one other received more than 50 per-

cent in one area. Furthermore, the substantive areas listed in Table III are highly significant areas from the legislators' standpoint. When Senators were asked to rate their preferences among committee assignments, Education ranked first, Finance fourth, Labor fifth, and Benevolent and Penal Institutions tenth in a listing of twenty-nine committees.

*Tentative Hypotheses.* The terms utilized to specify substantive areas of policy (taxation, labor, education, etc.) may perhaps more realistically be described as interviewing stimuli which represented different contexts of ideas; then legislators responded to these terms by naming those they regarded as influential within the context of ideas represented by each term. Alternatively, legislators responded by naming those they had heard of as influential within the same contexts.

The foregoing data then suggest that: (1) legislators generally become recognized as influential within certain policy-making areas before they achieve general influence; (2) organizational skills, falling outside the context of ideas relating to specific policy-making areas, give legislators recognition as having general influence; (3) in the terms utilized in the interviews, legislators become recognized as competent or influential in more than one context of ideas before becoming recognized as generally influential (i.e., among the top ten general influencers).

Specialization in the Indiana Senate is not as complete as one might find in other legislative bodies, such as Congress. Members of the 1961 Indiana Senate served on a minimum of three and a maximum of eight committees. When the tasks are more complex, when the stakes are higher, and when the institutional arrangements enforce a greater division of work, the emergence of influence may change accordingly. A legislator may then find that the path of least resistance calls for a demonstration of competence in a single context of ideas relating to policy and a greater emphasis upon organizational skills.

## Exercise of Influence

Influence is exercised through interaction, along patterns related to the proximity of issues, ideas, and people, and via certain styles. These facets of influence are the concern of this section. More specifically, I have devised and applied an interaction scale, an index to influence transferability, and indices to bill success and formal position success, to analyze them.

*Influence and Interaction.* Influence is exercised through interaction in one form or another. Like influence, interaction is an elusive concept. Ambiguity is reduced, it may be hoped, when such concepts are applied to specific sets of data. In this chapter "interaction" is described in a scale administered to forty-eight of fifty members of the Indiana Senate while the 1961 session was in progress. Every Senator was asked to rate every other Senator according to the following items and scale of weights:

0—Do not connect the name with the face
1—Recognize him, but have only a greeting acquaintance
2—Stop and talk with him regularly
3—Aid each other in common activities through actual personal contact
4—Visit or entertain in each other's house, apartment, or rooms, or eat meals together frequently, as well as aid each other in common activities

The total of scores that each Senator received was calculated and utilized as a rough measure of his degree of interaction. For this immediate research Senators were then grouped into quartiles by ranking their interaction scores.[4]

TABLE IV

RELATIONSHIP BETWEEN GENERAL INFLUENCE
AND LEGISLATIVE INTERACTION

|                           | INTERACTORS | | | |
|---------------------------|:-----------:|:----:|:---:|:-----------:|
|                           | VERY HIGH | HIGH | LOW | VERY LOW |
| High general influencers  | 11 | 10 | 3 | 1 |
| Low general influencers   | 1 | 3 | 9 | 12 |

$x^2 = 23.12$, p $<$ .001, when df $=$ 1.

Both influence and interaction scores are calculated from responses to interview items; however, the judgments necessitated by the two types of questions are quite different. The interaction scale called for a judgment applying only to the respondent when paired with each colleague in turn. The influence questions called for a judgment of each colleague's impact on the entire chamber. From these very different judgments comes the relationship between interaction scores and influence totals.

High legislative interactors (those falling above the median) tend to be high general influencers, and low legislative interactors tend to be low general influencers (Table IV). High legislative interactors

also tend to be high specific area influencers and low legislative interactors tend to be low specific area influencers.[5] The distribution of
Democrats and Republicans into high and low on these variables ap-
proximates the distribution in the chamber as a whole and can be
ruled out as an explanatory factor.

In order to exert influence, Senators must communicate either directly or indirectly with other Senators. Those who are recognized as
most influential interact at a higher rate than others; furthermore, the
items of the scale indicate that the interaction is direct and face-to-
face. Influence tends to be exerted or exercised through that type of interaction.

*Index of Influence Transferability.* The exercise of influence follows
patterns partly determined by the nature of the tasks a group must
perform. A task-diversified organization requires a number of skills,
many of which the members of the organization can recognize. Over
time skills build up priorities in relation to specific tasks. In a legislature the skills are not always easily identified, and their priorities in relation to policy-making follow no rigid standard. However, certain
patterns are distinguishable through the use of attribution data. Substantive areas of policy can be identified. The top influencers in each
area can be compared with the top influencers in every other area. Legislators with recognized skills in one area can influence other areas
with varying degrees of difficulty. Certain types of influence, that is,
are more transferable than others. For instance, influence in the area
of taxation may be more transferable than influence in the area of agriculture.

The term "transferable" is employed in place of a lengthy explanation of assumptions concerning the reasons why legislators with influence in certain areas tend to have influence in certain other areas. The
patterns along which influence is exercised are the major concern here.
The immediate and central questions are: (1) from which substantive
areas is a legislator most likely to transfer his influence to what other
substantive areas; and (2) which areas appear to be characterized by
high general influence? Rough answers to these questions can be calculated through a percentage matrix (Table V) .

The top ten influencers from each influence category are compared
with the top ten influencers of every other category.[6] In those substantive areas in which a greater percentage of top influencers overlap into
other influence categories there is also a tendency to overlap more frequently into the general influence category. For example, of the ten
members rated as having the highest influence in the area of taxation,
seven fall into the top ten in the general influence category, an overlap

which is as high as, or higher than, the overlap between general influence and any other substantive area. Correspondingly, members of the taxation influence area also fall more frequently into other substantive areas ($\bar{x} = .40$). The rank correlation coefficient of .84 demonstrates the more general nature of this tendency.

Several hypotheses can be drawn from the matrix analysis of the index of influence transferability, bearing in mind again that the matrix is composed from attribution data, while the discussion runs in terms of influence. One underlying assumption concerning the matrix

TABLE V

MATRIX OF AN INDEX OF INFLUENCE TRANSFERABILITY

| | Gen. Infl. | Tax. | Appr. | Bus. | Educ. | Agr. | Ben. | Lab. | Loc. | Area $\bar{x}$ | Area Rank | Gen. Area Infl. Rank |
|---|---|---|---|---|---|---|---|---|---|---|---|---|
| Gen. Infl. | X | .7 | .6 | .7 | .4 | .3 | .3 | .3 | .5 | | | |
| Tax. | .7 | X | .7 | .6 | .4 | .4 | .3 | .2 | .2 | .40 | 1 | 1.5 |
| Appr. | .6 | .7 | X | .4 | .5 | .4 | .2 | .3 | .2 | .39 | 2 | 3 |
| Bus. | .7 | .6 | .4 | X | .3 | .2 | .1 | .4 | .4 | .34 | 3 | 1.5 |
| Educ. | .4 | .4 | .5 | .3 | X | .2 | .3 | .2 | .2 | .30 | 4 | 5 |
| Agr. | .3 | .4 | .4 | .2 | .2 | X | .1 | .2 | .1 | .23 | 7 | 7 |
| Ben. | .3 | .3 | .2 | .1 | .3 | .1 | X | .1 | .1 | .19 | 8 | 7 |
| Lab. | .3 | .2 | .3 | .4 | .2 | .2 | .1 | X | .5 | .27 | 5 | 7 |
| Loc. | .5 | .2 | .2 | .4 | .2 | .1 | .1 | .5 | X | .26 | 6 | 4 |

$r' = .84$ *

* Rank correlation coefficient computed from formula (10.19) appearing in Allen L. Edwards, *Statistical Methods for the Behavioral Sciences* (New York, 1960), p. 195.

should be made clear. It is assumed that the substantive areas in the matrix do overlap, but that they nevertheless connote different meanings to respondents. No two substantive areas follow entirely consistent patterns when compared against other substantive areas and general influence, and no two substantive areas demonstrate a one-to-one correspondence when compared against each other. This assumption allows one to make tentative statements concerning the nature of influence transferability:

1. The higher the index of influence transferability between any two substantive areas, the easier it is for a legislator to transfer his influence from one area to the other area.
2. Conversely, the lower the index of influence transferability between any two substantive areas, the more difficult it is for a legislator to transfer his influence from one area to the other.
   EXAMPLE: It is easier for a legislator with a high influence in the area of

taxation to transfer his influence to the area of appropriations than to the area of labor.

3. At any given level of influence transferability between two substantive areas, a legislator with high influence in the area more closely associated with general influence can more easily transfer his influence to the other area than a legislator with high influence in the area less closely associated with general influence.

EXAMPLE: It is easier for a legislator with high influence in the area of taxation to transfer his influence to the area of benevolent institutions than it is for a legislator with high influence in the area of benevolent institutions to transfer his influence to the area of taxation.

4. If two substantive areas A and B have the same index value in relation to area C, and if area A is more closely associated with general influence than area B, a legislator who is identified with area A will find it easier to transfer his influence to area C than will a legislator identified with area B.

EXAMPLE: It is easier for a legislator with high influence in the area of taxation to transfer his influence to the area of labor than it is for a legislator with high influence in the area of agriculture, even though both taxation and agriculture demonstrate an index value of .2 in relation to the area of labor.

Certainly there are factors not fully taken into account when applying the index and stating the consequent hypotheses. For example, the index does not account for differences resulting from the influence rank of legislators within a given substantive area. Will a legislator with the highest rank in the area of taxation find it easier to transfer his influence to the area of education than the fifth ranking legislator in the area of taxation, assuming their ranks are equal in the area of education? Or if the answer is self-evident, then how much easier is it for him to transfer his influence to the area of education? The latter question opens up the old problem of how to measure the relative influence of individuals in a problem-solving situation, an answer for which this research will lay no claim to provide.

The index of influence transferability is further limited in the sense that it does not pinpoint the substantive and environmental complexities encountered in any specific piece of legislation, nor does it account for personality differences which might have an effect upon the influence structure.[7] Such limitations, however, do not prevent more general probability statements. Although the index may not apply to a specific legislator in regard to a specific piece of legislation, it is not so unreasonable to apply it to a group of legislators in regard to a large number of bills that fall more or less within a certain substantive area. Or it might be reasonable to advise a legislator to become recognized as competent in the areas of taxation and appropriations rather than in the areas of agriculture, benevolent institutions, or labor if he wishes to have the best chance of influencing all areas of legislation at some date in the future. Finally, the index lends itself to a more precise way of stating common-sense judgments concerning the associations between substantive areas of legislative activity as they relate to the influence structure.

*Styles of Influence.* The previous analysis, as explained, rests upon attribution data acquired through interviews. The data so gathered can be supported and supplemented by specific legislative facts, and, in turn, the arrangement of specific legislative facts can be supported by the judgments of qualified interview respondents. In this section two sets of facts are analyzed, bill sponsorship and passage data, and formal or official position data. The data are arranged into two indices: (1) the index to bill success; and (2) the index to formal position success.

The index to bill success for each legislator is defined as:

$$\frac{(\text{Number of his sponsored bills passing chamber})^2}{\text{Number of bills he sponsored}}$$

The index is the ratio of bills passed to bills sponsored, the numerator squared because of a J-distribution of bill sponsorship among Senators.

The index to formal position success for the minority party member is defined as:

$$\frac{\text{Committee assignment total}}{\text{Number of assigned committees}}$$

The committee assignment total is calculated by assigning group weights to a list of all committees ranked on the basis of the questionnaire previously mentioned, and then determining the committees to which each minority party member belongs. The same calculation is made for the majority party members, except that an allowance is made for those Senators with official chamber positions by totaling the official position weight of each (President Pro Tem = 10; Conference Chairman = 5; Committee Chairman = 3; Ranking Majority Member = 1). Thus the index to formal position success for these majority party senators is defined as:

Official Position Weight

$$X \frac{\text{Committee assignment total}}{\text{Number of assigned committees}}$$

Minority and majority party members are then ranked separately and distributed proportionally into four Senate quartiles.

Six classifications of legislators are relevant at this point. Legislators have been classified according to general influence, specific area influence, degree of interaction, the index to bill success, and the index to formal position success. The latter two are treated as indices to styles of influence. Some legislators exercise influence by actively and personally sponsoring legislation. Others seek and obtain strategic committee assignments and positions of authority, and exercise the sorts of influence that flow from these positions. Some legislators practice both styles effectively. To accommodate the third group, a sixth classification will be based upon a combination of the bill and formal position indices.[8]

Since the number of legislators involved in each classification is constant $(N = 50)$, though small, it is practical to employ the phi-coeffi-

TABLE VI

DEGREE OF ASSOCIATION BETWEEN VARIABLES

|  | GENERAL INFLUENCE | SPECIFIC AREA IN-FLUENCE | INTER-ACTION |
|---|---|---|---|
| Bill success | .20 | .36 | .44 |
| Formal position success | .20 | .44 | .28 |
| Bill and formal position success | .32 | .64 | .48 |

Phi Coefficients, $N = 50$

cient $(r\phi)$ to measure the observed degree of association between the various classifications.[9] Three relationships were considered earlier: (1) the significant relationship between general influence and specific area influence $(r = .68)$; (2) the significant relationship between general influence and degree of interaction $(r\phi = .68)$; and (3) the significant relationship between specific area influence and degree of interaction $(r\phi = .60)$. These strongly related variables can be given greater meaning when they are compared with the remaining classifications.

The index to bill success is significantly related to specific area influence and degree of interaction, but not significantly related to general influence (Table VI). Senators who sponsor a substantial number of bills which pass the chamber tend to be Senators who are high interactors. In the Indiana Senate, sponsors are generally responsible for their own bills, since no bill may have more than two named sponsors. The sponsors generally explain their own bills on the floor and quite often in committee. That they should of necessity interact with other Senators at a high rate in order to have high bill success seems quite reasonable; however, there are certainly offsetting factors such as the aid of lobbyists or the Governor's support, either of which might diminish the need for interaction by the sponsor.

Senators who have high bill success also tend to have high specific area influence. Their influence is felt within vital substantive areas of legislation. However, they are not necessarily recognized as generally influential in the chamber. The bills they sponsor may be narrow in scope, falling predominantly into one area of legislation. To be recognized as generally influential may require activities in addition to those required by bill sponsorship.

The index to bill success does not relate significantly to the index to formal position success.[10] Senators who sponsor a relatively large number of bills which pass the chamber do not necessarily achieve formal positions of authority or serve on the most sought-after committees. One type of activity neither precludes nor necessitates the other; yet, like Senators with high bill success, Senators with high formal position success tend to be high specific area influencers, high interactors, but not necessarily recognized as high general influencers. High formal position success (defined above) is not sufficient for high general influence.

Senators who have high bill and formal position success tend to be high interactors, high specific area influencers, and high general influencers. When the bill and formal position indices are combined the phi values rise in each case (Table VI). Bill and formal position success is most closely related to specific area influence $(r\phi = .64)$. Senators who serve on the most preferred committees, who hold such positions as committee chairman, and who sponsor a large number of bills which pass the chamber, are mentioned frequently as the most influential within substantive areas of legislation. Senators who practice both styles of influence effectively also tend to be recognized as generally influential $(r\phi = .32)$.

## Analysis of Exceptions

The brief analysis below attempts to explain exceptions to observed relationships, through the use of variables and relationships already considered, and with a minimum of recourse to other related variables.

In Table IV eight legislators did not fit the predominant pattern. Four were high general influencers but low interactors, and four were low general influencers and high interactors. Of the former, three were serving in at least their seventh session of the legislature and were members of the middle age group (born between 1900 and 1919) for members serving in the 1961 Senate. Experienced Senators tend to be high general influencers, as previously noted. Senators born between 1900 and 1919 also tend to be high general influencers (Table VII). But why do a few highly experienced Senators approaching the age norm of the chamber have a tendency to interact at a low rate?

Perhaps they have learned to communicate efficiently in order to fulfill their policy desires, or possibly the mere fact that they do approach the age norm has an effect which reduces the need for high interaction. It should be stressed, however, that the interaction questionnaire was designed to test interaction for only the 1961 session. Past interaction in previous sessions may very well carry over into the influence structure of the session under study, yet this past interaction would not nec-

### TABLE VII

RELATIONSHIP BETWEEN AGE
AND GENERAL INFLUENCE

| DATE OF BIRTH | HIGH GENERAL INFLUENCERS | LOW GENERAL INFLUENCERS |
|---|---|---|
| 1900–1919 | 17 | 9 |
| Before 1900 or After 1919 | 8 | 16 |

$x^2 = 5.12$, $p < .05$.

essarily register for certain items on the questionnaire. Finally, there is the possibility that the Senators had outside sources of influence which minimized the need for high interaction with other Senators. All but the last of these suggestions prove too much: they are as applicable to the normal as to the deviant cases.

The fourth Senator who was characterized as having high general influence and low interaction was a freshman Senator who interacted at a higher rate, at least, than any other freshman Senator—a borderline case.

Of the four Senators who were characterized as having low general influence but high interaction rates, one fell into the oldest age group and was serving in his sixth session, one was a female legislator, and the remaining two were in their second and third sessions of service. The latter two were rated high in specific area influence and would conform to the previous hypothesis on the emergence of influence if they should become recognized as general influencers in future sessions of the legislature. The other two evidently were content to talk without action.

The exceptions to the direct relationship between specific area influence and degree of interaction can to a large extent be accounted for by the same reasoning, partly because many of the same legislators are involved. Four of the ten exceptions to this second relationship appear to be of a different character, however, all four were in either their second or third session of service which appears to be a transitional phase of interaction and influence in the Indiana Senate.

There are eight exceptions to the direct relationship between general influence and specific area influence. All but one were in their second or third session. These exceptions did not support the hypothesis that specific area influence precedes general influence, nor did they support the contrary. On the other hand, the evidence did suggest that those classified as high specific area influencers but low general influencers were named significantly more frequently in one single substantive area than were those classified as low specific area influencers but high general influencers.

## Further Research on Influence and Interaction

What has the previous analysis accomplished? And what are the new avenues of research for studying the influential and the influenced? These are the questions to be explored in this final section.

Fifty state legislators of the Indiana Senate come together to settle their official business about every two years. Approximately 80 percent of them will have served at least one previous session in the Senate. They must rely upon each other, in part, to satisfy their official purposes. They will inevitably accumulate knowledge of their legislative environment, through firsthand observation, and by word of mouth. Much of this knowledge will be related to influence. The results of this research show that there is a conclusive and positive relationship between legislators' perceptions of influence and specific indices of legislative action.

The legislative environment is much more complex than this work can hope to portray. Many of the most important elements of legislative politics have been ignored. The governor and his staff, administrative agencies, news media, and pressure groups certainly have a profound effect upon policy in the state, not to mention the second chamber of the legislature. A full analysis of influence must take all major elements into account, and not just the activity of one subset whose elements are members of the Indiana Senate. In the long run, it is the policies of government (the output) that must be understood in relation to the behavior of policy-making participants (the input).

The previous analysis also demonstrates that the nature of influence can vary markedly from policy area to policy area. Any larger study of influence may need to account for these differences. One explanation has been offered. Legislative specialization has led to the growth of expertise in complex policy-making areas, such as the area of taxation, or finance. The locus of expertise will be a locus of influence, a base from which messages of instruction can be sent out to the larger legislative community. Does the legislature form its own brand of expertise? Or does it leave it up to the executive branch? Or does this depend upon the area of policy? Perhaps expertise does not exist in some areas.

Now I have suggested that: (1) the scope of research may be expanded by including all of the important participants in the Indiana legislative process, and (2) the character of influence may be better understood if its differentiation by policy area is examined more intensely. One step further, probably all facets of influence would be comprehended more fully if more than one state were studied. Indiana may be typical or it may be unique in its legislative practices. Learning proceeds by comparing one thing to another, or by comparing many things to each other simultaneously. Comparing the Indiana General Assembly with other state legislatures would be enlightening. In fact, why not compare all state legislatures and their environs at once? Contemporary correlation procedures invite this type of research and analysis. Causal inference, for example, is made possible through the use of simultaneous equations.[11]

It is useless to discuss any further the study of influence, however, unless the very term "influence" is recognized for what it is. Influence is a general term, a term that designates many kinds of interactions among people. "A causes B to act" is perhaps the most descriptive statement of influence available. What causes A to cause B to act? If it is C, and if A, B, and C are people, then we are describing interpersonal influence. C can also be some particular goal in the mind of A. Then we might begin to talk about drives, desires, or perhaps an entire array of things in the background of A that caused him to seek goal C. Perhaps these things in the background of A are constituents, parents, or friends. Perhaps they are environmental (e.g., a virus that caused A to become very ill in an earlier year, and now A tells B to support a health bill to finance medical research).

By saying that A causes B to act, it is meant, in the simplest sense, that two events have occurred, and that the occurrence of the first event contributes to the occurrence of the second event. Such a relationship can only be implied, or inferred, and cannot be proven. Yet it is something that people experience all their lives, the hand moving the apple, one person telling another what to do. The political scientist hopes that even without formal training in the art, the human mind will record the sequences of events before it, and that the human mind will draw reasonable inferences from them. For this reason legislators and others may be petitioned to evaluate the patterns of influence (A causing B), or events, to which they are exposed.

DIAGRAM 1

CAUSAL NET STRUCTURE IN TIME DIMENSION
FOR SINGLE INDIVIDUAL

TIME ZONES

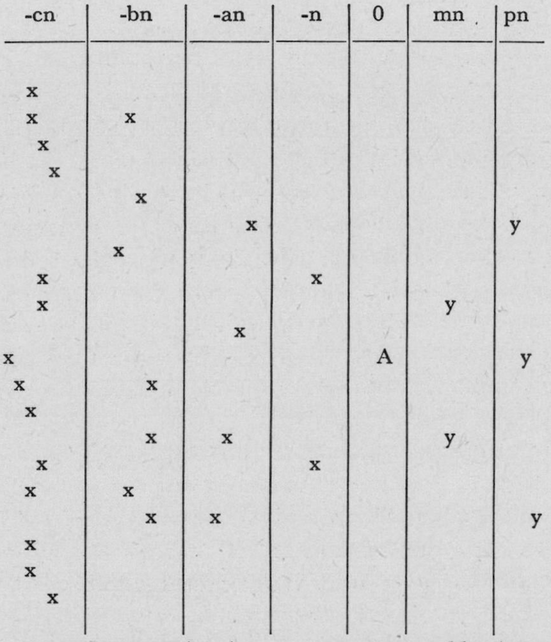

| -cn | -bn | -an | -n | 0 | mn | pn |
|-----|-----|-----|-----|-----|-----|-----|
| x | | | | | | |
| x | x | | | | | |
| x | | | | | | |
| x | | | | | | |
| | | x | | | | |
| | | x | | | | y |
| | x | | | | | |
| x | | | x | | | |
| x | | | | | y | |
| | | x | | | | |
| x | | | | A | | y |
| x | x | | | | | |
| x | | | | | | |
| | x | x | | | y | |
| x | | | x | | | |
| x | x | | | | | |
| | x | x | | | | y |
| x | | | | | | |
| x | | | | | | |
| | x | | | | | |

x = events causing A.    y = events caused by A.

The study of influence is a study of causal sequence. Causal sequences are often described by a net structure, as illustrated in Diagram I. A net structure oversimplifies reality for the purposes of analysis. It is a way of simulating, or modelling, the environment. In the diagram, the event of interest occurs at time zero (o). Let us assume that it is the action of a single legislator on a roll call vote. The event must take the form of either "Yes" or "No." Its form should be predicted from knowledge of its causes, symbolized by "x" in each case. Events caused by A are symbolized by "y." The x's (or causes) are classified into rough time zones. Any given x may cause A either directly, indirectly, or both. For purposes of analysis one can assume that an x cannot cause another x unless it is another time zone, and, of course, in an earlier time zone.

For causal analysis, I think it is helpful to think in terms of time zones. Basic time zones related to legislative processes are easily distinguishable. The researcher could begin delineating early childhood experiences (social background) , then in turn early career experience, primary and election experience before the session under study, leadership selection and committee assignments, the introduction of bills, committee action and the interaction of legislative participants, and the roll call voting act. The more intense the research, the more refined are the distinctions.

How intense does research need to be? Certainly it is impossible to trace every relevant event. Net structures are not sufficiently economical to incorporate the almost infinite complexity of even a single legislative session. Again it would seem that the answer lies in inference. It can be inferred that certain events will occur without observing them directly. Interaction and influence processes can be inferred. The task is to gather enough information that probability inference is appropriate. Inferences can be tested by predicting real events, such as roll call votes.

How much needs to be known to infer interaction and influence processes? No a priori answer can be given, of course, but the specific types of knowledge to be sought can be suggested. In a cross-national study it might be necessary to begin with cultural norms and a fairly high-level organizational theory. Representative bodies vary so markedly from country to country that it would be impossible to overlook many assumptions which now seem too obvious to repeat when describing American legislatures. But if our attention is confined to American legislatures, top priority knowledge takes more specific form. First, legislative participants must, in the abstract, be assigned goals. For only then can inferences about their goal-seeking behavior be drawn. Second, they must also be assigned propensities. When seeking goals, legislators will be inclined to act in certain ways. So will lobbyists and administrators. Knowledge of goals and propensities makes it possible to draw inferences about interaction and influence, and thus causal sequence. Recent literature has cast much light upon this subject. In particular, the studies of legislative role typologies have provided many important insights into the goals and propensities of legislative participants.[12] In a recent article, I have tried to point out how this type of knowledge might be applied when the goal of the legislative participant is to remove his uncertainty about an issue.[13]

Once sufficient data have been gathered to make reasonable inferences about legislative behavior, there is still the work of putting it together into systematic form. One of the more intriguing possibilities is found in the recent uses of computers for simulation and modelling. Large amounts of information can be stored and processed in a way that is analogous to real-life processes. Computer predictions of roll call votes, for example, can be employed to test the validity of the analogy, or model.

# 4 / Party Responsibility: Fact or Fiction in an American State Legislature?

*M. Margaret Conway*

THE IDEA OF PARTY RESPONSIBILITY HAS INTERESTED MANY POLITICAL scientists in recent years. Basic tenets of party responsibility theory, as stated by Thomas A. Flinn, include the following three conditions: "(a) intra-party cohesion and inter-party conflict in legislative situations; (b) communication of the facts of legislative combat; and (c) an attentive public."[1] Flinn hypothesized that the presence of these conditions are related to the presence of a number of independent variables. This study deals with only the first component of party responsibility, and, more specifically, considers whether the first component of party responsibility—intra-party cohesion and inter-party conflict—existed in Indiana's legislative system during the 1963 Indiana General Assembly.[2]

In 1963, the Indiana House of Representatives had fifty-six Republican and forty-four Democratic members; neither party had a constitutional majority in the Senate because one Republican Senator died after the election and prior to the convening of the legislature. His death left the Republicans with a working majority of twenty-five votes (to twenty-four Democratic ones) but without the required constitutional majority of twenty-six votes needed for final passage of legislation on third reading. A constitutional majority is one-half plus one of the elected members, or twenty-six votes in the Senate and fifty-one votes in the House. The Governor, a Democrat, was in the second legislative session of his four-year term and ineligible for re-election. The Lieutenant Governor (and thus also President of the Senate) was a Republican, as were the Senate Majority Leader and the Speaker of the House of Representatives.

At least two political scientists have attributed considerable influence in maintaining party cohesion in the legislature to party machinery within the legislature and throughout the state.[3] The Republican party's behavior in the 1963 Indiana General Assembly did not conform to this expectation.

The breakdown in party machinery within the legislature can be considered a result of deliberate attempts by potential rivals for the 1964 Republican nominations for state-wide office and by their supporters to embarrass those Republican legislative leaders who were potential nominees for these offices. The Lieutenant Governor was the most prominent potential nominee for Governor; and the Senate Majority Leader was a prominent potential candidate for U.S. Senator. The Speaker of the House, an ally of the Lieutenant Governor in his quest for the governorship, was rumored to desire the nomination for Lieutenant Governor.[4] Although some jockeying for future political advantage took place in the House, the Senate was the main arena, since the opponents of the Republican leadership in the House and in the Senate could attribute lack of accomplishment by Senate Republicans to insufficient leadership ability on the part of the Lieutenant Governor and the Senate Majority Leader. Of course, the fact that Republicans did not have a constitutional majority in the Senate was advantageous to Senate Republicans engaged in intra-party warfare.

Thus, two anti-leadership factions[5] encouraged Republican Senators to oppose policy stands taken by the Senate Republican leaders. Their tactics were successful in undermining the influence of the party leadership. Their success is understandable. For in Indiana if a legislator wishes to obstruct the aims of his party's leadership, the sanctions the leadership can apply are generally insufficient to hold him to support the program of the legislative leadership, particularly if he believes his actions can contribute to the future nomination for higher office of a member of another faction more acceptable to him. The possibility of future advantages from the nomination or election of a person more pleasing to a legislator's personal or political tastes are probably of greater value than the positive or negative results of any sanction the current leadership can apply.

The primary positive sanctions available are appointments to desired legislative committees, hiring of legislative patronage employees recommended by a legislator, and appointments to the Legislative Advisory Commission or to one of its committees. The first two sanctions are used prior to or at the beginning of the session; thus they are often ineffective because they are too soon used up. During the session the leadership may be able to exert some influence by threatening to assign a legislator's bill to an unfavorable committee or by promising to assign it to a favorable committee; in the Indiana General Assembly, however, this influence is quite limited.

The party machinery throughout the state was also ineffective in maintaining party cohesion because it was split by the same factions which disrupted the party machinery within the legislature. The state committee did make an attempt to maintain cohesion by establishing a special liaison committee to coordinate party legislative efforts. A special effort was needed since the party had a majority in the legislature, but did not control the governorship. The committee was relatively inactive, however, and had almost no effect on legislation.

Traditionally, the state chairman of the party not controlling the governorship is not expected to take a role in policy-making. The state chairman of the party controlling the governorship is completely dominated by the Governor. In 1963 the Republican state chairman tried but was unable to dictate policy or voting decisions to the majority of Republican legislators.[8] The Republican legislators did consult frequently with the state chairman and state committee, but these consultations were primarily for the purpose of explaining tax legislation, legislation in other substantive areas, and assessing possible consequences of the enactment of such legislation. A subcommittee of the Republican state committee did draft a series of legislative proposals on the subject of election laws but most of the proposals were defeated in the Senate since no Democrat would vote for the proposals and the Republicans lacked a constitutional majority. With the exception of these election proposals, unified proposals for legislative programs were developed by Republican legislative leaders and not by the state chairman or state committee.

The state chairman did, however, exert some influence on policy because he was also county chairman of the Republican party in Marion County, the most populous county in the state. In his own county, he was reputed to control or greatly influence the precinct committeemen, the nominating process, and campaign finances. Before the recent reapportionment, Marion County had six Senators and twelve House members, who, because they are elected at large and not by district usually are all of one party. This bloc election of representatives and the large number of representatives apportioned to the county made these delegations very influential within their party. In 1963 these delegations were Republican. The loyal-to-the-county-chairman element in them was large enough to impede any Republican proposal unless some Democrats voted for it. Most other local party officials and party organizations did not try to influence the legislators' voting behavior and those who tried weren't successful.

Thus, neither state nor local nor legislative party organizations appeared to contribute to the maintenance of Republican party cohesion in the 1963 Indiana legislature—and probably various elements of the party contributed to party conflict. Different elements of the party, at times, were divided in their policy preferences. This division was based on differences in policy preferences and rivalry for the 1964 nominations for state-wide offices.

It is assumed that the existence of intra-party cohesion and interparty conflict can be shown by the amount of conflict on roll call votes on Republican Party platform legislation in the 1963 General Assembly.[7] The ninety legislative measures were selected by the Republican Party's 1963 legislative leadership to carry out commitments made in the 1962 Indiana Republican Party Platform. That platform consisted of nineteen planks, but only thirteen of them could be implemented by the Indiana Republican legislators. Some could not be implemented because they required Republican control of the executive branch; others could be carried out only by Congressmen and not by state legislators. Thus, the platform contained thirteen planks capable of being executed by Republican state legislators. Since the platform statements were relatively unspecific, the Republican legislative leaders had some latitude in both the number and the details of the measures they could select to comply with the platform commitments. The Republican legislative leadership involved in selecting legislative vehicles to accomplish platform objectives included the Speaker of the House, the House Majority Leader, the President of the Senate (Lieutenant Governor), and the Senate Majority Leader.

These specific legislative proposals selected by the legislative leadership had several sources of origin: the Republican State Central Committee; the Republican-dominated Legislative Advisory Commission; Republican Policy committees of the legislature; individual members of the legislature; and bi-partisan agencies of the state government.

## Method

The data analyzed are all roll call votes on the ninety legislative measures alluded to previously. Both substantive and procedural roll calls were examined because procedural maneuvering is an essential element of the legislative struggle. Two indices were applied to each roll call: the index of cohesion and the index of likeness. The index of cohesion measures intra-party cohesion and is calculated "by dividing the number of votes cast by party members who were in the majority in the party on a roll call by the total number of party members who voted. The percentage thus obtained will range from 50 to 100, and is converted, for convenience of presentation, to a scale of 0 to 100." The index of likeness measures the difference in the degree of support given a measure by two groups—in this study, Republicans and Democrats; thus, the index of likeness measures the opposite of inter-party conflict. The index of likeness is calculated by "subtracting the percentage of 'yea' votes cast by one group from the percentage of 'yea' votes cast by the other, and subtracting the result from 100." [8]

After each index was calculated for each roll call, an average index of cohesion and an average index of likeness were calculated for each of the thirteen subject-matter areas of the party platform support list. On the basis of these data, generalizations can be made about the nature of intra-party cohesion and inter-party conflict. Factors which might be related to differences in cohesion and likeness are also examined.

## Findings

The index of cohesion is zero on a roll call if the parties are evenly divided. The analysis of roll call votes in Tables I and II shows that both parties displayed a relatively high degree of cohesion, but that there was less intra-party cohesion in the Republican party than in the Democratic party. In the Senate the Republicans had an average index of cohesion of 80 or higher in six of the thirteen issue areas while the Democrats had an average index of cohesion of 80 or higher in eight issue areas. In the House the Republicans had an average index of 80 or higher in eight issue areas while the Democrats had an average index of 80 or higher in eleven areas.

The analysis of the roll call votes rejects the hypothesis that there was high inter-party conflict on Republican platform bills and resolutions. In each chamber the average index of likeness fell below 80 in only four of the thirteen issue areas: In the Senate these areas were Crime and Penal Institutions, Elections, Limited Tax Reform, and Reapportionment; in the House these areas were Navigation, Elections, Urban Affairs, and Reapportionment. That the average index of likeness was high in nine of the thirteen issue areas in each chamber indicates a relative absence of inter-party conflict.

Malcolm Jewell points out that certain types of issues are more likely to create party conflict. The two major types of issues on which party conflict is more likely to occur are those indicative of socioeconomic conflict and those based on party interest.[9]

It is suggested that the first type of issue may arise because Republicans in theory represent districts with certain socioeconomic characteristics and Democrats represent districts with other socioeconomic characteristics. The only party platform issue of this nature on which low party likeness occurred was that of limited tax reform in the Senate.

Several other measures involved socioeconomic problems, including a proposed constitutional amendment permitting the classification of property for tax purposes. This resolution was amended in the Senate to prohibit a graduated net income tax, to change the distribution of gasoline tax revenues, and to tighten the assessment and collection of local property taxes.

The second type of issue, one of party interest, covers a variety of subjects, including control of state patronage, support or opposition to

TABLE I

AVERAGE INDICES OF COHESION AND LIKENESS AND PARTY VOTES
REPUBLICAN PLATFORM MEASURES, SENATE

| SUBJECT AREA | INDEX OF LIKENESS | INDICES OF COHESION REPUBLICAN-DEMOCRAT | |
|---|---|---|---|
| State Government | 100 | 100 | 100 |
| Crime and Penal Institutions | 70 | 69 | 82 |
| Labor | 98 | 72 | 84 |
| Highways | 83 | 73 | 79 |
| Agriculture | 88 | 68 | 82 |
| Conservation and Recreation | 90 | 81 | 100 |
| Navigation | 100 | 100 | 100 |
| Elections | 43 | 79 | 96 |
| Urban Affairs | 86 | 49 | 69 |
| Mental Health | 97 | 94 | 100 |
| Limited Tax Reform | 29 | 90 | 97 |
| Reapportionment | 39 | 89 | 80 |
| Education | 83 | 52 | 95 |

the incumbent administration by a particular political party, revision of the election laws, change in the administrative structure of key municipalities, and control of the apportionment of the state legislature.[10] Certainly in the 1963 Indiana General Assembly these areas of party interest were the subject of conflict. Election laws were the subject of several conflicts characterized by low party likeness. However, Republican party cohesion on election law roll calls was not as high as might be expected, possibly because some legislators voted to support revisions which would be most advantageous to their own re-election, regardless of the impact on their party. Several roll calls can be evaluated as tests of the opposition to the administration. The roll calls in the House on the proposal to construct a deep-water port on Lake Michigan were of this nature. Another party-interest issue on which low party likeness occurred was reapportionment. However, intraparty cohesion was low on those roll calls held during the special ses-

sion in the House of Representatives, when desperation forced many
seeking to preserve their political careers to deviate from the party
stands preferred by the leadership of both parties. A bill concerned
with metropolitan transportation problems in the capital city became
involved in inter-party politics in the House and also generated conflict within the Republican party. In summary, that part of Jewell's
hypothesis which predicts that low party likeness and party conflict
will occur on issues defined by legislators as party-interest measures is

TABLE II

AVERAGE INDICES OF COHESION AND LIKENESS AND PARTY VOTES
REPUBLICAN PLATFORM MEASURES, HOUSE

| SUBJECT | INDEX OF LIKENESS | INDICES OF COHESION | |
|---|---|---|---|
| | | REPUBLICAN-DEMOCRAT | |
| State Government | 100 | 100 | 100 |
| Crime and Penal | | | |
| Institutions | 85 | 93 | 90 |
| Labor | 98 | 96 | 100 |
| Highways | 92 | 75 | 85 |
| Agriculture | 95 | 100 | 90 |
| Conservation and | | | |
| Recreation | 88 | 74 | 97 |
| Navigation | 12 | 94 | 82 |
| Elections | 62 | 69 | 88 |
| Urban Affairs | 56 | 51 | 83 |
| Mental Health | 98 | 100 | 96 |
| Limited Tax Reform | 96 | 99 | 94 |
| Reapportionment | 38 | 66 | 61 |
| Education | 93 | 82 | 74 |

confirmed by the study of voting behavior on Republican platform
measures. Those issues relating to opposition or support of the administration, to revision of the election laws, to reapportionment of the
state legislature, and to regulation of urban municipal affairs in one of
the major urban areas generated higher party conflict than that which
occurred in most other platform support areas.

While these two types of issues were found to generate inter-party
conflict, in other areas inter-party likeness and lower party cohesion
existed. What factors might be related to such a pattern of legislative
voting behavior? Eulau discussed several explanations of the absence
of party conflict developed by political scientists concerned with problems relating to the explanation of unanimity in legislative voting behavior.[11] Keefe's contention that legislators are likeminded [12] is at-
tacked by Eulau as tautological, as is Truman's explanation that the
process of consensus building occurs outside the legislative chambers.[13]

Nevertheless, to some extent Truman's explanation of absence of conflict might account for the high party likeness on some Republican platform measures, since thirty of the ninety bills originated with the Legislative Advisory Commission. However, the label of origin was to some extent a convenient façade covering Republican maneuvering of contents to conform to the preferences of Republican legislative leadership. The fact that ten of the thirty bills failed to pass indicates that while conflict over some types of legislation is resolved by pre-session activities, this is not possible on all issues. Explanatory hypotheses proposed by other studies include one that conflict is concealed by false unanimity, but Eulau argues such unanimity by concealment would be difficult in a state legislature. Eulau proposes that unanimity exists where the area of disagreement is so large and the alternatives so ambiguous that a party cannot function as a cue-giver. An alternative hypothesis is that the party leadership acts as cue-giver on legislation where the alternatives are ambiguous to most legislators. The party leaders are, as other research indicates, generally expert in special fields and accorded high general influence.[14] In the absence of alternatives in the form of other bills or amendments to existing bills, little or no conflict will occur. A political party in control of the machinery of the legislature can be expected to push through its legislation with little conflict unless the opposing leadership proposes or vigorously supports amendments or alternative legislation.

What factors might be related to the variations in legislative voting behavior between the two parties on Republican platform legislation? This section will discuss several possible independent variables: constituency differences; electoral margin; legislative experience; social background regarding religion and occupation; relative availability of patronage from the state's chief executive; and majority-minority status.

The first independent variable considered is constituency differences. To test whether this variable is related to the different voting patterns of the legislators, it is necessary to find out the extent to which differences in platform support existed among legislators from different types of constituencies. Correlation analysis was used to indicate the degree of relationship between the voting behavior of legislators on Republican platform proposals (measured by their platform support score) and constituency differences (measured by four indices). The four indices used to separate the constituencies into types were: percent of the labor force employed in manufacturing in 1960; percent of the district's population living in urban areas in 1960; percent of owner-occupied residences; and population increase or decrease in the district from 1950 to 1960. These characteristics were selected because other studies found them to be related to legislative voting behavior. The percent of the labor force employed indicates the economic character of the district and the partisan nature of the constituency.[15] The percent of the district living in urban areas indicates the economic character of the district and the type of economy of the district. Some political scientists have found the urbanization of a district is also related to the party preference of the district. The percent of owner-occupied residences has been used by other researchers as indicative of both socioeconomic status and of party affiliation. The percent of population increase indicates the state of the economy in terms of growth-decline characteristics.[16] A declining or stagnant economy is re-

TABLE III

MULTIPLE CORRELATION AND PARTIAL CORRELATION COEFFICIENTS
REPUBLICAN PLATFORM VOTE SCORE AND CONSTITUENCY CHARACTERISTICS

| | PER CENT EMPLOYED IN MANU-FACTURING | PER CENT LIVING IN URBAN AREAS | PER CENT OWNER-OCCUPIED RESIDENCES | POPULATION INCREASE-DECREASE | ry .1234 |
|---|---|---|---|---|---|
| Senate: | | | | | |
|   Republicans | 0.103 | 0.308 | 0.332 | 0.246 | 0.504 |
|   Democrats | −0.059 | −0.404 | −0.283 | 0.002 | 0.477 |
| House: | | | | | |
|   Republicans | −0.191 | 0.558 | −0.004 | 0.069 | 0.635 |
|   Democrats | −0.003 | 0.249 | 0.012 | −0.014 | 0.324 |

flected in a rate of growth slower than the state average or by a decrease in the population of the legislative district.

The platform support score computed for each legislator indicates the extent of his support for measures proposed by the Republican leadership to carry out the party platform. One point was assigned each legislator for each of his roll call votes which support the Republican platform proposals. A legislator was given no point if he voted against a Republican platform proposal or was absent when a roll call vote on a Republican platform proposal was held. The Speaker of the House was not given a score because Indiana custom dictates that the Speaker does not vote unless his vote is needed to pass or defeat important legislation. In 1963 the Speaker did not vote on any of the Republican platform proposals.

In Table III, three types of statistical measurement were used: partial correlation coefficient, correlation analysis, and coefficient of multiple correlation. A partial correlation coefficient measures "the extent to which that part of the variation in the dependent variable which was not explained by the addition of new other independent factors can be explained by the addition of the new factor." [17] From the analysis using the partial correlation coefficient, it is apparent that the most significant constituency factor of the four used for explaining variation in legislators' votes for Republican platform proposals is percent of the district's population living in urban areas. The coefficient of multiple correlation estimates the relative variation of several independent variables associated with variation in the dependent variable. As can be seen from Table III, constituency factors account for approximately 40 percent of the variation in support for Republican platform measures among Republicans in the House, but only 10 percent of the variation among House Democrats. The amount of variation explained in the Senate by constituency influence is considerably less than for House Republicans and approximately the same for both parties. In the Senate these four variables account for about 25 percent of the variation in the vote score among Republicans and about 23 percent of the variation in the dependent variable among Democrats.

Another factor which might influence voting behavior is that of electoral margin. To determine whether there is a significant relationship between party loyalty and electoral margin, analysis of variance procedures were utilized. The index of party loyalty in this analysis is the platform score used previously. (It measures the number of roll call votes on which the legislator voted to support the legislation selected by the Republican party legislative leadership to carry out the 1962 Indiana Republican party platform.) Legislators in each party in each house were divided into three groups on the basis of the percent of total vote cast for that legislative office which the legislator received in the preceding election. This was the 1962 election for all House members and for twenty-five senators, and the 1960 election for the remaining senators. The following categories were used: received less than 54.9 percent of the total vote; received 55 to 59.9 percent of the total vote; received 60 percent or more of the total vote. The results of analysis of variance procedures (Tables IV, V, VI, and VII) indicate no significant relationship between party loyalty and electoral margin.

The amount of prior legislative experience also has been suggested as a factor influencing legislative voting behavior.[18] To test whether this is so, legislative experience of members of the 1963 Indiana General Assembly was analyzed in terms of the number of previous sessions in which the legislator served, including previous service in the House by members of the Senate. (No House member previously served in the Senate, but a number of Senators had served in the House.) Utilizing the criterion that a legislator usually is not experienced until he has served three terms, legislators were divided into two groups within each party in each house—those who had served more than three terms and those who had served three terms or less. Members of each party

TABLE IV

ELECTORAL MARGIN AND PLATFORM SUPPORT, ALL PLATFORM ROLL CALLS
HOUSE REPUBLICANS

PERCENT OF TOTAL VOTE

|  | 50–54.9 | 55.0–59.9 | 60 or more |
|---|---|---|---|
| Number of Constituencies | 34 | 12 | 9 |
| Mean Score | 54.794 | 55.167 | 49.000 |
| Standard Deviation | 6.623 | 6.088 | 9.899 |

ANALYSIS OF VARIANCE

|  | Sum of Squares | DF | Mean Square | F. Ratio |
|---|---|---|---|---|
| Between Groups | 262.4836 | 2 | 131.2418 | 2.5858 ª |
| Within Groups | 2639.2253 | 52 | 50.7543 |  |
| Total | 2901.7089 | 54 |  |  |

ª Not significant at the 5 percent level.

were also divided into groups on the basis of whether their vote for Republican platform legislation was less than the mean vote support score of their party in that legislative chamber or equal to or more than the mean vote support score. As Tables VIII, IX, X, and XI indicate, no significant differences were found within either party in voting support by legislators for Republican platform legislation when analyzed on the basis of legislative experience.

TABLE V

ELECTORAL MARGIN AND PLATFORM SUPPORT, ALL PLATFORM ROLL CALLS
HOUSE DEMOCRATS

PERCENT OF TOTAL VOTE

|  | 50–54.9 | 55–59.9 | 60 or more |
|---|---|---|---|
| Number of Constituencies | 27 | 11 | 6 |
| Mean Score | 41.630 | 42.455 | 44.167 |
| Standard Deviation | 7.001 | 6.089 | 8.612 |

ANALYSIS OF VARIANCE

|  | Sum of Squares | DF | Mean Square | F. Ratio |
|---|---|---|---|---|
| Between Groups | 32.6885 | 2 | 16.3443 | 0.3324 ª |
| Within Groups | 2015.8567 | 41 | 49.1672 |  |
| Total | 2048.5452 | 43 |  |  |

ª Not significant at the 5 percent level.

TABLE VI

ELECTORAL MARGIN AND PLATFORM SUPPORT, ALL PLATFORM ROLL CALLS
SENATE REPUBLICANS

PERCENT OF TOTAL VOTE

|  | 50–54.9 | 55.0–59.9 | 60 or more |
|---|---|---|---|
| Number of Constituencies | 18 | 4 | 3 |
| Mean Score | 51.167 | 51.750 | 51.333 |
| Standard Deviation | 8.611 | 9.500 | 4.726 |

ANALYSIS OF VARIANCE

|  | Sum of Squares | DF | Mean Square | F. Ratio |
|---|---|---|---|---|
| Between Groups | 1.1233 | 2 | 0.5617 | 0.0078 [a] |
| Within Groups | 1575.9166 | 22 | 71.6326 |  |
| Total | 1577.0399 | 24 |  |  |

[a] Not significant at the 5 percent level.

Another factor frequently thought to influence legislative voting behavior is a legislator's social background, although no direct connection between social background characteristics and voting behavior has been established.[19] However, legislators themselves tend to believe social background characteristics influence voting behavior. One Senator stated the common belief that the Democrats have greater cohesion than Republicans because of social background characteristics. He

TABLE VII

ELECTORAL MARGIN AND PLATFORM SUPPORT, ALL PLATFORM ROLL CALLS
SENATE DEMOCRATS

PERCENT OF TOTAL VOTE

|  | 50–54.9 | 55–59.9 | 60 or more |
|---|---|---|---|
| Number of Constituencies | 16 | 7 | 1 |
| Mean Score | 42.375 | 40.714 | 32.000 |
| Standard Deviation | 4.689 | 6.291 | 0. |

ANALYSIS OF VARIANCE

|  | Sum of Squares | DF | Mean Square | F. Ratio |
|---|---|---|---|---|
| Between Groups | 106.7798 | 2 | 53.3899 | 1.9768 [a] |
| Within Groups | 567.1786 | 21 | 27.0085 |  |
| Total | 673.9584 | 23 |  |  |

[a] Not significant at the 5 percent level.

## TABLE VIII

LEGISLATIVE EXPERIENCE AND VOTE SCORE, SENATE DEMOCRATS

| Vote Score | Number of Sessions Served | |
|---|---|---|
| | 1–3 | 4 or more |
| Equal to or more than the Mean Vote | 8 | 4 |
| Less than the Mean Vote | 8 | 4 |
| | P = .175 [a] | |

[a] Calculated using Fisher's exact probability test, Formula 6.1, Sidney Siegel, *Non-Parametric Statistics* (New York: McGraw-Hill Book Company, Inc., 1956), p. 96.

thought Democrats more frequently have religious backgrounds which emphasize greater dependence on figures of authority and that they are less frequently engaged in occupations in which independence from authority is tolerated. He stated that Republicans are more likely to pursue occupations where greater independence is permitted, such as the practice of law, real estate, or insurance or owner-operated businesses. If the Senator's explanations are correct, significant differences in occupation and religious affiliations would have occurred in the Senate, where the Democrats exhibited greater cohesion than the Republicans on ten of the thirteen subject-matter issues. However, an examination of a modification of these hypotheses, utilizing chi-square tests, indicated that there are no significant differences in occupational or religious patterns among the two parties in the Senate.[20]

In the House the Democrats were only slightly more cohesive than Republicans: The Democrats had a cohesion of 80 or above on eleven platform areas; the Republicans, on eight. However, the Republicans voted with greater average cohesion in seven areas, the Democrats in five, and on one the party members exhibited equal cohesion.

Another variable sometimes seen as exerting considerable influence on legislative party cohesion is the relative availability of patronage

## TABLE IX

LEGISLATIVE EXPERIENCE AND VOTE SCORE, SENATE REPUBLICANS

| Vote Score | Number of Sessions Served | |
|---|---|---|
| | 1–3 | 4 or more |
| Equal to or more than the Mean Vote | 4 | 11 |
| Less than the Mean Vote | 5 | 5 |
| | $X^2 = 1.42$, df = 1 | |
| | .30 < P > .20 | |

TABLE X

LEGISLATIVE EXPERIENCE AND VOTE SCORE, HOUSE DEMOCRATS

|  | Number of Sessions Served | |
| --- | --- | --- |
| Vote Score | 1–3 | 4 or more |
| Equal to or more than the Mean Vote | 20 | 4 |
| Less than the Mean Vote | 18 | 2 |
|  | P = .284 [a] | |

[a] Calculated using Fisher's exact probability test.

from the State's chief executive.[21] The fact that the Republicans did not control the governorship might explain in part lower cohesion among Republicans than among Democrats, as the patronage powers of the chief executive were unavailable to maintain discipline. Republican politicians maintain that this is one explanation for Republican dissension. One might also argue that cohesion among Democrats was lower than would have occurred during the Democratic governor's first legislative session because fewer and lower paying jobs were available to reward cooperative Democratic legislators and their friends and relatives. (Most of the jobs—especially the high-paying ones—were distributed primarily after the 1961 session, which was the first held during Governor Welsh's term in office. Since an Indiana Governor may not succeed himself, support for the Governor tends to diminish during the second legislative session held during his term.)

TABLE XI

LEGISLATIVE EXPERIENCE AND VOTE SCORE, HOUSE REPUBLICANS

|  | Number of Sessions Served | |
| --- | --- | --- |
| Vote Score | 1–3 | 4 or more |
| Equal to or more than the Mean Vote | 26 | 6 |
| Less than the Mean Vote | 18 | 5 |
|  | $X^2 = .2751$ | |
|  | $.70 < P > .50$ | |

Another explanation offered by political scientists for the differences in cohesion between the two parties in a legislature is that of majority-minority status. Wahlke, Eulau, Ferguson, and Buchanan found that "analysis of roll call votes in competitive systems shows that the majority party is generally more cohesive than the minority, though there may be exceptions, such as the instance where the minority party controls the governorship. The ratio of majority-minority strength may be an additional factor influencing legislators' party orientations."[22] In

### TABLE XII

OCCUPATIONAL DIFFERENCES AMONG PARTY DELEGATIONS, SENATE

| | WHITE COLLAR [a] | OTHER |
|---|---|---|
| Republican | 21 | 4 |
| Democrat | 17 | 7 |

$$X^2 = .6295 \qquad p = .5$$

[a] The following occupations were classified as white-collar ones: attorney; real estate agent; merchant; manufacturer; small businessman; contractor; salesman; clerk; news media employer; or professional person, such as teacher or doctor.

### TABLE XIII

RELIGIOUS DIFFERENCES AMONG PARTY DELEGATIONS, SENATE

| | CATHOLIC | NON-CATHOLIC |
|---|---|---|
| Republican | 1 | 24 |
| Democrat | 5 | 19 |

$$X^2 = .0258 \qquad p = .9$$

### TABLE XIV

OCCUPATIONAL DIFFERENCES AMONG PARTY DELEGATIONS, HOUSE

| | WHITE COLLAR | OTHER |
|---|---|---|
| Republican | 40 | 16 |
| Democrat | 30 | 14 |

$$X^2 = .0476 \qquad p = .9$$

### TABLE XV

RELIGIOUS DIFFERENCES AMONG PARTY DELEGATIONS, HOUSE

| | CATHOLIC | OTHER |
|---|---|---|
| Republican | 1 | 55 |
| Democrat | 10 | 34 |

$$X^2 = 10.938 \qquad p = .001$$

the 1963 General Assembly the author found no clear confirmation of any of these hypotheses. In the Senate the minority party had greater cohesion than the majority on ten of the thirteen subject-matter average indices of cohesion. On two subject-matter areas the average indices of cohesion were equal, and on reapportionment the Republicans displayed greater cohesion. In the House the majority party voted with greater average cohesion in seven areas, the minority in five; on one subject there was equal cohesion within the two parties.

Malcolm Jewell attributed party cohesion in some cases to the fact that "A legislative party accustomed to minority status may develop considerable unity, despite the diverse constituencies of its members, when the party elects a governor and wins a majority or a large minority in the legislature." [23] This might have been the case in the Indiana Senate, but it does not account for the differences between House and Senate patterns of voting on Republican platform measures.

Two explanations were given by the politicians for the patterns of cohesion found in the Senate. One hypothesis was that the best margin between parties for good party cohesion is a 2 to 5 majority. In such a situation no one man can determine the legislative results by changing his vote, yet the margin is close so that each legislator feels obligated to vote with his party; other party members will regard a legislator who does not vote with his party as a maverick and apply sanctions. Another explanation is that the Democrats in the Senate viewed many of the roll calls as votes in support of the Governor. This support was obligated not only because he was a Democratic Governor, the party's most visible spokesman, and the chief dispenser of future patronage and campaign support, but also because he was a former member of the Senate, a former colleague, and a personal friend.

## Conclusions

The first requirement for party responsibility—intra-party cohesion and inter-party conflict—was not met by the Republican party in the 1963 Indiana General Assembly. The average index of cohesion (which measures intra-party cohesion) fell below 80 on several of the thirteen issue areas in both legislative chambers; the average index of likeness (which measures inter-party conflict) fell below 80 on only four of the thirteen issue areas in each legislative chamber.

A number of factors thought by some political scientists to be related to the existence of intra-party cohesion and inter-party conflict were examined earlier in this article to see what contributions they make. Intra-party rivalry, higher political ambitions, the structure of party organization, and the process of making nominations to statewide office appear to contribute to lack of party cohesion among Republicans in the legislative session studied.

The hypothesis of Eulau that the party acts as a cue-giver might account in part for high party likeness, with the party leaders at the legislative, local, or state level not providing opposing cues which would generate party conflict as analyzed by low party likeness on platform roll calls. Party cohesion was less than 80 on several issue sets of roll calls. Within the Republican legislative delegations, this can be attributed in part to the activities of certain cue-givers; these tended however not to be the local constituency leaders, with one major exception, in which the size of the Republican county delegation involved was such that it could affect significantly outcomes on roll call votes. Jewell's suggestion that two major types of issues generate party conflict—those representing socioeconomic interest differences and those indicative of party interest—is only partially confirmed. On some issues inter-party conflict did occur, but on others intra-party conflict prevailed.

Eight factors were examined to determine their relationship to the variations in legislative voting behavior. Some variation was found to be based on constituency differences (determined by socioeconomic variables), with the variation being greater among Republicans than among Democrats. Electoral margin in the preceding election contest, evaluated using analysis of variance techniques, was not related significantly to vote score in either house or in either party. Legislative experience was not related to differences in voting behavior. Social background characteristics of religion and occupation did not differ significantly between the two parties; an exception was religious affiliation of members of the House, but the differences did not fit the expected pattern. Other factors considered included availability of patronage, majority-minority status, and the majority party's margin of control in each house. Of the factors examined, constituency differences and those related to personal ambitions, intra-party rivalries, party nominating processes, and party organization relations appear to have had some effect on levels of party cohesion and party likeness in voting on platform legislation.

## Suggestions for Further Research

Testing one hypothesis about the operation of the political system always raises other questions and leads to other hypotheses that need to be tested.

Efforts of a political party to meet the commitments of its platform have not been studied extensively in analyses of state politics or state governmental decision-making, nor has there been an analysis of the drafting of state party platforms. Creating a party platform may be viewed as recording whatever consensus exists at the time the platform is drafted. The platform may be dictated by the governor to his party or by the assured nominee for the highest office to be contested. A question that needs to be answered is: What is the role of the platform as an instrument of consensus building within the party and between the party and its clientele?

The analysis of the influence of various levels of party organization on party cohesion indicates that the extent and direction of influence varies with the particular nominating structure for local, state, or national offices which exists within a state. Comparative studies among states would make possible more precise evaluation of local party influence on the nominating process and its relationship to legislative voting behavior. Such studies might try to answer such questions as this: Are ambitious state legislators in states using direct primaries for nomination to higher office more responsive or less responsive to urban county chairmen than those in states using the convention system? In some states legislative service is not the avenue for advancement to higher state or national office. Another study might examine or try to define the characteristic patterns of party authority in these states and their relationship to legislative voting behavior and to patterns of political career advancement.

Another hypothesis, which might be tested comparatively among several states, is that local party influence on legislative voting behavior varies with the urbanization and competitiveness of the district, the local party leaders having greater influence in the more urban and the more competitive districts. The studies by Sorauf and by Wahlke, Eulau, Ferguson, and Buchanan present confirming evidence of this hypothesis about the role of local party leadership in recruiting candidates for legislative office, but that of Seligman presents nonconfirming evidence.[24] A study on this subject might try to determine under what conditions the local party leadership in politically competitive districts becomes active in legislative recruitment and selection.

The subject of the political influence of local party leaders raises many questions, such as these: What are the perceptions of county chairmen of their influence on legislators of their party who serve the legislative district in which their county is located? How do county chairmen seek to influence legislative voting behavior? When a legislative party leader tries to influence the voting behavior of a legislator, to what extent does he seek to exercise influence indirectly and in the man's constituency does he contact the party leader or some other type of local influence wielder?

While a person gains certain advantages in terms of access to particular types of information by being a participant-observer, he loses the ability to use other forms of observation such as systematic survey research because of the role he plays in the political process. In combination with roll call analysis, systematic field observation through the interviewing process should be used to test the hypotheses considered in this chapter in other legislative sessions and in several states.

## 5 / A Comparison of Rural and Urban State Legislators in Iowa and Indiana

### George W. Carey

THIS CHAPTER HAS TWO PURPOSES IN MIND: (1) TO COMPARE RURAL AND urban state legislators in Iowa and Indiana with respect to occupation, age at entry into legislative service, length of service, educational achievement, and cause of retirement; (2) to provide some measure of the existence or nonexistence of rural-urban conflict by comparing the number and nature of committee chairmanships held by the rural legislators with the number and nature of those held by urban legislators in each of these states.

Because this study was conducted some four years before the Supreme Court's first reapportionment decision in *Baker* vs. *Carr,* a few words are in order concerning its utility in the present controversies surrounding urban-rural representation in state legislative assemblies. This comparison was predicated on the assumption that reapportionment, designed to redress the representational imbalance between rural and urban areas, was not far in the offing. Indeed, some states had already undertaken such reapportionment on their own initiative. Certain questions necessarily arose—questions of far greater significance today in light of the Court's recent rulings—concerning the effects of reapportionment. Other studies have utilized a variety of approaches in seeking answers to these questions.[1] This material is presented as a supplement to these studies, so that political scientists might have a clearer picture of certain presumably significant differences between urban and rural legislators, the extent to which rural "forces" have heretofore dominated the internal organization of the legislative assemblies in question, and the possible consequences of reapportionment based on the "one man, one vote" formula designed to give the urban areas greater representation in the state legislatures. And while this data cannot provide direct answers to most of the questions that have since arisen concerning the supposed rural-urban conflict and the changes to be wrought by reapportionment, they nevertheless provide some basis for intelligent speculation.

## Method and Procedure

This chapter compares legislators from the most rural and the most urban districts. It is felt that contrasting legislators from extreme rural and extreme urban categories makes more obvious differences which exist with respect to the characteristics measured in this study. Legislators representing districts in between the rural and urban extremes are not included, and references to rural and urban legislators, districts, or whatever mean the most rural and the most urban in each instance.

The following table shows for each session the number of legislators representing the most rural and the most urban districts, who are included in this research, and the number of legislators representing districts in between the rural and urban extremes, who are excluded from it.

|  | *Most Rural*<br>(Included in<br>study) | *Most Urban*<br>(Included in<br>study) | *In Between*<br>(Excluded from<br>study) |
|---|---|---|---|
| Iowa House | 53 | 14 | 41 |
| Iowa Senate | 18 | 7 | 25 |
| Indiana House | 45 | 29 | 26 |
| Indiana Senate | 21 | 15 | 14 |

Population concentration within a district is used as the criterion of the district's urban or rural character for two reasons: First, there is general agreement that rural-urban character is in large measure related to population concentrations; and second, no other measurable characteristics have been suggested which provide a more meaningful measure of rural and urban character.

For Iowa, the most rural districts are defined as districts (i.e., counties) that have not contained a city as large as 5,000 according to the 1930, 1940, and 1950 censuses. The 53 Representatives from the 53 most rural counties comprised 49 percent of the total lower chamber membership of 108. According to the 1950 census these 53 counties contained 31 percent of the total population of Iowa. Districts considered the most urban in Iowa were those with two Representatives in the lower chamber. All other districts had one Representative. These two-member districts contained the seven largest cities of Iowa: Des

Moines, Sioux City, Davenport, Cedar Rapids, Waterloo, Council
Bluffs, and Dubuque. The fourteen Representatives from these seven
districts represented thirteen percent of the total lower house membership while the population of these districts represented 31 percent of
Iowa's total population. In the Iowa Senate (total membership 50),
there were eighteen Senators from the most rural districts and seven
from the most urban.

For Indiana, the most rural districts included all districts in which
50 percent of the population at no time resided in cities as big as 5,000.
These districts held forty-five lower chamber seats and 33 percent of
the total population. In the Indiana Senate (total membership 50),
there were fifteen Senators from the most urban districts and twenty-
one from the most rural. Districts which contained cities classified as
"first class" for legislative purposes are considered the most urban in
Indiana. These districts contained the five largest population centers
in the state: Marion County (Indianapolis), Allen County (Fort
Wayne), Vanderburgh County (Evansville), Lake County (Gary,
Hammond, and East Chicago), and St. Joseph County (South Bend).
In addition, there were four multi-county districts that contained one
of these population centers. These multi-county districts are also considered as most urban. These urban districts held 29 of the 100 seats in
the lower chamber and contained 41 percent of Indiana's total population (1950 census).[2]

The following analysis includes rural and urban legislators who
served in the Iowa House at any time during the period from 1925 to
1959 and all those who served in the Iowa Senate at any time from
1937 to 1959. For the Indiana legislature all rural and urban legislators who served from 1925 to 1959 are included. This period includes
eighteen regular sessions for the Iowa House and the Indiana House
and Senate. Most of the data presented here are concerned with the
lower chambers of the Iowa and Indiana legislatures because they provided a greater number of cases from which to generalize than the
upper chambers. However, significant differences which existed between the rural and urban legislators of the lower and upper chambers
are noted in the text.

## Characteristics of Rural and Urban Legislators

*Age at Entry.* Table I presents the ages at entry for rural and urban
members of the Iowa and Indiana lower chambers. In Iowa, the median age of entry for rural legislators was 52, while for urban legislators the median was 45. For Indiana rural and urban legislators the

medians were, respectively, 51 and 47. A comparison of medians, however, does not give the full picture of the age distributions. In Iowa, proportionately twice as many rural legislators entered after 55; and conversely, proportionally more than twice as many urban legislators as rural legislators entered before the age of 40. A contrast of Indiana rural and urban legislators presents much the same picture. In Indiana, 23 percent of the rural legislators compared with 42 percent of urban legislators started their legislative service before the age of 40. A more striking contrast is that only 14 percent of the urban legislators in Indiana entered after the age of 55, while 32 percent of the rural legislators did.

TABLE I

AGES AT ENTRY INTO HOUSE FOR THE MOST RURAL
AND THE MOST URBAN LEGISLATORS
Iowa and Indiana, 1925–1959

|  | AGE AT ENTRY | | | | | | |
|---|---|---|---|---|---|---|---|
|  | 20–29 | 30–39 | 40–49 | 50–59 | 60+ | Unk | N |
| *Iowa House* | | | | | | | |
| (%) Most Rural | 3 | 12 | 29 | 33 | 22 | 1 | 449 |
| (%) Most Urban | 8 | 29 | 25 | 22 | 15 | 1 | 115 |
| *Indiana House* | | | | | | | |
| (%) Most Rural | 4 | 19 | 25 | 24 | 20 | 8 | 378 |
| (%) Most Urban | 13 | 29 | 26 | 12 | 11 | 9 | 312 |

The marked differences in age at entry between rural and urban legislators is attributable to the fact that urban districts sent to the legislature proportionally far more lawyers, and lawyers, as a group, entered the legislature at a much earlier age than farmers.[3] A comparison of the age at entry for farmers and lawyers of Iowa reveals the medians for rural and urban lawyers were 43 and 37 respectively, and for both rural and urban were 55. Again, Indiana presents a similar picture: The median ages at entry for rural and urban lawyers were 42 and 37 respectively, and the median age for rural and urban farmers was 57 and 56, respectively.

*Occupation.* As expected, farmers represented the largest single occupational group among the most rural legislators while lawyers composed the largest occupational group among the most urban legislators. From Table II it can be seen that in the Iowa lower chamber the ratio of rural farmers to rural lawyers was in excess of 4 to 1 and in the Indiana lower chamber the ratio of rural farmers to rural lawyers, though considerably less than in Iowa, was still in excess of 2 to 1. For the most urban legislators, as would be expected, the ratios of lawyers to farmers was about 2.6 to 1 in the Iowa lower chamber and over 4 to 1 in the Indiana lower chamber.

Though the proportion of farmers and lawyers differed sharply between the rural and urban legislators, the proportion of businessmen in both states for both groups remained relatively stable. Only among the urban legislators of Indiana could laborers be said to constitute anything near a significant occupational group. Professional people, other than lawyers, were most numerous among the rural legislators of Indiana, although even here they constituted only 10 percent of the total. Among those occupational groups in the residual category were, in order of their size, (a) insurance and real estate; (b) salesmen,

TABLE II

OCCUPATIONS OF THE MOST RURAL AND THE MOST URBAN LEGISLATORS
Iowa and Indiana, 1925–1959

| *Iowa House* | FARMER | LAW-YER | BUSINESS-MEN | LA-BORERS | PROFES-SIONAL (OTHER THAN LAWYERS) | UN-KNOWN AND OTHER | N |
|---|---|---|---|---|---|---|---|
| (%) Most Rural | 53 | 12 | 10 | * | 1 | 24 | 449 |
| (%) Most Urban | 16 | 42 | 13 | 3 | 2 | 24 | 115 |
| *Indiana House* | | | | | | | |
| (%) Most Rural | 36 | 16 | 18 | 4 | 9 | 17 | 378 |
| (%) Most Urban | 7 | 32 | 16 | 10 | 6 | 29 | 312 |

* Less than 1%

clerks, and white-collar workers; and (c) newspapermen, editors, and publishers. Except for individuals in insurance and real estate, who composed 5 percent of the most rural legislators and 9 percent of the urban legislators in Indiana, in no instance did any of these groups represent as much as 4 percent of the rural or urban legislators in either state.

The same occupational analysis of the Iowa and Indiana Senates reveals that the rural areas sent proportionally far more lawyers to the Senate than to the lower chamber. In Iowa, the rural regions, for the period of 1937–59, sent 22 farmers and 18 lawyers, while in Indiana, from 1925–59, the rural districts sent 30 farmers and 40 lawyers. These data suggest that there is no deep-seated reluctance on the part of the people of the rural areas to send lawyers to the legislature. These findings also suggest that proportionally fewer farmers and proportionally more lawyers had the desire, political contacts, and/or resources to seek election from the senatorial districts which, in the case of the rural districts, included two or more lower chamber districts.

*Educational Achievement.* The data in Table III show that urban legislators, on the whole had a higher degree of educational achievement than rural legislators. Approximately 1 out of every 4 rural legislators in Iowa and Indiana possessed a college degree. Among the Iowa urban legislators about 1 in 2 had a college degree, and among Indiana's urban legislators 1 in 3 held a college degree. Obviously, the difference between the educational achievements of rural and urban legislators reflects the fact that there was a higher proportion of lawyers among the urban legislators.

Of those who did not attend college, there were twenty-five individuals from Indiana's rural districts and thirteen from the urban who

TABLE III

EDUCATIONAL ACHIEVEMENT OF THE MOST RURAL
AND THE MOST URBAN LEGISLATORS
Iowa and Indiana, 1925–1959

| | EDUCATIONAL ACHIEVEMENT | | | | |
| | Possess College Degree | Attended College May Have Degree | Did Not Attend College | Unknown and not Otherwise Classified | N |
|---|---|---|---|---|---|
| *Iowa House* | | | | | |
| (%) Most Rural | 27 | 27 | 32 | 14 | 449 |
| (%) Most Urban | 50 | 18 | 16 | 16 | 115 |
| *Indiana House* | | | | | |
| (%) Most Rural | 25 | 25 | 36 | 14 | 378 |
| (%) Most Urban | 34 | 25 | 31 | 10 | 312 |

were known to have not completed high school. Among the rural Representatives of Iowa, there were twenty who were known to have not graduated from high school; but among the urban Representatives of Iowa, there was not one known case of a Representative's not completing high school. Since this information was gathered from the biographical data offered by the legislators, it is difficult in the vast majority of cases to determine at what exact point those legislators who did not attend college terminated their formal education. Probably the number of legislators known to have not graduated from high school would be increased if more information were available concerning their formal educational achievement.

The proportion of urban legislators with college degrees in the Iowa and Indiana Senates was the same as that among the urban legislators of the lower chambers. The percentage of rural legislators with college degrees in the Iowa Senate was appreciably higher (42%) than it was in the lower chamber (27%). The same was true in the Indiana Senate: Rural legislators who had college degrees comprised 31 percent of the total rural delegation. However, in both the Iowa and Indiana Senates, proportionally more urban Senators had college degrees than did their rural counterparts.

*Length of Service.* There was a high degree of turnover among both the rural and urban Representatives in Iowa and Indiana. Table IV shows that a large majority of urban and rural legislators did not serve more than two sessions. In one extreme case—Indiana's urban Representatives—62 percent did not go beyond one session of service and 84 percent did not go beyond two sessions. Furthermore, in neither state did more than 31 percent of the rural or urban legislators go on to three sessions of service.

As would be expected, the rate of turnover varied according to party. One uniformity to be noted is that more Republicans than Democrats served four or more sessions before retiring. This fact is most noticeable among the urban legislators of Iowa where 27 percent of the Republicans and only 9 percent of the Democrats served four or more sessions.

Several reasons may be offered for the higher proportion of Republicans serving four or more sessions. It might be assumed that Republicans had greater success at the polls than Democrats; but as the subsequent section on cause of retirement will demonstrate, there is considerable evidence to show that this was not entirely the case. A more plausible explanation may be that more Republicans were better able to afford the financial burden of campaigning and legislative service—particularly in Iowa and Indiana, where the pay for legislative service was relatively low.[4] Another logical explanation may be that Republicans had a greater incentive to seek re-election to the legislature because Republicans controlled the lower chambers in these two states for a majority of the sessions and positions of leadership were naturally awarded to Republicans.

*Cause of Retirement.* The high turnover of rural and urban legislators in Iowa and Indiana could not be attributed to a particularly strong inter-party or intra-party competition for legislative seats. Table V shows that except for rural Representatives of Iowa, the majority of those who retired from legislative service did not seek re-election. Among Iowa's rural legislators, 45 percent did not seek re-election, while among Iowa's urban legislators 59 percent did not seek re-election. Among both the rural and urban Representatives in Indiana, 53 percent did not seek re-election to the lower chamber.

An analysis of these data by party shows that among the rural Indiana legislators and the urban Indiana and Iowa legislators proportionally fewer Democrats sought re-election and proportionally more Re-

## TABLE IV

### NUMBER OF SESSIONS SERVED BEFORE RETIREMENT FROM HOUSE BY THE MOST RURAL AND THE MOST URBAN LEGISLATORS

#### Iowa and Indiana, 1925–1957

| Sessions Served before Retirement from House | IOWA | | | | | | INDIANA | | | | | |
| --- | --- | --- | --- | --- | --- | --- | --- | --- | --- | --- | --- | --- |
| | Most Rural | | | Most Urban | | | Most Rural | | | Most Urban | | |
| | R (%) | D (%) | Both R&D (%) | R (%) | D (%) | Both R&D (%) | R (%) | D (%) | Both R&D (%) | R (%) | D (%) | Both R&D (%) |
| 1 Session | 29 | 53 | 36 | 31 | 58 | 41 | 39 | 43 | 41 | 59 | 66 | 62 |
| 2 Sessions | 37 | 26 | 34 | 31 | 25 | 29 | 24 | 33 | 28 | 24 | 20 | 22 |
| 3 Sessions | 17 | 13 | 16 | 11 | 8 | 9 | 15 | 14 | 15 | 6 | 7 | 7 |
| 4 Sessions | 11 | 4 | 9 | 8 | 3 | 6 | 11 | 5 | 8 | 6 | 4 | 5 |
| 5+ Sessions | 6 | 4 | 5 | 19 | 6 | 15 | 11 | 5 | 8 | 5 | 3 | 4 |
| N | 285 | 111 | 396 | 65 | 36 | 101 | 185 | 148 | 333 | 146 | 137 | |

## TABLE V

### Cause of Retirement for the Most Rural and the Most Urban Legislators from House Iowa and Indiana, 1925–1957

| Cause of Retirement | IOWA | | | | | | INDIANA | | | | | |
|---|---|---|---|---|---|---|---|---|---|---|---|---|
| | Most Rural | | | Most Urban | | | Most Rural | | | Most Urban | | |
| | R (%) | D (%) | Both R&D (%) | R (%) | D (%) | Both R&D (%) | R (%) | D (%) | Both R&D (%) | R (%) | D (%) | Both R&D (%) |
| Defeated Primary | 20 | 6 | 16 | 15 | 14 | 15 | 15 | 12 | 14 | 27 | 21 | 24 |
| Defeated General Election | 21 | 43 | 27 | 11 | 8 | 10 | 28 | 26 | 27 | 18 | 9 | 14 |
| Went other Chamber | 7 | 2 | 5 | 8 | 8 | 8 | 3 | 3 | 3 | 4 | 7 | 6 |
| Other Known Cause * | 5 | 9 | 7 | 9 | 8 | 8 | 4 | 3 | 3 | 2 | 4 | 3 |
| Did not Seek Re-election | 47 | 40 | 45 | 57 | 62 | 59 | 50 | 56 | 53 | 49 | 59 | 53 |
| N | 285 | 111 | 396 | 65 | 36 | 101 | 185 | 148 | 333 | 146 | 137 | 283 |

* Includes death, resignation, defeat in general election or primary for other chamber.

publicans were defeated at the polls in seeking re-election. Among the rural legislators of Iowa, 47 percent of the Republicans and 40 percent of the Democrats who retired did not seek re-election. Additionally, 49 percent of the rural Democrats compared with 41 percent of the rural Republicans were defeated in the primary and general elections in Iowa.

The general election provided the chief obstacle for rural Republicans and Democrats seeking re-election in Iowa and Indiana. It is to be noted, however, that the primary elections and the general elections accounted for about an equal number of defeats among rural Republicans in Iowa. The primary election, on the other hand, was the chief stumbling block for urban Republicans and Democrats in both states. Among both the rural and urban Representatives in both states who unsuccessfully sought re-election, the primary election was the means of defeat for a higher percentage of Republicans than Democrats. This tends to support the proposition that the primary is a more important obstacle to candidates of the party having the best chance of winning the general election. In rural Iowa, for example, 20 percent of the Republican incumbents were defeated in the primary, while only 6 percent of the Democratic incumbents shared the same fate. However, clearly other variables were operating in Iowa's urban districts, for despite the fact that the Republicans had far greater success in electing Representatives from these areas, Democratic incumbents were defeated in the primary election in almost the same proportion as Republicans.[5]

## Rural and Urban Legislators and Committee Chairmanships

An axiom of political science concerning the operations of American legislatures is that the bulk of legislative work is performed in standing committees. In this regard, the Iowa and Indiana legislatures are no exceptions. We have good reason, therefore, to expect rural-urban conflict (presuming, of course, that it does exist) to manifest itself both in the number and the nature of committee chairmanships held by rural and urban legislators.

Table VI shows that for the lower chamber the number of chairmanships per individual for Iowa's rural legislators (.86) was less than that for its urban legislators (1.09). A totally different picture is presented for Indiana's rural and urban lower chamber legislators: 1.05 chairmanships per rural Representative compared with .80 for each urban Representative. However, these gross figures overlook two highly important factors: First, urban Representatives in Iowa and

## TABLE VI

TOTAL NUMBER OF CHAIRMANSHIPS HELD AND NUMBER HELD PER INDIVIDUAL
FOR THE MOST RURAL AND THE MOST URBAN LEGISLATORS
Iowa, 1925–1959; Indiana, 1925–1957

|  | IOWA HOUSE | | INDIANA HOUSE | |
|---|---|---|---|---|
|  | Most Rural | Most Urban | Most Rural | Most Urban |
| Total Number of Chairmanships | 385 | 125 | 349 | 222 |
| Number of Chairmanships per Individual | .86 | 1.09 | 1.05 | .80 |
| Number of Legislators | 449 | 115 | 333 | 283 |

rural Representatives in Indiana served longer before retiring and thus accumulated more chairmanships per individual than their counterparts; [6] second, since proportionally more Democrats were found among the urban legislators of both states and since Republicans had been in control of both lower chambers for most of the sessions under analysis, the average number of chairmanships was necessarily lower for urban legislators.

Table VII presents the data necessary to determine more accurately whether urban legislators were discriminated against in the committee chairmanships awarded them. In this table the lower-chamber legislators are differentiated by state, by party, and by type of district (Iowa rural Republicans, Iowa rural Democrats, Iowa urban Republicans, etc.).

## TABLE VII

TOTAL NUMBER OF CHAIRMANSHIPS HELD FOR THE MOST RURAL AND THE
MOST URBAN REPUBLICAN AND DEMOCRATIC LEGISLATORS
Iowa, 1925–1959; Indiana, 1925–1957

|  | IOWA HOUSE (1925–1959) | | | | INDIANA HOUSE (1925–1957) | | | |
|---|---|---|---|---|---|---|---|---|
|  | Most Rural | | Most Urban | | Most Rural | | Most Urban | |
|  | R | D | R | D | R | D | R | D |
| Number of Seats Held | 738 | 216 | 169 | 83 | 473 | 292 | 263 | 230 |
| Number of Chairmanships Held | 355 | 30 | 109 | 16 | 253 | 96 | 127 | 95 |
| Number of Chairmanships per Individual | 1.12 | .23 | 1.46 | .34 | 1.36 | .65 | .87 | .69 |
| Number of Chairmanships per Seat | .47 | .14 | .65 | .19 | .53 | .33 | .48 | .41 |
| Number of Legislators | 317 | 132 | 68 | 47 | 185 | 148 | 146 | 137 |

From Table VII it can readily be seen that in Indiana the differences between the average number of chairmanships held by each Republican rural Representative was 1.36 compared with .87 for each urban Republican in Iowa, each Republican rural Representative held 1.12 chairmanships compared with 1.46 for each Republican urban Representative. In Indiana, rural and urban Democrats held approximately the same average number of chairmanships per individual: .65 for each rural Democrat compared with .69 for each urban Democrat. In Iowa, each rural Democrat held .23 chairmanships, and each urban Democrat held .34.

However, as previously noted, a higher proportion of urban Republicans in Iowa and rural Republicans in Indiana served longer before retiring, and for this reason their average number of chairmanships per individual was higher. By calculating the average number of chairmanships per seat for Republicans and Democrats from the rural and urban districts of Iowa and Indiana, this variable can be taken into account. In Iowa the rural Republicans still held fewer chairmanships per seat (.47) than urban Republicans (.65). Iowa rural Democrats held .14 chairmanships per seat compared with .19 for Iowa urban Democrats. Rural and urban Republicans in Indiana were very close in the number of chairmanships per seat with .53 for rural Republicans and .48 for urban Republicans.

Finally, if the average number of committee chairmanships is calculated for rural and urban Representatives of both states regardless of party affiliation (Table VIII), it is found that Iowa rural Representatives held .40 chairmanships per seat compared with .50 chairmanships per seat for Iowa urban Representatives and Indiana rural Representatives held .46 chairmanships per seat compared with .45 chairmanships per seat for Indiana urban Representatives.

A similar analysis of the Iowa and Indiana Senates did not yield any evidence of discrimination against urban Senators in the committee chairmanships awarded them. An analysis of the Iowa Senate from 1937 to 1959 shows that 69 rural Senators held 147 chairmanships or slightly less than 2.1 per man. A closer analysis shows each urban Republican held, on the average, 2.6 chairmanships and each rural Republican 2.4 chairmanships. This difference is explained in large measure by the fact that urban Republican Senators served slightly longer before retiring than rural Republicans.

Indiana rural Senators from 1925 to 1957 held on the average 2.6 chairmanships compared with 2.2 chairmanships per Indiana urban Senator. The fact that a higher proportion of urban Senators were Democrats while 13 of the 17 sessions were controlled by Republicans does not account for this difference: Each rural Republican Senator

## TABLE VIII

### Average Number of Chairmanships Held For Rural and Urban Legislators Iowa, 1925–1959; Indiana, 1925–1957

| | Iowa House (1925–1959) | | | Indiana House (1925–1957) | | |
|---|---|---|---|---|---|---|
| | Number of Seats | Number of Chmps. | Average Chmps. per seat | Average Chmps. per seat | Number of Chmps. | Number of Seats |
| 115 Urban Reps. | 252 | 125 | .50 | .45 | 222 | 493 | 312 Urban Reps. |
| 449 Rural Reps. | 954 | 385 | .40 | .46 | 349 | 765 | 378 Rural Reps. |

held on the average 3.62 chairmanships compared with 3.18 for urban Republican Senators. This difference is accounted for, however, by the fact that rural Republicans served longer than urban Republicans. The average number of committee chairmanships for each seat in the Indiana Senate shows that both rural and urban Republicans held about 1.6 chairmanships per seat.

The data presented thus far do not provide any evidence of rural legislators' discriminating against urban legislators in awarding committee chairmanships. On the contrary, these data show that length of service and party affiliation were the variables which accounted most for the differences in the proportionate number of chairmanships held

TABLE IX

NUMBER OF IMPORTANT COMMITTEES HEADED BY THE MOST RURAL
AND THE MOST URBAN LEGISLATORS
Iowa and Indiana, 1949–1959

| | IOWA | | | | INDIANA | | | |
|---|---|---|---|---|---|---|---|---|
| | House | | Senate | | House | | Senate | |
| | Most Rural | Most Urban | Most Rural | Most Urban | Most Rural | Most Urban | Most Rural | Most Urban |
| Republicans | 30 | 13 | 14 | 12 | 20 | 13 | 28 | 21 |
| Democrats | X | X | X | X | 9 | 11 | X | X |
| Total | 30 | 13 | 14 | 12 | 29 | 24 | 28 | 21 |

X = No Important Committee Headed. Republicans controlled the Iowa House and Senate and the Indiana Senate from 1949–59. Democrats controlled two sessions of the Indiana House during this period.

by rural and urban legislators. However, the quantitative methods employed so far treated all committees on the basis of equal importance. Obviously, some committees were far more important than others; if rural-urban conflict did exist, it might be supposed that the rural legislators held proportionately more of the important committee chairmanships than urban legislators. To investigate this possibility, appraisals of the most important committees were obtained from individuals familiar with the operation of both legislatures; the criteria for a committee to be selected most important were the number of bills referred to committee, the importance of bills referred to committee, and the competition which existed among the legislators for the position of chairman.[7]

The data in Table IX, the number of important committees headed by rural and urban legislators in both states, hardly supports the thesis of rural-urban conflict. The important committees of the Iowa House divided thirty for the most rural Representatives and thirteen for the most urban (a ratio of 2.3 to 1) even though there were 3.8 times as many rural legislators as urban. In the Indiana House, where there were forty-five rural and twenty-nine urban Representatives each session, the important chairmanships, when the Republicans controlled this chamber, were held by rural and urban Representatives in proportion to their respective numbers. In the two sessions of the chamber (1949–1959) when the Democrats were in control, however, urban Democrats held more important committee chairmanships than rural

TABLE X

IMPORTANT COMMITTEES HEADED BY URBAN AND RURAL LEGISLATORS
Iowa and Indiana, 1949–1959

| IOWA | | IOWA | |
|---|---|---|---|
| *House*  (Most Rural) | | *Senate*  (Most Rural) | |
| Agriculture I & II | (7) | Appropriations | (3) |
| Judicial I & II | (6) | Judicial I & II | (4) |
| Ways and Means | (5) | (Most Urban) | |
| Tax Revision | (4) | Judicial I & II | (6) |
| (Most Urban) | | Cities and Towns | (5) |
| Cities and Towns | (5) | | |
| Schools | (4) | | |
| INDIANA | | INDIANA | |
| *House*  (Most Rural) | | *Senate*  (Most Rural) | |
| Agriculture | (3) | Agriculture | (4) |
| County and Township | (4) | Cities and Towns | (4) |
| Education | (3) | County and Township | (5) |
| Judiciary A | (3) | Education | (3) |
| Roads | (6) | Legislative Apportionment | (4) |
| (Most Urban) | | (Most Urban) | |
| Affairs Lake County | (3) | City of Indianapolis | (6) |
| Affairs Marion County | (5) | Organ. of Courts and | |
| Affairs 2nd Class Cities | (4) | Criminal Code | (3) |
| Legislative Apportionment | (4) | Public Policy | (6) |
| | | Benevolent & Penal Inst. | (4) |

Number in ( ) indicates the number of times committee was headed. Judicial I and II and Agriculture I and II are two committees which have been grouped together here.

Democrats. In the Iowa Senate, where in each session there were eighteen Senators from the most rural districts and only seven from the most urban, the most important committee chairmanships were divided about equally between the two groups. In each session of the Indiana Senate, there were twenty-one Senators from the most rural districts and fifteen from the most urban; of the most important committees, the urban Senators held slightly more chairmanships per individual than their rural colleagues.

On certain committees, in both Iowa and Indiana, there was a definite clustering of chairmanships by the type of district. Table X divides the committees into those most frequently headed by rural legislators and those most frequently headed by urban legislators and lists the number of times during the 1949–1959 period that each committee was headed by rural and urban legislators. As one would expect, urban legislators, in general, headed those committees concerned with urban affairs. The committees headed by rural legislators seem more diversified in subject matter, but again as would be expected, except for the Iowa Senate, rural legislators frequently headed committees concerned with agriculture. The Judicial 1 and 2 committees of the Iowa House and Senate were frequently headed by rural legislators, while the County and Township Affairs Committee in both the Indiana House and Senate was held predominantly by rural legislators.

## Some Conclusions

The following conclusions seem more or less obvious from the data presented here:

(1) The examination of the proportion of the committee chairmanships held by rural legislators to that held by urban legislators provides no evidence that urban legislators of either state were discriminated against by rural legislators. The differences in the average number of chairmanships held by urban legislators and the average number held by rural legislators appeared to be the result of party affiliations and length of service rather than the rural or urban character of legislators' districts. Nor does it appear that urban legislators, during the period under study, were denied their proportionate share of important committee chairmanships.

The data regarding committee chairmanships, then, add some support to the thesis advanced by others that the extensiveness of rural-urban conflict has been grossly exaggerated in political science literature. What the data do show is that there has been a high degree of specialization; rural and urban legislators chair those committees most immediately concerned with their interests. There is little reason to presume that even with reapportionment and greater urban representation this practice will cease.

(2) The data support the commonly held belief that reapportionment designed to increase the proportion of urban legislators will also result in a higher proportion of lawyers. Moreover, the average age of these lawyers will be considerably lower than that of the rural representatives. We may profitably ask, What difference is this likely to make in terms of legislative behavior? Derge's findings with respect to the legislative behavior of lawyers give these implications: (a) Insofar as sponsorship of bills which become law can be considered as an

index of their importance as policy formulators, lawyers are more important than non-lawyers. (b) Lawyers do not frequently vote together with high cohesion on roll call votes where 10 percent or more of the legislators are on the losing side. (c) The political and social attitudes of lawyers do not differ significantly from those of non-lawyers.[8]

There is, however, reason to believe that a higher proportion of lawyers will result in a higher turnover among legislative membership. While the evidence is far from conclusive on this matter, lawyers seem to begin their legislative service at an earlier age than other occupational groups and to terminate it sooner. We can only speculate why this is so. It may well be that lawyers seek political office for experience in lawmaking, as a means of enhancing their firm's or their own reputation, or as a stepping-stone for higher elective or appointive office. But whatever their motivation, it is reasonable to believe that reapportionment will result in younger legislators and will aggravate the already serious problem of high turnover among state legislators.

(3) If it is true that reapportionment will result in a younger group of legislators than we presently have, this question arises: After reapportionment, can we expect any significant changes in legislative behavior? Two theories are frequently advanced with respect to this question: (a) older individuals are likely to be more conservative (more resistant to change), and conversely, younger individuals are more likely to be liberal (more prone to favor change); and (b) the "generation thesis," which suggests that "the political frame of reference in terms of which one first begins to think seriously about politics may remain in force for the rest of one's life."[9] There is some evidence to suggest that the generation theory is more suitable in accounting for the legislator's political outlook. But, once again, the evidence is far from conclusive.

(4) A question related to (1), (2), and (3) above is this: How does reapportionment affect the strength of political parties in both of these states? Too many imponderables are associated with reapportionment for any definitive answer to this question. In the absence of any outrageous gerrymandering, the following conclusion seems warranted: In Iowa, Democrats certainly would become a more numerous and important minority than they have traditionally been; in Indiana, the prospects of Democratic control of both houses of the legislature are considerably improved.

## Suggestions For Further Research

Many have speculated about the effects of reapportionment along the guidelines set down by the Supreme Court. Certain propositions seem fairly well established: (1) That political party which controls at the time of reapportionment will seek to maximize its strength and to minimize the strength of the opposition party. (2) Even given the standard of "one man, one vote," the party that is dominant at the time of reapportionment has more than sufficient latitude to redistrict pretty much according to its will. In other words, the "one man, one vote" formula, by itself, is not a hindrance to those processes of gerrymandering so much deplored in political science literature. (3) The nature and extensiveness of rural-urban conflict has been grossly exaggerated in much political science literature dealing with state politics and processes. This particular study does little more than add another small piece of evidence to this effect.

Although empirical studies of almost every description are necessary to measure the effects of reapportionment, a more compelling need at this juncture is the development of a theory or theories that would place empirical findings in a meaningful perspective and indicate those areas and problems that need further exploration. A fruitful approach to this task would be to ask ourselves precisely what functions we want our representative assemblies to perform. For instance, most would probably agree with the broad proposition that legislatures should make intelligent and effective laws that are responsive in one fashion or another to the will of the people. We could then proceed to ask ourselves: What attributes must a legislature possess in order to fulfill these functions? And having asked this question, we are in a better position to fit our existing data into a more meaningful framework and to identify problem areas that demand more intensive research. Two examples of such areas will illustrate this point:

(1) We know from numerous studies that most state legislatures have high rates of turnover.[10] Presuming only that it takes several sessions for an individual to understand the working of the legislature and to gain an appreciable amount of knowledge in certain established legislative subject areas, we have reason to believe that a higher turnover rate would adversely affect the quality of legislative output. In any event, this is one factor that seems highly related to legislative performance and one worth investigation from several angles. If, for instance, higher turnover does result from reapportionment, would this tend to place greater power and influence in the hands of the few who do remain in the legislature for a long time? If so, how does this affect the responsiveness of legislators to the public will? Or is there any relationship between turnover and consistent public policy? These are but a few of the questions that might arise from such an approach.

(2) Intelligent, effective, and responsive public policy formation requires a certain amount of informational input into legislative systems. For instance, legislators many times must calculate what the

probable public reaction will be to the enactment of given policies. This reaction can, of course, range from overwhelming approval to wide-scale public disobedience. A legislator's estimation of probable reaction can easily have an influence on his final vote on any given issue, for while he may favor a given policy, information gained from a variety of sources, including his own reasoning and knowledge, may lead him to believe that enforcement of the policy would be too cumbersome and expensive. Clearly, reapportionment can have a bearing upon the formulation of an intelligent estimate of public reaction, since the channels through which groups and individuals have in the past oriented themselves will, in many cases, undergo varying degrees of changes.[11] Put otherwise, there is no a priori reason to assume that more relevant information necessary for rational calculation of costs of policy implementation will be available to decision-makers after reapportionment. Indeed, given the role of political parties in reapportionment and the fact that the focus of political activity and channels of communication for the citizens will be altered, there is reason to believe the opposite.

In the last analysis, however, the answers to these and a myriad of related questions depend upon a theory or theories that would place empirical findings in a meaningful perspective and indicate those problems and areas that need further exploration.

# 6 / Legislative Attitudes Toward Interest Groups

*Henry Teune*

THE CATEGORIES OF DISCOURSE ON THE SUCCESS OR POWER OF INTEREST groups include their internal characteristics, such as cohesiveness and leadership; their place in the social and political structure as indicated by wealth and numbers; their access to decision-making centers; and their acceptability to decision-makers with whom they register their claims.[1] Existing explanations of interest group influence could be improved upon by knowledge about the interrelationship of these categories and also by developing explanations of the categories themselves. Do wealthy, cohesive interest groups with large memberships have better access than those which have small treasuries, few members, and factions? Does a legislator respond more favorably toward interest groups with ubiquitous access than toward one with only a sporadic, ungrammatical newsletter? What explains the acceptability of interest groups to a legislator?

One finding of this research is that the general receptivity of legislative candidates to interest groups can be explained by the importance of interest groups not in society generally but in that part of it which is most relevant to the legislator—the constituency. This finding elaborates the tentative conclusion of Zeigler that the success of interest groups partially depends on the legitimacy accorded them by those in a position to make authoritative decisions.[2] The elaboration is that this legitimacy, interpreted as favorable attitudes toward interest groups, depends on the nature of interest group activity in the constituency.

Two not necessarily competitive factors are explored. One is that a favorable attitude toward interest groups is a function of the legislative candidate's need for financial, personal, and political support. This need will be labelled "insecurity" and is inferred from the candidate's present position, political record, and personal characteristics. The other is that a favorable stance toward interest groups is a consequence of the kind of constituency which he wants to represent and which can give or deny him the reward of office.

The two hypotheses to be examined are: (1) those legislative candidates who are more insecure in their personal and political positions will be more favorably disposed toward (more receptive to) interest groups than those who are more secure, and (2) those legislative candidates who come from or are standing for election in more heterogeneous districts and who experience greater contact with interest groups in their constituencies will be more favorably disposed toward interest groups than those from more homogeneous (often rural) constituencies.

## Design of the Research

In the summer of 1960, 238 of all of the legislative candidates and holdover Senators for the 1961 Indiana General Assembly were given a lengthy oral interview. This was 86.5 percent of the total universe of 275 candidates and holdover Senators.[3] The questionnaire (see Appendix B) was designed to cover three substantive areas: (1) attitudes toward interest groups, (2) relationships between the legislator and his constituency, and (3) opinions and appraisals of the then controversial Indiana "right to work" law.[4] Data on the legislator himself, his personal activities and roles, and his relationship to the party were also obtained.

The questionnaire was designed for many purposes. Because of this rather omnibus approach, several kinds of secondary analyses are possible. Although the original interest-group attitude questions were designed to examine another "theory" or set of hypotheses, this present test of hypotheses was designed after the completion of the first research. Because of the ex post facto analyses of the data, two major concepts, "insecurity" and "interest group activity in the district" were not assessed as efficiently or as effectively as they might have been.

## Defining Attitudes Toward Interest Groups

Two measures of favorable-unfavorable attitudes toward interest groups were used. The primary measure was a summary rank of responses to a set of general statements about interest groups. The second measure was a summary rank of agreement or disagreement with the "policies and activities" of some specific interest groups with lobbyists who were active in the previous legislative session. Both sets of items required the legislative candidate or holdover Senator to check one of the following categories: "agree," "tend to agree," "undecided," "tend to disagree," and "disagree." [5]

There were twelve general statements which related to interest groups in general. They were all designed to elicit the respondent's feelings on the usefulness of interest groups for himself as a politician, for the legislative process in general, and for effective democratic government. It was intended that all of the items together would reflect the legitimacy of interest groups as an integral part of state politics.

Several dozen items were written. Many of these items were suggested by examination of other questionnaires, particularly that of Wahlke, Eulau, Buchanan, and Ferguson.[6] Each item was placed on an evaluation sheet for informal comment by people acquainted with either attitude scale construction or with Indiana state politics. The items selected were:

(1) Allowing interest groups to operate in the legislature is a desirable way of allowing the people to get at the legislature.

(2) The operations of interest groups provide an inexpensive means of giving the legislature information.

(3) Interest groups aid the democratic processes by communicating to the legislator what the people want.

(4) [The job of the legislator is to work out compromises among conflicting interests.]

(5) It is necessary for legislators to explain their vote to interest group leaders.

(6) It would be desirable for opposing interest groups to get together and iron out their differences on proposed legislation rather than throw the issue open in the legislature.

(7) A legislator can decide how to vote on most issues by asking himself if the proposed law is fair to groups which will be affected by the law.

(8) It is difficult for a legislator to distinguish between what interest groups want and what is in the best interest of the state of Indiana.

(9) Interest groups in general make unreasonable demands on public officials. (negative)

(10) [Under our form of government, every individual should take an interest in government directly, not through interest group organizations.] (negative)

(11) Even if a legislator suspects that the leadership of an interest group is not representative of the membership, it is generally too difficult to find out how well the leadership represents the membership.

(12) [So many groups want so many different things that it is often difficult to know what stand to take.] (negative)

The items in brackets are from the questionnaire of Wahlke, Eulau, Buchanan, and Ferguson. "Negative" in parentheses indicates that disagree reflects a favorable or positive attitude. Unfortunately, not enough negatively worded items were included to reduce possible response set.

Each of the response categories was arbitrarily weighted from one to five consistent with the positive or negative nature of the item. Every respondent received a total summated score. By plotting each of the respondent scores, a highly normalized distribution was obtained. They were then divided into quartiles for analysis.

Eight interest groups were listed. The legislators and candidates were asked to respond with varying degrees of agreement or disagreement with the policies and activities of these groups. The groups were: Indiana Farm Bureau, Indiana AFL-CIO, Indiana Conference of Teamsters, Indiana State Teachers Association, Indiana State Medical Association, Indiana Manufacturers Association, Indiana State Chamber of Commerce, and Taxpayers Federation. Only the last of these was perhaps not well known. The other seven are part of the everyday scene in the General Assembly. Taken together they represent two labor union organizations, two professional organizations, two business associations, the major farm organization in the state, and one organization dedicated to low taxes.

Again the responses to these organizations were summated with weights of one to five. The candidates and legislators were separated into four groups for analysis. Although a normal distribution of respondents was approximated, the scores tended to be high, reflecting a large degree of agreement.

The question of the validity of these measures of interest group orientation remains. Because of severe time limitations, the questionnaire was not adequately pre-tested. Thus there were neither data nor general information to purify the scales sufficiently before interviewing. A large number of items were administered so that it is possible to purify the present twelve-item interest-group orientation scale. This could be done by intercorrelating each of the items and by discarding the five or six items with the lowest average correlation. This was done, but it is not reflected in this analysis.[7] Purifying the scale by discarding items that perhaps tend to measure something other than a single homogeneous dimension of interest group attitudes would perhaps increase some of the relationships presented in this study.

Because of the simplicity of the specific interest group items, it was not necessary to perform an inter-item analysis on these responses. However, some doubt should remain about whether responses to specific interest groups can be summated into a score of agreement with interest groups in general. Whether these responses can be properly summated depends, of course, on the representativeness of the specific interest groups and on the equality in familiarity of each of the respondents with the groups in question. Most of the interest groups that were included should have been familiar to all but the most naïve candidates. Further, the range of political opinion represented by these groups is substantial enough so that it is likely that a high agreement score reflects a disposition to agree with interest groups in general rather than with specific policies being promoted by some of them.

If these two measures both assess a single dimension of agreement-disagreement with or favorable-unfavorable attitudes toward interest groups, then they should be significantly correlated. Although it would be desirable to have more than two measures of the same attribute for validation, these two measures do correlate significantly. The summated scores on the general interest-group attitude scale and the specific interest-group agreement items were transformed into standard scores. The correlation between these two scores for all respondents was .24 ( significant at the .01 level).

Which of these two measures is the better measure of the "real" feelings of the candidate toward interest groups? Because of a lack of a third independent, distinct measure of interest group attitudes, this question cannot be answered. Because the responses to these two measures are significantly correlated, each measure is validated to some extent by the other. If the two did not correlate, then the general items, designed as the direct measures, would perhaps have been interpreted as the valid ones.

Although party differences are often cited as the critical variable for legislative behavior, there is no significant Republican and Democratic difference on the general interest group scale. In the findings reported below, party was always held constant for each variable; that is, Democrats and Republicans were examined independently. However, with one or two exceptions, no better relationship could be found by holding party constant than by lumping both Democrats and Republicans together. This is a consequence in part of the fact that legislative candidates were interviewed and not elected legislators alone, and apparently the universe of Republican and Democratic candidates differs from that which is elected.

Party differences on agreement with individual, specific interest groups were substantial. Democrats were more favorable toward labor unions; Republicans toward business organizations. In the total scores for agreement-disagreement with all of the interest groups together, party differences are not significant. As a matter of fact, Democrats and

Republicans fall about equally into each of the four categories of high and low agreement with specific interest groups.[8]

## Defining Insecurity

Insecurity was not directly assessed in the questionnaire. Thus, it was necessary to use several indicators of insecurity. If several "reasonable" indicators of insecurity do not significantly relate to either of the two assessments of interest group attitudes, then the insecurity hypothesis, at least as far as these indicators of insecurity are concerned, can be rejected. The approach is to give several indicators of insecurity. These are categorized into the following: (1) individual characteristics of the candidate or legislator, (2) his perceptions of his political situation, and (3) his experiences. Each of these indicators is compared with the scores on the two scales of interest group attitudes.

*Individual Characteristics.* Each indicator should have a hypothesis or proposition which links it to the attribute which the indicator supposedly indicates. Because the attribute of insecurity was not directly assessed, none of the hypotheses linking the attribute to the indicators can be demonstrated in this research. Although it would be possible to argue for each linking hypothesis by presenting substantiating evidence from other research, this will not be done in this report.

The first assumption was that the longer the period of residence of a candidate in the district in which he was standing for election, the more secure he would be. Thus, length of residence in the district is one indicator of security or insecurity. The second hypothesis was that the less the legislative experience of a candidate or legislator, the greater would be his insecurity. The third assumption was that low educational attainment would be related to insecurity. Educational attainment would be an indicator of knowledge. People with more knowledge should have greater confidence in making choices, or so it will be assumed here, than those with less knowledge. The fourth assumption was that high personal income would be related to security; low income would, in turn, be related to dependence and insecurity.

*Perceptions.* All of the measures of perceptions are based on the legislators' and candidates' judgment about the strength of his party and party organization in his district. The assumption, a general one, is that the greater the strength of the party and the more vigorous the party organization in the district, the more secure the candidate and legislator will feel in his political position. In turn, the politician's perception of weakness of his own party in the district would be tied to greater dependence on interest groups for political support.

The questions that relate to a politician's perceptions of how important his party is as a base of political strength are the following: (1) "How about the relative strength of the parties in your district—over the years has the district been safe Republican, or Democratic, fairly close, or what?" (These responses were coded by the interviewer into the following: (a) safe Democratic, (b) mostly Democratic, (c) competitive, (d) mostly Republican, and (e) safe Republican.) (2) "How strong is the political party organization in your legislative district?" (The responses were coded by the interviewer as (a) very weak, (b) pretty weak, (c) about average, (d) pretty strong, and (e) very strong. This analysis reports findings for single-member single-county districts.) (3) "How important is the party organization in determining the outcome of a general election for the legislature in your district?" (The interviewer coded into the following categories: (a) totally unimportant, (b) unimportant, (c) somewhat important, (d) quite important, and (e) most important.) (4) "In general, within your legislative district is there much competition in your party's primary?" (The interviewer code was (a) no competition, (b) little, (c) moderate, (d) a lot, and (e) very competitive.)

*Experiences.* A set of questions tapped the legislative politician's experiences. The first was about the competition in the primary, "Did you have opposition in the primary this year?" (The number of opponents was coded. This question was, of course, not asked of holdover Senators.) Here the assumption is, although a weak one, that the greater the number of opponents in the primary, the less secure the candidate will be in seeking and obtaining office.

The question that perhaps assesses the amount of insecurity of the candidate most directly is one that asked about his reaction to his primary competition. If the candidate had opposition, he was asked, "How much were you worried about it?" (The responses were categorized by the interviewer into the following: (a) not worried at all, (b) only a little, (c) moderately, (d) a lot, and (e) extremely so.) A single question, however, that purports to assess a complex past psychological state, such as worry, will probably have little validity.

The final question about the experience of the legislators and candidates was a rather lengthy one: "It has been said that interest groups sometimes try to exert political influence by threatening to provide the legislator with an opposition candidate in the primary. Have you ever known cases in which opposition was provided in this manner?" (The code here was a simple "yes" or "no.")

*Defining Interest Group Activity in the District*

Interest group activity in a political district can be either inferred from certain socioeconomic characteristics or observed directly. Whether the stimuli of interest group activity actually penetrate the selective shield of a politician is another matter. Three kinds of indicators are used to assess interest group activity in the district: (1) the socioeconomic character of the district as expressed in census data, (2) the legislator's and the legislative aspirant's perceptions of interest group activity, and (3) the experiences of the legislative candidate with interest groups.

*District Characteristics.* Many combinations of socioeconomic data on legislative districts are possible. Most of them are related to economic factors; many are aspects of urbanization. Only urbanization is used. On the basis of 1960 census data, all legislative districts were classified according to the percentage of the population living in urban areas and the size of the urban concentrations. Out of the nine categories developed, the three used in this analysis are: (1) districts containing Ft. Wayne, Gary, Hammond, East Chicago, South Bend, and Evansville with always more than 50 percent of the population living in one of these cities, (2) districts, not classified as more urban, containing cities of over 20,000, and (3) districts containing no cities of over 10,000 with always more than 50 percent of the population living in cities of under 5,000.

*Perceptions.* Several questions related to the social, economic, and religious nature of the district. In a series of questions about the district two produced responses sufficiently distributed for analysis: "How about the religious composition of the district?" and "How about the main economic activity of the district?" Both of these questions were coded after the questionnaires were completed.

Three questions concerned the political activity of local organizations. In two of these questions the number of local organizations mentioned was recorded: "Aside from the party itself, what local organizations would you say are important in determining the outcome of an election in your district?" and "Are there any interest groups or lobbies that are particularly strong in your own district?" ("Which ones are these?") The third question was about local union political activity: "Is there much union political activity (in the district)?" (These responses were coded (a) yes, strong; (b) yes, quite a lot; (c) some; (d) not too much; (e) yes, but confined to one area; and (f) no.[9]

*Experiences.* Two questions called for information about the legislator's and the candidate's experiences with interest groups. Perhaps the questions are more related to attitudes toward interest groups than to experiences. The first question was "How important a part do interest groups play in telling you what you want to know about your constituency?" (These responses were coded by the interviewers as (a) totally unimportant, (b) unimportant, (c) some importance, (d) important, and (e) very important.) The second question only indirectly assesses experiences: "Are there any specific groups of voters whose preferences you think you know particularly well?" ("What groups are these?") The number of groups mentioned is used in this report.

## Findings

Because the relationships between the indicators and the attributes of insecurity and interest group activity in the district have not been demonstrated, it is possible to interpret the findings either as a test of the two hypotheses or as a set of individual relationships. If none or only a few of the indicators are related to the attributes, then, of course, the hypotheses have not been tested. If all or most of the indicators are related to the attributes, then to some extent the hypotheses have been tested. Because multiple indicators for both of the explanatory variables were used, it is possible to assume that some of them are, in fact, indicators of the attributes. Because there is a validity measure for the interest group scale and because of the multiple items in each of the two measures, there can be confidence in the adequacy of the measures of interest group attitudes.

The table below summarizes the findings. It gives predicted relationships, derived from the two hypotheses, the direction of the findings with a chi-square significance level for relationships observed, and the categories used in the analysis. It is recognized that other statistical tests could have been used, but generally the relationships cited should hold under other tests of significance. Only by taking members of one party was it possible to get relationships for two of the indicators noted in the table. If members of both parties were combined, the relationships disappeared. It is difficult to interpret the findings for single parties except in a very speculative way.

There are twenty-two positive predictions derived from the insecur-

# TABLE I

## ATTITUDES TOWARD INTEREST GROUPS AND INDICATORS OF INSECURITY AND OF INTEREST GROUP ACTIVITY

| INSECURITY INDICATORS | Prediction from Hypotheses | The General Interest Group Items | | | Agreement with Specific Interest Groups | | |
|---|---|---|---|---|---|---|---|
| | | Observed Relation | Chi-Square Level | Categories | Observed Relation | Chi-Square Level | Categories |
| *Individual Characteristics* | | | | | | | |
| 1. brief residence in the district | positive | none | — | | none | — | |
| 2. little legislative experience | positive | negative | .05 | no session vs. 3 or 4 sessions | negative | .05 | none vs. 3 or more sessions |
| 3. low formal educational attainment | positive | none | — | | negative | .05 | college or more vs. high school & less |
| 4. low income | positive | none | — | | none | — | |
| *Perceptions* | | | | | | | |
| 1. weakness of own party in elections in district | positive | none | — | | none | — | |
| 2. weakness of party organization in district (single county districts only) | positive | negative | .05 | very strong vs. very and pretty weak | negative | .01 | strong and very average and less vs. strong (Republicans only) |
| 3. highly competitive primary | positive | negative | .05 | very competitive vs. moderate or less | none | — | |
| 4. unimportance of party in outcome of elections | positive | negative | .05 | most important vs. important & somewhat important | none | — | |
| *Experiences* | | | | | | | |
| 1. large number of opponents in primary | positive | none | — | | none | — | |

TABLE I (continued)

ATTITUDES TOWARD INTEREST GROUPS AND INDICATORS OF INSECURITY AND OF INTEREST GROUP ACTIVITY

| INDICATORS OF INTEREST GROUP ACTIVITY IN DISTRICT | Prediction from Hypotheses | The General Interest Group Items | | | Agreement with Specific Interest Groups | | |
|---|---|---|---|---|---|---|---|
| | | Observed Relation | Chi-Square Level | Categories | Observed Relation | Chi-Square Level | Categories |
| 2. worried about primary competition | positive | none | — | — | *negative* | .01 | not at all and a little vs. extremely |
| 3. heard interest groups provided opposition in primaries | positive | none | — | — | none | — | — |
| *District Characteristics* | | | | | | | |
| urban district | positive | *positive* | .05 | (see text for categories) | none | — | — |
| *Perceptions* | | | | | | | |
| 1. several organizations important in district | positive | *positive* | .01 | none vs. 1 or 2 vs. 3 or 4 | none | — | — |
| 2. several organizations important in elections in district | positive | *positive* | .01 | none vs. 3 or more | none | — | — |
| 3. commercial and industrial activity | positive | *positive* | .05 | farming, small retail vs. commercial and industrial (Democrats only) | none | — | — |
| 4. mixed Catholic-Protestants | positive | *positive* | .05 | all or predominant Protestant vs. 25%–50% Catholic | *positive* | .05 | all or predominant Protestant vs. 25%–50% Catholic |
| 5. unions active in politics | positive | *positive* | .01 | much and a lot vs. some vs. none and not too much | none | — | — |

## TABLE I (continued)

### ATTITUDES TOWARD INTEREST GROUPS AND INDICATORS OF INSECURITY AND OF INTEREST GROUP ACTIVITY

| INDICATORS OF INTEREST GROUP ACTIVITY IN DISTRICT | Prediction from Hypotheses | The General Interest Group Items | | | Agreement with Specific Interest Groups | | |
|---|---|---|---|---|---|---|---|
| | | Observed Relation | Chi-Square Level | Categories | Observed Relation | Chi-Square Level | Categories |
| *Experiences* | | | | | | | |
| 1. several groups whose preferences are well known | positive | positive | .02 | none vs. 1 or 2 | positive | .01 | two and less vs. 3 and more |
| 2. interest groups important in telling about constituency | positive | positive | .01 | very important vs. somewhat and unimportant vs. totally unimportant | positive | .02 | somewhat important and less vs. important and very important |

ity hypothesis for the eleven indicators. Not a single one of these was positive in support of this hypothesis. Eight of the predicted positive relationships turned out to be negative. There was no relationship for the remaining predictions. Sixteen positive predictions were made for the eight indicators of interest group activity in the district. Of these eleven were positive and none negative. If the indicators are valid

## TABLE II

### Urban-Rural Districts, Strength of Party Organization, and Number of Interest Groups Active in District

| Districts | Party Organization (single-county districts only) | | No. of Lobbies and Interest Groups Active in District | |
|---|---|---|---|---|
| | very weak, pretty weak & average | pretty strong and very strong | 0, 1, 2, or 3 | 4 or more |
| URBAN 50% or more of population in cities over 20,000 | 16 | 61 | 57 | 32 |
| RURAL 50% or more of population not in cities | 36 | 30 | 106 | 18 |
| | $X^2 = 6.22$, significant at .02 level | | $X^2 = 13.24$, significant at .001 level | |

NOTE: The number of cases does not equal 238 because some districts were not classified and because of no response. The question on party organization was asked only in single county districts because of the involvement of two or more county party organizations in multi-county districts.

ones, then the insecurity hypothesis should be rejected and the interest group activity hypothesis accepted.

The general interest group items are related to more indicators of interest group activity in the district than the items measuring agreement with specific interest groups. This may be because of greater contamination in the specific interest group items, resulting from responses to the policies of particular interest groups. There are no contradictions, however, in the relationships found for the two measures of interest group attitudes.

The findings show more than an absence of relationships with the indicators of insecurity. In fact eight out of twenty-two predictions from the insecurity hypothesis are disconfirmed. The data would to some extent support a contention that the more legislative candidates are firmly based personally and politically, the more receptive they are to the role of interest groups. In particular, weakness of party organization was not related to reliance on interest groups, whereas the presence of a viable political organization was associated with candidates who were receptive to interest groups.

There is a relatively clear pattern. Legislative candidates from urban districts perceived their party organizations as strong and having many active interest groups; rural districts were seen as having weak party organizations and few active interest groups. This is shown in Table II. The pattern is somewhat obscured because of the unsatisfactory definitions of urban and rural and perhaps because the relationships are not linear.

Consistent with the relationships between urban districts and strong

TABLE III

STRENGTH OF PARTY ORGANIZATION (SINGLE-COUNTY DISTRICTS) AND NUMBER OF INTEREST GROUPS ACTIVE IN DISTRICT

| | NUMBER OF LOBBIES AND INTEREST GROUPS ACTIVE IN DISTRICT | |
| --- | --- | --- |
| Strength of Party Organization | 0, 1, 2, or 3 | 4 or more |
| Very weak, pretty weak, and average | 41 | 8 |
| Pretty strong and strong | 61 | 39 |

$X^2 = 7.91$, significant at .01 level

party organizations and many active interest groups was the relationship between perceptions of strong party organization and the number of interest groups. This is presented in Table III.

This evidence, if the sample of indicators is indeed an adequate reflection of the attributes of insecurity and the extent of interest group activity in legislative districts, supports the hypothesis that favorable attitudes toward interest groups are a function of interest group activity in the pivot of a politician's career, the district. Even perhaps more strongly supported by the evidence is the rejection of the hypothesis that personal and political insecurity predisposes legislative candidates toward interest groups.

## Conclusions and Implications

The legislative candidate who is favorably disposed toward interest groups and their functions in the political process has most probably had substantial contact with a variety of groups in his constituency. Experienced candidates are significantly more approving of interest groups than inexperienced candidates. This is probably the result of longer associations with interest groups operating in constituencies.

What is surprising is that candidates who have the backing of a strong party organization and substantial support in the voting habits of the public are also favorably inclined toward interest groups. In the same questionnaire a set of items, similar to the interest group items, was administered to assess orientations to the political party. There was a strong relationship between commitment to the political party and favorable attitudes toward interest groups.[10] Strong orientations to both the political party and interest groups are not incompatible. Strong parties do not lessen ties with interest groups.

The data show that interest group activity in the constituency stands out as the most important set of variables for explaining attitudes toward interest groups. Interest group activities important for the legislative process are those which occur in legislative districts. What interest groups do in the legislative halls, hotel rooms, and in committee hearings seems to be of less significance in shaping attitudes than activity in the constituency which the legislator or the candidate is going to represent. In turn, the economic and social structure largely determines what interest groups can do in the constituencies. The disposition to respond to interest groups is a component of the complex of factors that prompt a legislator to respond to his constituency. Interest groups are important to him as part of the constituency that he feels he should or must represent. The constituency is an integral part of the political world of the legislator, and insofar as interest groups are meshed into this part of his political world, the legislator will be receptive to them.

If the constituency is the focal point of interest group influence, then a variety of research tasks can be set forth. Specifically, the number, intensity, and kind of interest group contacts with legislators, the fusion of the interest group with the party organization (which is suggested by the relationship between reported strong political organization and favorable attitudes toward interest groups), and the general mobilization of interest groups into the political system at the local or district level should prove to be highly predictive of attitudes toward interest groups. Rather than asking legislators about their associations with lobbyists and interest group spokesmen within and about the legislative meetings, questions should be directed to the subtle and seemingly critical part interest groups play within the constituency.

# PART III

# Theory Building About Legislative Behavior

# 7 / Some Theory and Data on Representational Roles and Legislative Behavior

*Kenneth Janda*

EDMUND BURKE'S SPEECH IN 1774 TO HIS CONSTITUENTS AT BRISTOL HAS had a lasting impact upon the study of representative-constituency relationships. Traditional inquiry into this topic had accepted Burke's approach as exemplified by the question, "How ought a representative act in reference to constituency demands?" Thus phrased, the topic is a normative problem and does not invite empirical inquiry. For almost two hundred years, the study of representative-constituency relationships focused on this classic normative question, as scholars built a literature of opinions and arguments about the proper role of the representative.[1]

In recent years, however, research in representative-constituency relationships has shown a concern for empirical questions, which ask not how representatives ought to act but how they do act. This redirection is due largely to the work of Eulau, Wahlke, Buchanan, and Ferguson, who in 1959 published an article that distinguished between the style and focus of representational roles.[2] They used the style of representation to refer to the particular criterion of judgment the legislator might use in deciding on legislative issues. A representative who feels that he ought to decide on the basis of his own values and evaluation of the facts is labeled a trustee. One who feels that he ought to disregard his personal opinions and to obey his constituents is called a delegate. Trustees and delegates differ in the norms they have internalized concerning the proper style of representational behavior.

In addition to representational style, Eulau and his co-authors, formulated the concept of representational focus, which refers to the particular group of persons whose welfare the representative feels he ought to consider in making his decisions. A representative who feels that he ought to consider primarily the welfare of his constituents is labeled as district-oriented. One who feels that he ought to consider the welfare of all the people in the state is called state-oriented.

The authors employed these conceptual distinctions in a comparative study of legislators in four states: Ohio, California, New Jersey, and Tennessee.[3] They sought to determine the style and focus of legislators' representational roles by analyzing responses to the question, "How would you describe the job of being a legislator; what are the most important things you should do here?"[4] Responses were coded in terms of both the style and the focus of representation. For the style of representation, the category of politico was added to accommodate answers which contained a mixture of delegate and trustee elements. Similarly, the hybrid category of district-and-state-oriented was used to code responses which reflected both elements of the focus of representation.

These categories were then employed in studying the distribution and interrelation of role orientations across the four states. The initial analysis seemed to confirm the face validity of their operationalization: legislators' responses to the question could be categorized in terms of the authors' concepts of representational roles. The applicability of these concepts to elected representatives at the national level was later confirmed in Jones' case study of the Agriculture Committee in the U. S. House of Representatives.[5]

The final report of the four-state study disclosed additional data which not only supported the face validity of their operationalization but also indicated the relevance of their conceptualization for explaining legislative behavior. The authors found that legislators with different representational roles (delegate—trustee) also differed in their attitudes toward the legislative process.[6] Further support for the validity and relevance of the authors' conceptualization is contained in at least two subsequent studies. McMurray and Parsons disclosed results of a survey that showed clear differences in the public's attitudes toward representational roles of legislators and judges.[7] And in their comparison of the role orientations of Michigan legislators with elected delegates to the Michigan Constitutional Convention, Friedman and Stokes found significant differences between the groups, at least with respect to the focus of representation.[8]

The conceptual distinctions and terminology of Eulau and his co-authors have won general acceptance within contemporary literature on legislative behavior.[9] But research using these concepts has not gone much beyond reaffirming the validity of operationalizations and suggesting the relevance of the concepts for explaining legislative behavior. As yet we have no proof that delegates are more responsive to constituency opinions than trustees are. We have no proof that district-oriented legislators do resolve decisions in favor of their constituents while state-oriented legislators subordinate local interests to state interests. In fact, we do not even have any systematic statements of hypotheses relating representational roles to legislative behavior. Research on representational behavior has not progressed much since its auspicious beginning.

## Research Obstacles and Strategies

By far the greatest obstacle to empirical research on representative-constituency relationships is the tremendous cost and complexity involved in gathering the necessary data. At a minimum, data are needed on both sides of the relationship: on representatives and their constituencies.[10] Data on representatives—including their backgrounds, attitudes, and official behavior—are relatively accessible. Indeed, most of the studies on representational roles have focused exclusively on the legislator's side of the representative-constituency relationship. Data on the representatives' constituencies, however, are far more costly to obtain and therefore less available.

Demographic or census-type data on constituencies, which have been used in many studies of legislative behavior, are simply not adequate for research on representational behavior. Comparing legislators' behavior with constituents' opinions requires precise information about individuals' opinions within the districts. The most suitable research method yet developed for obtaining reliable information about the nature and distribution of personal opinions among large populations is the sample survey. An appropriately drawn sample of about 2,000 respondents furnishes an adequate basis for making confident statements about opinions held by 70 million voters in the United States. But the science of probability sampling is such that a sample roughly the same size is needed to make statements at a similar level of confidence about the much smaller electorates of a U. S. Congressman or even the average state legislator. Because careful sample surveys are expensive to conduct and complex to administer, sampling techniques have not been used for systematic research in representational behavior until very recently.

A pioneering effort in research on representative-constituency relationships was undertaken in 1958 by the University of Michigan's Survey Research Center, which designed its national sample of the electorate in a manner that permitted limited analyses of constituency opinions in about 100 congressional districts, thereby resulting in the first direct comparisons between representatives' behavior and their constituents' opinions.[11] Despite this breakthrough, sample survey methodology in the study of representational behavior remains complex and expensive, and research on the topic in the foreseeable future is unlikely to employ sample surveys to any large extent.

Pending the availability of appropriate data on constituents' opinions, what strategy promises the greatest payoff for studying representational behavior? A two-step procedure seems to be in order: The first step should be to formulate and codify propositions relating representational roles to legislative behavior; the second step should be to test propositions that utilize interview data on legislators.

Relatively few explicit propositions are set forth in the literature on representational behavior, which is richer by far in implicit consequences of representational roles. A systematic presentation of these hypotheses would help determine research priorities and provide a base for the cumulation of knowledge about representational behavior. Not all the propositions in such a theoretical framework would link representational roles with legislative behavior; some would relate representational roles to psychological, sociological, and political variables associated with the individual. In the absence of appropriate data to test propositions between roles and behavior, remaining propositions could at least be tested with interview data on legislators; this is the second step in the suggested strategy. Assuming some coherence among sets of propositions in the theoretical framework, validation of some sets would support, but not prove, the validity of the others. This indirect attack on the problem will build up our knowledge while we await appropriate sample survey data for testing the remaining propositions.

This chapter attempts to follow the research strategy briefly outlined above. It will first set forth a systematic statement of hypotheses relating representational role orientations to legislators' behavior, attitudes, and perceptions. It will then test some of the propositions with available data. After evaluating the results of these exercises, it will make some suggestions about the needs of future research on representational behavior.

## Theoretical Framework

The sets of propositions presented below are referred to as a theoretical framework instead of as a theory because they are not interrelated in a rigorous deductive system. Whether or not these propositions prove to be deducible from a smaller number of propositions and thus constitute a theory of representational behavior is a subject for later study. At present, there is a need for straight forward formulation and codification of individual propositions. Extensive revisions and refinements of the hypotheses undoubtedly will be prompted by bringing them into the open and organizing them for critical review.

The theoretical framework will be limited only to propositions employing the four representational role concepts: delegate, trustee, district-oriented, and state-oriented. The two hybrid concepts of politico, for the style of representation, and district-and-state-oriented, for the focus of representation, will not be incorporated into these propositions. This limitation is imposed both because of the unclear nature of the hybrid concepts and because of a desire to simplify the task of constructing the theoretical framework by dealing only with the "polar" concepts for each role orientation. But as Hyman and Sheatsley point out in their methodological critique of "The Authoritarian Personality," which also studied only extreme groups on both sides of the authoritarianism scale, the middle group may differ from the extremes in unexpected ways.[12] Therefore, legislators in the hybrid or middle categories cannot always be expected to occupy a place in the propositions between the delegates and trustees or between the district-oriented and state-oriented representatives.

In fact, despite the past treatment of these hybrid categories as role orientations, there is reason to regard them as indicating the absence of any role orientation, using the term "role" in its technical sense to refer to normative expectations of behavior. The individual legislators' normative expectations of the behavior they think ought to be demonstrated by one who occupies a legislative office can serve as a motivational basis for their official behavior. This conception is similar to Simon's definition of role in terms of "the premises that are to guide the decisions of the actor as to his course of behavior." [13] These premises are normative in nature. In representational behavior, they state how the representative ought to act, using "ought" in the sense of duty.[14]

The legislator's personal norms about the proper style and focus of representation are acquired and internalized through a process of verbal learning and political socialization. The argumentative literature which has arisen over the "proper" role of the representative indicates that social norms are ambiguous or contradictory concerning representational behavior in the face of constituency demands. Political socialization may cause some individuals to internalize behavioral norms concerning their relationships with their constituencies and may not cause others to internalize such norms.

It is sufficient to say that (1) the internalization of behavioral norms of role performance derives from a complex process of political socialization, (2) not all individuals will internalize norms for representational behavior, and (3) those who do may reveal differences in the specific nature of the norms internalized. By recognizing that some individuals do not internalize behavioral norms of role performance (i.e., that some individuals do not act according to self-defined standards of behavior), we are not required to fit every legislator into a representational "role." Thus the hybrid categories of politico and district-and-state-oriented are omitted from the theoretical framework of propositions relating representational roles to legislative behavior.

Several assumptions underlie the formulation of these propositions. It is assumed, for example, that legislators with internalized norms will behave consistently with those norms and that legislators will not incur behavior costs unless they judge the rewards worth the costs of acting. Assumptions are also made about the political socialization process in American culture and about the need to achieve consistency among roles, attitudes, and behavior.

The theoretical framework will follow this format: classification of dependent variables in terms of roles, attitudes, and behavior; separation of propositions within each classification to compare delegates with trustees and to compare district-oriented with state-oriented legislators; explanation of reasoning underlying specific propositions; and presentation of the propositions.

## Dependent Variables: Representational Roles

I. Style of Representation

A. Because representational roles will be internalized as a result of idiosyncratic factors in political socialization, there is no a priori reason to expect role orientations to be related to standard sociological variables. This produces the following propositions.

1. Style of representation is unrelated to education.
2. Style of representation is unrelated to occupation.
3. Style of representation is unrelated to age.
4. Style of representation is unrelated to income.
5. Style of representation is unrelated to urbanization.

B. There is no apparent conflict between representational style and positions on broad public policy issues.

6. Style of representation is unrelated to party affiliation.
7. Style of representation is unrelated to liberal-conservative ideology.

C. One who has held public office has experienced the problems of obtaining information for making decisions, and he is aware of the communication problems between the representative and his constituency.

      8. In comparison with candidates who have not served in the legislature, incumbent legislators are more likely to be trustees than delegates.

  D. An elected official's style of representation depends on the nature of the office to which he is elected: higher offices encourage greater reliance on personal judgment in decisions.

      9. In comparison with representatives, senators are more likely to be trustees than delegates.

  E. The political socialization process operates in the context of constituency politics to affect the style of representation: the threat of political reprisal reduces reliance on personal values in decisions.

      10. In comparison with legislators from safe districts, those from competitive districts are more likely to be delegates than trustees.

II. Focus of Representation

  A. Because representational roles will be internalized as a result of idiosyncratic factors in political socialization, there is no a priori reason to expect role orientations to be related to standard sociological variables.

      11. Focus of representation is unrelated to education.

      12. Focus of representation is unrelated to occupation.

      13. Focus of representation is unrelated to age.

      14. Focus of representation is unrelated to income.

      15. Focus of representation is unrelated to urbanization.

  B. There will be no apparent conflict between representational focus and positions on broad public policy issues, unless support and opposition for such issues are defined along geographical lines. *If geographical regionalism is not a political factor:*

      16. Focus of representation is unrelated to party affiliation.

      17. Focus of representation is unrelated to liberal-conservative ideology.

  *If geographical regionalism is a political factor:*

      18. Members of the minority party, in comparison with members of the majority party, are more likely to be district-oriented than state-oriented.

      19. Members of the minority ideological position, in comparison with members of the majority position, are more likely to be district-oriented than state-oriented.

  C. Service in the legislature is unlikely to disclose any impracticalities in pursuing either focus of representation.

    20. Focus of representation is unrelated to the absence or presence of previous legislative service.

D. An elected official's focus of representation depends upon his personal identification with his district.

    21. In comparison with others, legislators representing single political units (e.g., a county or a whole city) are more likely to be district-oriented than state-oriented.

    22. In comparison with others, legislators who went to public school in the district are more likely to be district-oriented than state-oriented.

E. The political socialization process operates in the context of constituency politics to affect the focus of representation: the threat of political reprisal draws attention to the district.

    23. In comparison with legislators from safe districts, legislators from competitive districts are more likely to be district-oriented than state-oriented.

III. Interrelationships between Style and Focus of Representation

A. Although the style and focus of representational roles are analytically distinct, they are empirically related because political responsibility is enforced through elections on the basis of districts.

    24. Delegates are more likely to be district-oriented than state-oriented.

    25. Trustees are more likely to be state-oriented than district-oriented.

    26. District-oriented legislators are more likely to be delegates than trustees.

    27. State-oriented legislators are more likely to be trustees than delegates.

## Dependent Variables: Attitudes toward Constituency

I. Comparison of Delegates and Trustees

A. In order to maintain consistency between their personal norms of conduct and their attitudes toward their constituency, delegates must believe that their constituents are informed about politics. Therefore, in comparison with trustees, delegates are more likely to believe that

    28. their constituents possess opinions on legislative issues.

    29. their constituents know what goes on in the legislature.

    30. their constituents know about their stands on issues.

31. their constituents know about their election opponents' stands on issues.

B. Not only must delegates believe that their constituents are informed about the legislative process, they also must believe that they can determine their constituents' opinions. Therefore, in comparison with trustees, delegates are more likely to believe that

32. they know their constituents' opinions.
33. they can find out their constituents' opinions.

II. Comparison of District-oriented and State-oriented Representatives

A. In order to maintain consistency between their personal norms of conduct and their attitudes toward their constituency, district-oriented representatives must believe that their districts have special interests that may conflict with those of the state. Therefore, in comparison with state-oriented legislators, district-oriented representatives are more likely to believe that

34. their districts have special interests to be represented in questions of public policy.
35. the interests of their districts may conflict with the interests of the state.

B. In order to maintain consistency between their personal norms of conduct and attitudes toward their constituency, district-oriented representatives must believe that they are well informed about their districts. Therefore, in comparison with state-oriented legislators, district-oriented representatives are more likely to believe that

36. they know their constituents' interests.
37. they can find out their constituents' interests.

*Dependent Variables: Behavior To Determine Constituency Opinions*

I. Comparison of Delegates and Trustees

A. Because of their motivation to act in accordance with their constituents' wishes, delegates will readily incur behavior costs in attempts to determine constituency opinions. More specifically, in comparison with trustees, delegates are more likely to

38. conduct public opinion polls.
39. visit their constituencies more frequently.
40. pay more attention to their mail.

41. use a wider variety of methods to determine constituency opinions.
42. consult representatives of local interest groups.

B. Because they are not committed to constituency opinions as a basis for their decisions, trustees are more likely than delegates to incur behavior costs in getting information from non-constituency sources. More specifically, in comparison with delegates, trustees are more likely to seek information and advice from

43. party leaders.
44. representatives of state-wide interest groups.
45. experts from the executive branch, especially if they are of the same party.
46. friends in the legislature outside of the local delegation (if there are multi-member districts) or outside of the same region (if regionalism is a political factor).

II. Comparison of District-oriented and State-oriented Representatives

A. Because of their motivation to promote their constituents' welfare, district-oriented representatives will readily incur behavior costs attempting to determine constituency interests. More specifically, in comparison with state-oriented representatives, district-oriented representatives are more likely to

47. conduct opinion polls in their districts.
48. visit their constituencies more frequently.
49. pay more attention to their mail.
50. use a wider variety of methods to determine constituency interests.
51. consult representatives of local interest groups.

B. Because state-oriented representatives are not committed to constitutency interests as a basis for their decisions, they are more likely to incur behavior costs in getting information from non-constituency sources. More specifically, in comparison with district-oriented representatives, state-oriented representatives are more likely to seek information and advice from

52. state-wide polls.
53. party leaders.
54. representatives of statewide interest groups.
55. experts from the executive branch, especially if they are of the same party.
56. friends in the legislature outside of the local delegation (if there are multi-member districts) or outside of the same region (if regionalism is a political factor).

## Dependent Variables: Behavior in Support of Legislation

I. Comparison of Delegates and Trustees

A. By definition, delegates are motivated to behave in accordance with their perceptions of constituency opinions. In comparison with trustees, therefore, delegates are more likely to

57. introduce bills which they believe are favored by a plurality of their constituents.
58. speak on behalf of bills which they believe are favored by a plurality of their constituents.
59. vote for bills which they believe are favored by a plurality of their constituents.

B. By definition, trustees are motivated to behave in accordance with their own values and evaluation of the facts. In comparison with delegates, therefore, trustees are more likely to

60. support legislation which they feel is morally right.
61. reflect their own political attitudes in their actions.
62. support legislation favored by their party.

C. For delegates, the probability of acting in accordance with their perceptions of constituency opinions is a direct function of their confidence in the accuracy of those perceptions. Given a conflict between sources of information on constituency opinions, delegates are more likely to follow constituency opinions expressed

63. in polls over those expressed in their mail.
64. in firsthand visits to the constituency over those expressed by interest group representatives visiting the legislature.

II. Comparison of District-oriented and State-oriented Representatives

A. By definition, district-oriented legislators are motivated to promote their districts' interests in the legislature. In comparison with state-oriented representatives, therefore, district-oriented representatives are more likely to

65. introduce bills which they believe promote the interests of their districts.
66. speak on behalf of bills which they believe promote the interests of their districts.
67. vote for bills which they believe promote the interests of their districts.

B. By definition, state-oriented legislators are motivated to decide in accordance with their perceptions of the state's interests. In comparison with district-oriented representatives, therefore, state-oriented representatives are more likely to

68. introduce bills which they believe promote the interests of the state.
69. speak on behalf of bills which they believe promote the interests of the state.
70. vote for bills which they believe promote the interests of the state.
71. reflect their own political attitudes in their actions.

The above theoretical framework obviously does not exhaust the possible relationships between representational roles and various aspects of legislative behavior; many other dependent variables could be brought into the framework. Moreover, it does not present propositions cutting across the style and focus of representation, stating, for example, whether a delegate is more likely to conduct opinion polls than a district-oriented legislator. The framework was severely limited in scope to simplify this initial attempt at building a theoretical framework. Even with its limitations, the framework encompasses seventy-one propositions which suggest the magnitude of the task involved in building theory about political behavior.

Despite the complexity and frustration involved in constructing propositions or theoretical frameworks for inquiry, this task must be done as a part of systematic empirical research in political behavior. The above propositions may seem arbitrary or downright wrong, but at least they are explicit; they are open for review, criticism, and validation. Initial attempts to codify propositions about an aspect of political behavior may be awkward or naïve, but they are also a necessary precursor to more sophisticated theory.

## Data to Test Some Propositions

Data from a previously unpublished study are available for testing some of the propositions in the theoretical framework.[15] The data were gathered during the summer of 1960 from 238 interviews with candidates for the 1961 Indiana Legislature and with holdover Senators from the 1959 session.[16] Although the Indiana research was inspired by the four-state study previously cited,[17] the studies differed substantially in the operations performed to identify legislators' representational roles.

The four-state study assigned representational role orientations to legislators by coding their free answer responses to the question, "How would you describe the job of being a legislator—what are the most important things you should do here?" The coding procedures are described as follows:

> In constructing stylistic and areal-focal role orientation types, the responses to the question were coded in terms of (a) characterization of the job; (b) objectives of the job; and (c) criteria of decision. . . . In general, data concerning criteria of decision yielded the stylistic orientation, and data concerning the objectives of the job yielded the areal orientation.[18]

The authors report that somewhat more than half of the 474 respondents could be assigned stylistic role orientations and about half could be assigned a real role orientations. In their words:

> The reduction in the number of respondents from the total samples is, of course, due to the open-endedness of the question. Hence not all respondents could be used in the construction of the role types as they emerged from representatives' own definitions, and in the analysis.[19]

Their experience in obtaining such a high proportion of unusable responses with an open-ended question prompted the formulation and use of closed questions in the Indiana study. Legislators' representational styles were tapped by having them disclose their attitudes toward two statements which advanced opposing views on the proper style of the representative. Each of the 238 respondents was handed these questions interspersed among ten other attitude items and asked to check the extent of his agreement with each statement. The items and the distribution of responses among the five available response categories are given in Table I.

## TABLE I

### STATEMENTS ABOUT THE STYLE OF REPRESENTATION AND THE DISTRIBUTION OF RESPONSES TO THOSE STATEMENTS

Delegate: "Even though the legislator is firmly convinced that his constituents are not properly evaluating the issues, it is his job to disregard his *own* views and vote the way they want."

Trustee: "Because his constituents seldom know all the various aspects of important issues, the legislator serves his constituency best if he is left alone to make careful decisions by himself."

|  | Agree | Tend to Agree | Unde-cided | Tend to Disagree | Disagree |  |
|---|---|---|---|---|---|---|
| Delegate | 28 | 32 | 10 | 58 | 106 | N = 234 [a] |
| Trustee | 32 | 33 | 7 | 70 | 94 | N = 236 [b] |

[a] Four persons gave no answer.          [b] Two persons gave no answer.

The assumption underlying the design of these items was that legislators who held clear conceptions of their representational roles would reveal their conceptions by responding in a consistent manner to the opposing statements. Legislators who agreed with the item favoring the delegate style of representation would demonstrate a consistent response by disagreeing with the item favoring the trustee style, and vice versa. Legislators who were undecided or inconsistent in their responses could be identified as not having internalized any personal norms concerning the style of representation—falling in the category of politico.

A scoring method was used to determine individual legislators' role orientations. Five response categories were weighted 1–2–3–4–5 from

TABLE II

ANALYTICAL CATEGORIES CONSTRUCTED FROM SCALE SCORES ABOUT THE STYLE
OF REPRESENTATION

| Scale Scores: [a] | 2 | 3 | 4 | 5 | 6 | 7 | 8 | 9 | 10 |
|---|---|---|---|---|---|---|---|---|---|
| Number of persons with scale score | 13 | 17 | 15 | 30 | 76 | 35 | 10 | 18 | 19 |
| Total number in each category | (Delegate) | | (Politico) | | | (Trustee) | | | |
| | 45 | | | 141 | | | 47 | | |

[a] Five persons failed to answer both items and therefore were not classified.

"agree" to "disagree" for the delegate item, while the weights were reversed for the trustee item. Each person's weighted responses for the pair were then summed. If a respondent's responses were strong and consistent for both items within a pair, he would receive either a minimum score of 2 or a maximum score of 10, depending upon which attitude he favored. If his responses were inconsistent or in the "undecided" category for both items, the individual received a score of 6. All possible response patterns were accommodated by a nine-point scale from 2 to 10. This scale was collapsed into three categories for the purpose of assigning representational roles to individuals. The distribution of scale scores along with the three analytical categories for the style of representation is given in Table II.

Categorizing legislators as delegates and trustees on the basis of their responses to two short attitude items is admittedly a crude operationalization. The forty-five delegates and forty-seven trustees produced by this process are at best imperfectly identified. Nevertheless, the responses probably tap the legislators' attitudes well enough to test some propositions with data from the Indiana study.

The above theoretical framework was formulated since the Indiana study was conducted, and not all the variables in the theoretical frame-work were covered by questions in the interview schedule. In all, data are available to test sixteen out of the thirty-five propositions dealing with delegate-trustee comparisons. Because of the relatively small num-bers of cases involved, the data have all been collapsed into dichoto-mies, with the exceptions of occupation and party competition in dis-trict. The chi-square statistic has been used throughout to test significance levels of the relationships.[20] The propositions will be pre-sented as stated in the theoretical framework. They will be followed by data tables and, when necessary, discussion of the data.

PROPOSITION 1: Style of representation is unrelated to education.

SUPPORTED

|  | Not College Graduate | College Graduate | (totals) |
|---|---|---|---|
| Delegates | 27 | 18 | 45 |
| Trustees | 31 | 16 | 47 |

$x^2 = 0.35$ 1 df. Not significant

PROPOSITION 2: Style of representation is unrelated to occupation.

SUPPORTED

|  | Law-yer | Farmer | Insur-ance | Busi-ness | Labor | White Collar | Profes-sional |
|---|---|---|---|---|---|---|---|
| Delegates | 8 | 8 | 4 | 4 | 11 | 3 | 7 |
| Trustees | 8 | 12 | 3 | 8 | 5 | 6 | 2 |

$x^2 = 8.29$ 7 df. Not significant

PROPOSITION 4: Style of representation is unrelated to income.

SUPPORTED

|  | Under $10,000 | Over $10,000 |
|---|---|---|
| Delegate | 29 | 14 |
| Trustee | 28 | 18 |

$x^2 = 0.45$ 1 df. Not significant

PROPOSITION 5: Style of representation is unrelated to urbanization.

SUPPORTED

|  | Over 50% of district in cities over 20,000 | Under 50% of district in cities over 20,000 |
|---|---|---|
| Delegate | 21 | 23 |
| Trustee | 16 | 26 |

$x^2 = 0.81$ 1 df. Not significant

PROPOSITION 6: Style of representation is unrelated to party affiliation.

SUPPORTED

|  | Democrat | Republican |
|---|---|---|
| Delegate | 22 | 23 |
| Trustee | 21 | 26 |

$x^2 = 0.16$ 1 df. Not significant

PROPOSITION 7: Style of representation is unrelated to political ideology.[a]

SUPPORTED

|  | Conservative | Liberal |
|---|---|---|
| Delegate | 21 | 24 |
| Trustee | 20 | 27 |

$x^2 = 0.16$ 1 df. Not significant

[a] Ideology was determined by separating legislators at the median according to their summated scores on three agree-disagree statements about government intervention in the economy, business' role in government, and labor's influence in politics

All six of the preceding propositions were supported by the Indiana data. In one sense, however, these propositions might be considered very trivial, for they state no relationships, only the absence of relationships. It is a fact that any number of nonsense variables with random values can be cross-classified to produce statistically insignificant relationships. But there are two reasons these propositions are not trivial. First, they do derive from the assumption that the political socialization process works upon individuals in idiosyncratic ways to produce representational role orientation and that the standard sociological and political variables do not account for role orientations. But perhaps more important, these null propositions establish that other existing differences between delegates and trustees cannot be due to spurious correlations on behalf of standard sociological and political variables. The force of this argument awaits the validation of propositions that state directional relationships.

PROPOSITION 8: In comparison with candidates who have not served in the legislature, incumbent legislators are more likely to be trustees than delegates.
SUPPORTED

|  | Inexperienced Candidates | Experienced Candidates |
|---|---|---|
| Delegates | 26 | 19 |
| Trustee | 17 | 30 |

$x^2 = 4.31$ 1 df. Significant at .025 level.
One-tailed test.

PROPOSITION 9: In comparison with representatives, senators are more likely to be trustees than delegates.
UNSUPPORTED

|  | Candidates for House | Candidates for Senate |
|---|---|---|
| Delegates | 32 | 13 |
| Trustees | 37 | 10 |

$x^2 = 0.71$ 1 df. Not significant

PROPOSITION 10: In comparison with legislators from safe districts, those from competitive districts are more likely to be delegates than trustees.

UNSUPPORTED

| | Candidates' perceptions of party competition [a] | | |
| | Safe one Party | Mostly one Party | Competi- tive |
| --- | --- | --- | --- |
| Delegates | 14 | 24 | 7 |
| Trustees | 13 | 21 | 13 |

$x^2 = 2.02$　2 df. Not significant

[a] Variable was formed from responses to the question: "How about the relative strength of the parties in your district—over the years has the district been safe Republican or Democratic, fairly close, or what?"

PROPOSITION 28: In comparison with trustees, delegates are more likely to believe that their constituents possess opinions on legislative issues.

SUPPORTED

| | Proportion of constituents seen to have preferences [a] | |
| | Almost none —a few | Some— almost all |
| --- | --- | --- |
| Delegates | 16 | 28 |
| Trustees | 28 | 19 |

$x^2 = 4.90$　1 df. Significant at .025 level.
One-tailed test.

[a] Variable was formed from responses to the question: "Do you think that the average voters in your district have any specific preferences concerning the more important bills you vote on in the legislature?"

PROPOSITION 29: In comparison with trustees, delegates are more likely to believe that their constituents know what goes on in the legislature.

## SUPPORTED

| | Amount known by voters about the legislature [a] | |
| | Almost nothing to very little | Some to almost everything |
| --- | --- | --- |
| Delegates [b] | 5 | 13 |
| Trustees | 18 | 11 |

$x^2 = 5.23$    1 df. Significant at .02 level.
One-tailed test.

[a] Variable was formed from responses to the question: "In general, how much would you say the average voter knows about what you do in the legislature?"

[b] The numbers of delegates and trustees are reduced because this question was asked only of candidates with previous legislative experience.

PROPOSITION 30: In comparison with trustees, delegates are more likely to believe that their constituents know their stands on issues.

## UNSUPPORTED

| | Voters' knowledge of his stands on issues [a] | |
| | Almost nothing to very little | Some to almost everything |
| --- | --- | --- |
| Delegates | 21 | 23 |
| Trustees | 26 | 21 |

$x^2 = 0.52$    1 df. Not significant

[a] Variable was formed from responses to the question: "How much do you think the average voter knows about your stands on issues like those we've talked about?"

PROPOSITION 31: In comparison with trustees, delegates are more likely to believe that their constituents know their election opponents' stands on issues.

SUPPORTED

| | Voters' knowledge of opponents' stands on issues [a] | |
| | Almost nothing to some | Quite a bit |
| --- | --- | --- |
| Delegates [b] | 18 | 10 |
| Trustees | 39 | — |

$x = 16.37$ 1 df. Significant at the .001 level.
One-tailed test.

[a] Variable was formed from responses to the question: "How much do the people of your district know about your opponents' stands on issues?"

[b] The numbers of delegates and trustees are reduced because this question was asked only of candidates in single member legislative districts.

PROPOSITION 32: In comparison with trustees, delegates are more likely to believe that they know their constituents' opinions.

UNSUPPORTED

| | When candidates know about preferences [a] | |
| | Hardly ever to sometimes | Quite often to almost always |
| --- | --- | --- |
| Delegates | 10 | 31 |
| Trustees | 18 | 29 |

$x^2 = 1.95$ 1 df. Not significant

[a] Variable was formed from responses to the question: "Do you think that you generally know how the rank-and-file voters in your district feel about issues that concern them?"

PROPOSITION 60: In comparison with delegates, trustees are more likely to support legislation which they feel is morally right.

SUPPORTED

|  | Extent of agreement with statement [a] | |
|  | Agree or tend to agree | Undecided to disagree |
| --- | --- | --- |
| Delegates | 29 | 16 |
| Trustees | 41 | 6 |

$x^2 = 6.56$     1 df. Significant at the .02 level.
One-tailed test.

[a] Variable was formed from responses to this attitude statement: "A legislator can decide how to vote on most issues by asking himself if the proposed law is morally right."

PROPOSITION 62: In comparison with delegates, trustees are more likely to support legislation supported by their party.
SUPPORTED

|  | Extent of agreement with statement [a] | |
|  | Agree or tend to agree | Undecided to disagree |
| --- | --- | --- |
| Delegates | 13 | 31 |
| Trustees | 24 | 23 |

$x^2 = 4.36$     1 df. Significant at the .025 level.
One-tailed test.

[a] Variable was formed from responses to this attitude statement: "If a bill is important for his party's record, a member should vote with his party even if it costs him some support in his district."

Of the sixteen propositions tested with data from the Indiana study, twelve were supported, including all six that predicted the variables to be unrelated. Of the ten propositions that predicted positive relationships between variables, six were supported. While evidence from this study validates most of the propositions tested, failure to support all the predictions suggests that parts of the theoretical framework need to be re-examined, considering the negative findings for four propositions. Each of the four will be discussed below.

Proposition 9, which states that in comparison with representatives, senators are more likely to be trustees than delegates, is flatly unsupported by the data. The reasoning behind this proposition is that the style of representation depends on the nature of the elected office and that higher office encourages greater reliance on personal judgment in decisions. Interestingly enough, Friedman's and Stokes' comparison of Michigan legislators with delegates to the state's recent constitutional convention also found no difference between the two groups of officials on the style of representation.[21] Where focus of representation was concerned, however, they found convention delegates more state-oriented than district-oriented. Despite the plausibility of the reasoning, this proposition should be seriously questioned. And the theoretical framework, which does not contain any proposition relating nature of office to focus of representation, might be re-examined in the light of Friedman's and Stokes' study.

Proposition 10, which states that in comparison with legislators from safe districts, those from competitive districts are more likely to be delegates than trustees, falls short of support in the data. The proposition derives from the idea that threat of political reprisal reduces reliance on personal values in decisions. Wahlke and his co-authors report a relationship between competitiveness and focus of representation, with competitive districts producing more district-oriented legislators (see Proposition 23).[22] Their failure to report such a finding for the style of representation may mean that the relationship also did not appear in their data. If this is true, Proposition 10 and its underlying reasoning are probably false.

Proposition 30, which states that in comparison with trustees, delegates are more likely to believe that their constituents know their stands on issues, is also unconfirmed. This might seem indeed unusual because of the apparent soundness of the reasoning behind the proposition. In order to maintain consistency between their role orientation and attitudes toward their constituency, delegates would be expected to believe that their constituents are informed about politics. One factor which might have smothered this expected relationship is the ego-involvement of candidates, who took pride in stating that they made sure their positions on issues were known. If ego-involvement is indeed a factor and the reasoning behind Proposition 30 is sound, then the relationship should be found in Proposition 31, which is limited to constituent's knowledge of their opponents' stands on issues. Proposition 31 is supported by the data at the .001 level of significance. The reasoning does appear to be correct, although Proposition 30 is probably false.

The final proposition unsupported by the Indiana data—Proposition 32—states that in comparison with trustees, delegates are more likely to believe that they know their constituents' opinions. The data lean in the expected direction but not at the .05 level of significance. The question that produced the data—"Do you think that you generally know how the rank-and-file voters in your district feel about issues that concern them?"—once again may have constituted a threat to the candidates' ego, causing them to claim omniscience rather than ignorance. Some subtler method should be devised for testing this proposition before it is regarded as false.

## Suggestions for Further Research

This article has attempted to follow a two-step strategy of research by (1) formulating and codifying propositions relating representational roles to legislative behavior and (2) testing them with available data. In general, theory construction and theory validation constitute the strategy of scientific inquiry. Variations on this theme for particular topics of research are sometimes dictated by the state of the theory and availability of data. Research on representational behavior has been conducted without much explicit theory and without the availability of crucial data. This article proposes no new method for acquiring the missing data on constituents' opinions, but it hopefully contributes to the development of explicit theory.

In addition to the ever-present need for continued development of theory, there are several immediate needs for future research on representational behavior. Perhaps most obvious and pressing is the need for better measures of representational roles. The single open-ended question used in the four-state study and the two closed-ended questions used in this study and in others [23] indicate that crude operationalizations are adequate for revealing the existence of relationships with other variables. But the goal of scientific research should be not only to establish the existence of relationships but also to specify the form of those relationships.[24] For this purpose, more precise measures are required.

Research should be undertaken on the operationalization of representational roles. Various methods ought to be investigated or, if necessary, created especially for the task. Even within the interview situation, many different techniques and procedures can be tried in an attempt to construct better measures of representational roles. For example, batteries of items might be prepared and administered to appropriate populations. Intercorrelations among items might be studied, and Guttman scales might be investigated. Other techniques or procedures found in the literature on attitude scaling and psychological measurement might be studied for application to representational roles. We ought to be able to develop measures of the focus and style of representation that improve considerably on those used in existing studies.

Research should also be undertaken to test propositions that relate roles to perceptions of constituency interests and opinions. Although sample survey data are necessary to determine the actual opinions and interests within constituencies, the representatives' perceptions of these variables can be determined through interviews. Complete understanding of representational behavior ultimately requires that constituency attitudes be matched against legislative behavior, but much can be learned about representational behavior without these data. In fact, none of the seventy-one propositions in the theoretical framework require data on actual constituency opinions and attitudes.

Miller and Stokes demonstrated the feasibility and fruitfulness of gathering data on legislators' perceptions of their constituents' opinions.[25] They showed that legislators vary considerably in the extent to which they execute their perceptions of constituency opinions. Moreover, correspondence between perceptions of opinions and legislators' behavior varies greatly with the issue. Miller and Stokes were fortunate in also having data on actual constituency opinions for comparison with legislators' perceptions; these data made their study the pioneering effort that it is. But even without these data, their study is important for its findings on behavior and perceptions.

Finally, future research should certainly seek to establish connections between representational roles and legislative behavior. Legislators' perceptions are important variables affecting representational behavior, but it is the behavior of the representatives which we are ultimately interested in explaining. Data on bill sponsorship and roll call voting, for example, should be included in research on representational behavior.

To summarize, further research on representational behavior should concentrate first on developing better measures of representational roles. These measures should then be related to data on legislators' perceptions and behavior in an attempt to validate propositions contained in the theoretical framework. And throughout the process, of course, careful attention should be given to the elaboration and refinement of theory on representational behaviors.

# 8 / Simulating Legislative Processes

*Wayne L. Francis*

THE OPEN AND COMPETITIVE LEGISLATIVE ENVIRONMENT IS AN INVITING subject for systematic, scholarly study; thus, there is a great deal of information about and analyses of legislative processes. The concentration of effort on political parties, elections, legislatures, and representation has moved the state of empirical inquiry on these subjects beyond that of most other political subjects. That legislative behavior is complex, few will deny. The outcome of a legislative session is the product of an intricate mixture of private and organized behavior. To understand its meaning within the context of a scientific theory would appear to many to be a wild-eyed premature goal. Still, if one judges by the amount of empirical work devoted to legislatures, progress toward scientific theory should be evident.

I would maintain that much scientific progress has been made and that this progress toward formal theory has several faces. The recognition of the significance of pressure groups and executive agencies in the formation of policy, the meaning of social background characteristics for legislative behavior, the significance of formal rules and informal norms associated with legislatures, an understanding of cognitive dispositions (attitudes) of legislators, and an appreciation of the attributes of power and friendship relations among legislative participants make up a substantial array of major advances in scientific knowledge.

In *The Legislative System,* Wahlke, Eulau, Buchanan, and Ferguson[1] sought to integrate these major advances by using the concept of a system to encompass all factors relevant to the behavior of a legislative body. The term "system" implies a multiplicity of variables (people and things) that are continuously changing, yet maintaining a semblance of constancy over time. The legislative system changes in response to demands from within the system and from the environment. These demands are called inputs. The results of the system changes are called outputs. Inputs and outputs are either internal or external. Each part of the system—such as legislators, pressure group leaders, and the governor—is called a component and has a description list, which is a list of its characteristics, also called inputs and outputs. All inputs and outputs represented on a description list of a component of the system are internal. All other inputs and outputs are external. A system may be misunderstood because the internal inputs and outputs are incorrectly described or because external inputs and outputs were not taken into account. As will be seen, these distinctions have their precise empirical counterparts in computer-based simulation exercises.

## Simulation and Modelling

A model is a symbolic construct whereby all relationships between symbols are totally explicit (either assumed or deducible), and thus exhibiting relational meaning in the absence of empirical content. Simulation, the process of building an analogy to complex parts of the real world, is often considered to be a special type of modelling. Some will argue that it isn't modelling at all, but a pre-model exercise. Those who argue that simulation is not modelling point out that simulations produce analogies, or synthetic universes, not formal mathematical equations. A formal mathematical model will rest upon a set of careful definitions and a set of axioms. Comparatively speaking, simulation exercises are loose attempts to imitate particular situations, formal models are constructs capable of yielding general theorems.

In view of the ambitious demands of formal mathematical modelling, the state of inquiry in political science looks relatively primitive. The field is not, however, without its partial successes. Ithiel de Sola Pool, Robert Abelson, and Samuel Popkin have created a satisfactory election model for the presidential election years of 1960 and 1964.[2] With a seven-factor model they are able to give reasonable predictions of party voting in 48 states. By employing three issue-clusters (civil rights, social welfare legislation, and nuclear responsibility), party identification, voter turnout, and two geographic considerations, they produced a ranking of states that correlated .90 with the actual outcome. Their formulae were developed from knowledge of early opinion poll results (taken at least two years in advance of election) and well-informed guesswork.

Is the Pool-Abelson-Popkin study a simulation or a formal model? The authors use the terms "simulation" and "model" interchangeably.

It is a simulation as I have used the term to the extent that the data bank of opinion polls is construed to be an analogy to public opinion on election day. It is a formal model to the extent that they have developed a set of equations based upon explicit definitions and assumptions. The study illustrates that simulation and formal modelling go hand in hand, that a simulation provides an empirical base from which a formal model can be created.

If an electorate can be simulated and modelled satisfactorily, so can a legislature and its participants. The procedure could be similar to the one used in the election study; that is, a sample of legislative participants could be drawn, a series of questions could be submitted to them, and the results could be recorded in a data bank. The outcome of a legislative vote depends upon party identification, geographic considerations, and relevant attitudes. Since a large number of roll call votes take place in a legislative session, tests on the outcome of several legislative measures would provide an excellent verification technique.

In the legislative project a sample may be unnecessary, since the total population of the system is relatively small. Yet the entire process in a legislative system may be much more complex than the legislative voting process. Considerations of bargaining and organization in the determination of voting patterns are much more prevalent in the legislative framework. So while the advantage of dealing with a small universe is apparent, the difficulty of dealing with complex goal-seeking behavior is eminent.

Although the purpose of modelling the legislative process may be to predict passage or failure of legislation and the concomitant roll call votes, attention may also be directed toward more explanation depth. An explanation takes on more depth as it extends over a greater number of causal links. In the beginning a model can be constructed to show that several factors contribute directly to the outcome, as illustrated by the Pool-Abelson-Popkin study. But these questions then arise: Why do those several factors exist? Can they be traced to earlier events? A legislative simulation will accommodate explanation depth if its description lists are generous of fact. Diverse considerations—such as social background, type of district, official positions, and cognitive structure—are helpful to this end.

A transition from simulation to modelling may be abrupt, or very gradual. A gradual transition will be accomplished through the simulation—by restructuring, condition-testing, and scoring. The scoring processes and their definitions provide the primary evidence for developing mathematical expressions suitable to a formal model. A model built from these basic processes is more likely to reflect the bargaining and organizational features of the legislative system.

*Simulating A Legislative System*

Scientific simulation is generally more successful when based upon extensive empirical research than when it is not based on such research. To simulate successfully a legislative system, a heavily researched legislature and legislative session should be selected. In constructing an argument for simulation and modelling, I have selected the 1961 legislative session of the Indiana General Assembly. In that year there were several studies going on simultaneously. The raw data for these studies were stored on punch cards convenient to computer analysis. The Indiana data collections of Professor Charles S. Hyneman of Indiana University included social background information, roll call votes, committee assignments, and a legislative history of bills. An extensive post-primary, pre-election interview study of 238 legislative candidates was administered prior to the legislative session.[3] An interaction and influence interview study was made by the author after the legislative session of 1961 began.[4] In addition, the Institute of Public Administration (then Bureau of Government Research) processed election returns and percentages for that year.[5] There were also several university faculty and staff members who participated in the session.

In simulating the Indiana legislature, I would include at least the following types of components:

A. Bills              D. Governor
B. Committees         E. Pressure Groups (or Representatives)
C. Legislators        F. Newspapers

Executive agencies may also be included, depending upon whether or not their impact upon the system finds expression through the governor. Each legislator, committee, pressure group, and newspaper may be placed in the system.

The second crucial step requires the assignment of description lists to the components of the system. Any factor that may affect the outcome of legislation should be found somewhere on one of the description lists. Purely for illustration, several description lists are presented below in Table I. These lists, as illustrated, are perhaps insufficient in detail, but, naturally, it is difficult to predict how much information is needed to simulate a legislature satisfactorily.

Every component of the system should have a description list comparable to those illustrated in Table I. A description list may be empty; that is, the proper information may not be available. Also, a compo-

## TABLE I

EXAMPLES OF DESCRIPTION LISTS FOR COMPONENTS OF A
SIMULATED LEGISLATIVE SYSTEM

| DESCRIPTION LISTS | INFORMATION SOURCES |
|---|---|

I. Bill A
  A. Formal Sponsors
    1. Legislator S
    2. Legislator NN
  B. Informal Sponsors
    1. Governor
    2. State Teachers Association
  C. Finance
    1. Yes
      a. $3,000,000
  D. Taxation
    1. No
      a. (type)
  E. Education
    1. Yes
      a. School construction
  F. Apportionment
    1. No
  G. Health
    1. No
      a. (type)
  H. Labor
    1. No
      a. (type)
  I. Business
    1. No
      a. (type)
  J. Civil Rights
    1. No
      a. (type)
  K. Transportation
    1. No
      a. (type)

II. Committee on Education
  A. Committee Chairman
    1. Legislator A
  B. Ranking Majority Member
    1. Legislator X
  C. Other Majority Members
    1. Legislator DD
    2. Legislator S
    3. Legislator T
    4. Legislator NN
    5. Legislator PP
  D. Minority Members
    1. Legislator W

Information Sources:

* Study 43 (Legislative History of Bills) or Official Journal

Information for B through K obtained from official records and interviews

* A-D, Study 13 (Committee Assignments)

| Description Lists | Information Sources |
|---|---|

2. Legislator Z
3. Legislator VV
4. Legislator TT
  E.  Committee Desirability Rating

* Study 16 (Senate Influence)

     1. 4.2 (5 point scale)
  F.  Amount of Business

Official Journal, Appendix

     1. 46 bills/session

III. Legislator A
  A.  Political Party
     1. Democrat
  B.  Legislative Chamber

* A-E2, Study 10, (Legislative Personnel)

     1. Senate
  C.  Occupation
     1. Lawyer
  D.  Length of Service
     1. 6 years
  E.  Type of District
     1. Part Urban—Part Rural
     2. Multi-member
       a. 2 members

* E3, Study 35 (Elections by County

     3. % vote last election
       a. 52.4
  F.  Official Positions
     1. Committee Chairman
       a. Education
       b.

* F-G, Study 13 (Committee Assignments)

     2. Ranking Majority Member
       a. Benevolent and Penal
       b.
  G.  Committee Assignments
     1. Education
     2. Benevolent and Penal Inst.
     3. Org. of Courts and Crim. Code
     4. Cities and Towns
     5. Finance
     6. Judiciary B
  H.  Attitude toward Pressure Groups
     1. Indiana Farm Bureau
       a. Neutral
     2. Indiana Conference of Teamsters
       a. Unfavorable
     3. Indiana Manufacturers Assoc.
       a. Unfavorable
     4. Indiana State Chamber of Comm.
       a. Neutral
     5. Indiana AFL–CIO
       a. Favorable

* H-K, Study 14 (Legislative Candidates)

     6. State Teachers Association
       a. Favorable

| DESCRIPTION LISTS | INFORMATION SOURCES |
|---|---|

    7. Taxpayers Federation
      a. Unfavorable
    8. State Medical Association
      a. Neutral
I.  Areal Orientation
    1. State
      a. 3.9 (Scale Range, 0–4)
J.  Propensity to Accept Instructions
    1. High
      a. 3.2 (Scale Range, 0–4)
K.  Liberal-Conservative Index
    1. Liberal
      a. .8 (Scale Range, 0–4)
L.  Closest Legislator Friends
    1. Legislator D
    2. Legislator M
    3. Legislator Y
    4. Legislator BB
    5. Legislator KK
M.  Other Legislator Friends
    1. Legislator B
    2. Legislator F
    3. Legislator L
    4. Legislator P
    5. Legislator W
    6. Legislator CC
    7. Legislator FF
    8. Legislator GG
N.  Calls "Influential"
    1. Generally
      a. Legislator D
      b. Legislator Y
      c. Legislator V
      d. Legislator CC
      e. Legislator FF
      f. Legislator MM
    2. Taxation
      a. Legislator FF
      b. Legislator Z
      c. Legislator J
    3. Local Government
      a. Legislator L
      b.
      c.
    4. Finance
      a. Legislator B
      b. Legislator W
      c. Legislator Q
    5. Education
      a. Legislator X

* L-N, Study 16 (Legislative Influence)

| DESCRIPTION LISTS | INFORMATION SOURCES |
|---|---|

    b. Legislator W
    c. Legislator S
  6. Labor
    a. Legislator S
    b. Legislator GG
    c. Legislator N
  7. Business
    a. Legislator N
    b. Legislator TT
    c.
  8. Agriculture
    a. Legislator QQ
    b. Legislator O
    c.
  9. Benevolent Institutions
    a. Legislator B
    b. Legislator M
    c. Legislator D

* Studies 10, 13, 14, 16, 35, and 43 are part of the Indiana Data Library on State Politics at Indiana University.

nent may have another component as an element of its description list; for example, a legislator may have on his description list the committees to which he belongs, and a committee may have on its list the members who serve on it. If all description lists were placed side by side before entering a simulation exercise, one would probably notice a fair amount of repetition among the lists. If a particular list structure is a necessary part of a simulation, then either it will be inserted before the simulation exercise begins or compiled during the exercise itself. The choice would appear to be one of personal preference.

A simulation exercise begins by asking a specific question about the system. The processes necessary to answer the question must then be implemented. Two obvious questions for a legislative system are the following: (1) Will Bill A pass or fail the chamber? and (2) By what vote will Bill A pass or fail the chamber? Three basic kinds of processes should lead to an answer. The first I have called condition-testing; the second, scoring; and the third, restructuring. Condition-testing is searching a description list for a piece of information. That information will either increase, decrease, or have no effect upon the likelihood that Bill A will pass. Its positive or negative impact must be stored on a scoring device. When new description lists are created or old ones changed as part of the simulation exercise, these changes are called restructuring processes. A complex simulation will have numerous restructuring, condition-testing, and scoring processes.

A simulation proceeds by having the analogue go through a series of condition-testing, scoring, and restructuring processes. These processes are stimulated by Bill A. They will, no doubt, be very complex if Bill A is a controversial measure that succeeds in reaching the passage stage. An appropriate analogy may require hundreds of separately identified processes and sub-processes. Near lunacy would be suspected if one were to conduct the simulation manually. There are, to my knowledge, two practical ways to run a complex simulation (the only kind likely to give results). The first is a laboratory experiment wherein people are asked to act out the parts that have been reconstructed from real-life situations.[6] The second is a computer experiment. Generally speaking, a legislature is too large to simulate in a laboratory experiment (not inherently, but given the present amount of resources known to exist). So the alternative is a computer simulation.

An enormous advantage to the system approach employed herein is its designed correspondence to modern technological concepts of computer science. Computer specialists often speak of inputs, outputs, and system. Locations in computer storage are analogous to the components in a social system. Program languages build in routines that are analogous to human thought processes and capacities. Electrical current supplies the "motion" characteristic of social systems. When you add to these analogies the great speed with which computers can operate, the goal of building sophisticated models of social systems draws within reach.

Perhaps for those not familiar with simulation it is difficult to imagine the precise steps of a simulation exercise, especially when the exercise is carried on within a computer. It is important to realize, first of all, that computer specialists have created program languages (forms of instructions) purposely designed for simulation work. They are called, appropriately, "list-processing" languages. IPL-V, LISP, COMIT, and SLIP are different programming versions of the same basic concepts.[7] IPL-V is probably the most widely used. When a researcher employs one of these languages, he is able to process lists like those presented in Table I with great ease. The description lists of legislators, pressure groups, committees, bills, newspapers, and executive leaders are stored in computer memory as the first part of a program written in a list-processing language. The real programming then begins; that is, the processing instructions are given. These instructions may restructure the description lists, test them for various conditions, and score the results.

To illustrate the procedure, I have created below a number of verbal instructions that could be written more briefly in a symbolic language:

Call a list of bills  (Bil)
Call first sponsor of first bill
Test for party of sponsor
Create a list of sponsor party affiliation
Store party of first sponsor on new list  (Spa)
Test for sponsor formal position
If committee chairman test for committee
Is bill in area of committee E
If not try ranking majority member
If not try committee assignments
If Yes call for close friends
Test for close friends on committee
Score number on Index $Z_1$
Call second sponsor of first bill
Test for party of sponsor
Store party of second sponsor on list *Spa*
Is second sponsor on committee E
If Yes call for close friends
Test for close friends on committee
Add number to score on Index $Z_1$

A simulation would pass through hundreds of such instructions. One side benefit of almost every program language is the capacity to handle repetitive processes without actually repeating the program instructions. For example, I have made separate but identical instructions for the two sponsors in the above series of verbal statements. This would not be necessary in a computer language. In fact, the description lists of 100 legislators could be processed with instructions almost no greater in number than the number necessary for one legislator.

The original question—whether Bill A will pass or fail the chamber and by what vote—must be kept in mind throughout the entire sequence of instructions. For ultimately the researcher is attempting to feed just enough information into his simulation to guarantee that his predictions will be within a desired range of accuracy. If the predictions are accurate, new explanations of legislative behavior should be forthcoming. The researcher would now know enough to match the inputs of a system with its outputs.

In modelling the Indiana legislative system, two questions are bound to arise: How generally does the model apply? and, What are the payoffs for policy-makers?

There is no a priori way of satisfactorily answering the question of how generally the model applies. It seems logical that states with contours similar to those of Indiana could be characterized by the same model. To decide if other states could be characterized by the model of Indiana (and if so, which ones) , it is important to know exactly where the state legislature ranks among all state legislatures on a number of significant variables. A 1963 survey of state legislators in every state indicates that Indiana had the following rankings: [8]

1. 3rd (among states) in inter-party conflict
2. 6th in intra-party conflict
3. 12th in regional conflict
4. 24th in pressure group conflict
5. 17th in decision-making centralization

The party of the governor and the party distribution of seats in the legislature would also be important factors. It is clear from these characteristics of Indiana that another simulation would be needed in a state where, for example, inter-party conflict was absent at the state legislative level. In my opinion, it is doubtful that one could foresee variations in all state legislatures by simulating a single session or single state legislative environment.

For pure research the pursuit of knowledge, not commercial payoff, is the primary goal. Nevertheless, early speculation about the payoff of innovative research can be informative to the researcher as well as to the outside observer. One thing is almost certain. If great strides in the pursuit of knowledge are made, people will apply that knowledge to satisfy their needs. Ample testimony lies in the widespread use of public opinion "experts" to assess voting tendencies and trends. In evaluating the commercial potential of innovative research, adjustments can be made to accommodate wider interest in what one must necessarily consider to be important. An eye to the applied aspects of a study can often lead to unanticipated returns in both pure and applied understanding.

Assume that a simulation advances to the point that a knowledgeable observer would say that it is behaving very much like the legislature did during the session. The same bills die in committee. Bills pass by the same vote. Computer components act or are acted upon in ways that are similar to the events of a real-life session. Would it not be reasonable then to argue that one could also reverse the procedure—could insert changes in the computer system and then suggest analogous changes in the real legislative system? Perhaps a governor or majority leader wishes to know what he must bargain away to gain passage for his major proposals. The computer system could suggest alternatives. Or perhaps a legislative commission has been empowered to develop proposals for legislative reorganization to avoid particular problems that have arisen in the past. The computer system could provide a means for testing the consequences of possible changes.

There is little reason for legislators to adhere to obsolete ways of arriving at decisions. The problems of legislatures are severe enough that new methods of decision-making are welcome when current decision-making procedures prove inadequate. Stalemate is frustrating for most legislators. Already they have implemented electronic voting machines, legislative service agencies, and advisory commissions, but researchers have not given them anything more exciting (except in a small number of states where computer apportionment has been employed). Researchers have done much more for the business firm. Now, at least some researchers can turn their attention to computer help for legislators.

# PART IV

# Recruitment of Political Leadership

# 9 / The Politicized Nature of the County Prosecutor's Office, Fact Or Fancy?—the Case in Indiana

*Kan Ori*

SALIENT TO THE DISCUSSION OF COUNTY PROSECUTORS IS A STANDARD remark concerning the political nature of the office. As Harold Alderfer puts it, "the office is often sought by younger members of the bar who view it as a stepping-stone to higher political or judicial preferment."[1] Robert Babcock similarly generalizes that "vigorous young lawyers" traditionally start their political careers as county prosecutors.[2] My purpose here is to ascertain—at least in the context of Indiana—whether or not prosecuting attorneys were young, inexperienced, and fired up with political aspirations when they began their service, and to what extent their office served as a springboard to higher political office.

## Youth and Inexperience

Assumptions regarding the youth and inexperience of county prosecutors are widely held, but seldom empirically shown. Did the Indiana prosecutors enter their offices young? Were they, when they became prosecuting attorneys, younger than most state legislators in Indiana? Table I contains data on the age of entry of incumbent prosecutors and of state legislators in 1959.[3] Striking differences may be observed between these two groups. Of the Hoosier prosecutors in Table I, 80 percent entered office before 40 years of age, compared with 30 percent of both House members and senators of the 1959 General Assembly. Since prosecuting attorneys are lawyers, more significant findings may be obtained if one compares them with lawyers in the Assembly. The research of David R. Derge of Indiana University shows that 61 percent of the lawyer-representatives and 39 percent of the lawyer-senators began their legislative service before 40 years of age, in contrast to 32 percent and 25 percent respectively of the whole

*157*

TABLE I

AGE GROUP AT ENTRY OF INCUMBENT (1963) COUNTY PROSECUTORS AND MEMBERS
OF THE 1959 INDIANA GENERAL ASSEMBLY

| | AGE GROUP AT ENTRY | | | | | |
| | 21–39 % | 40–54 % | 55+ % | Un-known % | TOTAL % | N |
| --- | --- | --- | --- | --- | --- | --- |
| County Prosecutors | 80 | 20 | — | — | 100 | 66 |
| House Members | 30 | 37 | 20 | 13 | 100 | 86 |
| Senators | 30 | 54 | 10 | 6 | 100 | 47 |

group.[4] Even compared with the lawyer-legislators, therefore, the incumbent prosecutors are demonstrably younger.

Table II shows findings on the age of entry and retirement of ex-prosecutors and ex-state legislators who have achieved the office of U. S. Senator, U. S. Representative, or the Governor of Indiana from 1900 to 1963.[5] Almost all (93%) of the ex-prosecutors left that office before reaching their fortieth birthday. Twice as many ex-prosecutors left their offices between the ages of 21 and 39 as did former members of the House, and three times as many left as did ex-state senators. Early coming and going of county prosecutors may be indicative of the role of that office in their public career pattern.

In his study of the lawyer in the Indiana General Assembly, Derge uses the length of law practice as a criterion for measuring the degree of legal experience of the lawyers.[6] Table III indicates the average number of years in practice by the Indiana prosecuting attorneys and by lawyer-members of the Indiana General Assembly, using a 3 percent random sample of the lawyer population of Indiana.[7] County prosecutors had considerably fewer years of legal experience than did lawyer-legislators, the experience difference between lawyer-senators and

TABLE II

AGE GROUP AT ENTRY TO AND RETIREMENT FROM COUNTY PROSECUTOR'S OFFICE
AND INDIANA GENERAL ASSEMBLY OF THOSE WHO BECAME U. S. SENATORS,
CONGRESSMEN, AND GOVERNORS, 1900–1963

| | No. WITH THIS AS EXPERI-ENCE | AGE GROUP AT ENTRY | | | | AGE GROUP AT RETIREMENT | | | |
| | | 21–39 % | 40–54 % | 55+ % | Total % | 21–39 % | 40–54 % | 55+ % | Total % |
| --- | --- | --- | --- | --- | --- | --- | --- | --- | --- |
| County Prosecutors | 29 | 100 | — | — | 100 | 93 | 7 | — | 100 |
| State Legislators | 37 | | | | | | | | |
| House | 22 | 64 | 31 | 5 | 100 | 45 | 41 | 14 | 100 |
| Senate | 17 | 65 | 35 | — | 100 | 29 | 65 | 6 | 100 |

prosecuting attorneys being nearly ten years, and that between lawyer-representatives and prosecutors about five years. The lawyer-members of the House were notably less experienced, and prosecuting attorneys much less experienced, on the basis of the years-in-practice criterion than the general lawyer population of Indiana. Derge observed that about one-fourth of the lawyer-representatives during the same period had practiced less than five years, as had one lawyer-senator.[8] In the three-term period (1955–63), about one-third of the county prosecutors had less than five years of law practice, and one in every seven of

TABLE III

AVERAGE NUMBER OF YEARS IN THE PRACTICE OF LAW FOR
COUNTY PROSECUTORS AND LAWYERS IN THE INDIANA GENERAL
ASSEMBLY, AND FOR A 3 PERCENT SAMPLE OF THE LAWYER
POPULATION OF INDIANA

|  |  | N | AVERAGE YEARS |
|---|---|---|---|
| County Prosecutor | 1963 | 75 | 10 |
|  | 1959 | 80 | 12 |
|  | 1955 | 77 | 11 |
| House | 1959 | 17 | 13 |
|  | 1957 | 16 | 19 |
|  | 1955 | 19 | 15 |
| Senate | 1959 | 19 | 23 |
|  | 1957 | 16 | 21 |
|  | 1955 | 16 | 21 |
| Random sample |  | 131 | 24 |

them had been in the practice of law less than three years. Thus, if the average number of years in the practice of law serves as an index of experience for lawyer-politicians, Indiana prosecutors have been less experienced than their House counterparts and much less experienced than the general lawyer population or Indiana lawyer-senators.

Professional ability is another ground for judging. Both Derge and Charles S. Hyneman of Indiana University used the rating of lawyers by Martindale-Hubbell as an indicator of a lawyer's quality.[9] The Martindale-Hubbell ratings cover only those lawyers with more than five years of law practice. Since one-third of the county prosecutors are thus ineligible, the Martindale-Hubbell rating is not used in this chapter.

How experienced have the prosecuting attorneys in Indiana been politically? Of the prosecutors in office in 1963, 91 percent had not been elected previously to any public office; conversely, 74 percent of the 1963 lawyer-legislators had held some elective public post. It should be noted, however, that one out of every three prosecuting at-

torneys serving at the time of the survey had held party office previously and that one out of every four of them had occupied appointive public offices. The overwhelming majority (96%) of these latter
offices were concerned with law enforcement.

## Political Ambition and Perception of the Office

There may be several indicators of a man's political ambition or
desire for political participation. One of these is family background.
Do the Indiana prosecutors come from families in which there has been
a higher degree of political involvement than those of state legislators?

TABLE IV

Family Political Background of 66 Indiana County Prosecutors and 133
Members of the 1959 General Assembly

| | | No Politi-cal Experi-ence | Held Party Office Only | Elected to Public Office Local County | State | Fed. | Unk. | Total |
|---|---|---|---|---|---|---|---|---|
| | N | % | % | % | % | % | % | % |
| County Prosecutors | 66 | 74.2 | 7.6 | 15.2 | — | 1.5 | 1.5 | 100 |
| State Legislators | 133 | 77 | 6 | 12 | 4 | 1 | — | 100 |
| Lawyers | 33 | 58 | 3 | 24 | 12 | 3 | — | 100 |
| Others | 100 | 83 | 7 | 9 | 1 | — | — | 100 |

Are more of them raised in politically conscious families than are lawyer-legislators? Table IV sets forth findings concerning family political
background of sixty-six prosecuting attorneys (79% of the total) and
133 state legislators (89% of the total) .

County prosecutors rated fairly close to state legislators in general as
far as parental political involvement in public life is concerned. About
one-fourth of the prosecutors and legislators claimed a parent who was
politically active in terms of election to public or party office. Approximately 17 percent of the parents of both groups were elected to public
office; parents of the prosecutor group served mostly at the local
county level, while more than one-third of the state legislators' parents
held state or national office.

On the other hand, it is apparent that more Indiana lawyer-legislators grew up in politically motivated families than did Indiana prosecuting attorneys: Twice as many lawyer-legislators reported family
backgrounds of a political nature.[10] Incumbent prosecutors came from

politically oriented families slightly more often than state legislators, whereas considerably more lawyer-legislators than prosecuting attorneys experienced political involvement at home.

Another measure of a man's ambition is his own assessment. When asked whether they would be interested in seeking any other public office in the future, the majority of county prosecutors responded in the affirmative, while 33 percent were negative and 14 percent were uncertain. Only 3 percent of the prosecutors who were incumbents in 1963 intended to make the office a lifetime career: the emphatic majority (91%) had other plans.[11]

Table V contains data regarding the political intentions of 66

TABLE V

AGE GROUP DISTRIBUTION OF 66 INDIANA COUNTY PROSECUTORS AND THEIR FUTURE
POLITICAL PLANS, 1963

|  | N | PRESENT AGE GROUP DISTRIBUTION | | | |
|  |  | 20–39 % | 40–54 % | 55+ % | Total % |
| --- | --- | --- | --- | --- | --- |
| County Prosecutors with a Plan to Seek Other Public Office in the Future | 35 | 77 | 23 | — | 100 |
| County Prosecutors Who Are Uncertain as to Their Future Plans | 9 | 78 | 22 | — | 100 |
| County Prosecutors with No Plans to Seek Other Public Office | 22 | 45.5 | 45.5 | 9 | 100 |
| Total | 66 | 67 | 30 | 3 | 100 |

county prosecutors. It is to be noted that there is a positive correlation between age group and future political plans. Two-thirds of both office-seeking and uncertain prosecuting attorneys were in the age distribution of 20 to 39. The majority of those who professed no political ambitions in terms of seeking other public office in the future were above 55 years of age.

How have Hoosier prosecutors perceived their office? Have the public-office aspirants differed from the others in their perceptions? Table VI provides a summary of responses given by the incumbent prosecutors regarding the effects of their service upon their future careers.

Two major considerations, one economic and one political, affected the thinking of county prosecutors as they evaluated the office in relation to their future careers: "Would my service as county prosecutor be of assistance in terms of law practice, thus accelerating my earning power?" and "Would my experience as prosecuting attorney help further my political career?" The overwhelming majority of respondents thought their experience as prosecutors would help (78.7%) or would not affect (10.6%) their future careers. Only 4.6 percent of them felt their service would hinder their future careers, and the remaining 6.1 percent did not know whether it would or not.

A slightly higher percentage of the public-office aspirants viewed their service as county prosecutors as being of assistance to their future careers than did nonaspirants. Perhaps they perceived their experience as prosecuting attorneys as a route to higher political office. On the other hand, only 9 percent of those interested in public office thought their service would affect them adversely if they sought other public positions; thus it can hardly be concluded that county prosecutors conceived their office as a hindrance to their future careers, public or pri-

TABLE VI

EFFECT OF SERVICE AS COUNTY PROSECUTOR ON THEIR FUTURE
CAREER AS EVALUATED BY 66 INCUMBENT PROSECUTORS
IN INDIANA, 1963

|  | PUBLIC OFFICE ASPIRANTS % | OTHERS % | ALL MEMBERS % |
| --- | --- | --- | --- |
| Will Help | 82.9 | 74 | 78.7 |
| Will Make No Difference | 5.7 | 16 | 10.6 |
| Will Hinder | 8.6 | — | 4.6 |
| Don't Know | 2.8 | 10 | 6.1 |

vate. In terms of gaining trial experience, service as county prosecutor is obviously professionally rewarding. This is conceivably a major reason why so many prosecuting attorneys felt their experience in the office would help their future careers.

A convincing majority of the prosecutors (83%) considered their office valuable to a public-service career, whereas only 6 percent thought it would not be valuable. It is significant that all of the public-office aspirants supported the proposition that the office of prosecutor is a good first elective public office for young lawyers who are interested in public service. Of the nonaspirants, 13 percent rejected the idea that the prosecutor's office is a sound initiation to public life for young attorneys, while two-thirds of them accepted the notion. For one-fifth of them, it made no difference.

Asked to rate the offices of prosecuting attorney and of state legislator, both groups—the public-office aspirants and the nonaspirants—claimed their office as a better means of achieving higher political and judicial positions. Two and one-half times as many public-office aspirants chose the prosecutor's office as chose the state legislature, and four

times as many people in the nonaspirants' group supported the prosecuting attorneyship as supported the state legislative post.

About two-thirds of the incumbent prosecutors responded affirma-
tively, as summarized in Table VII, when asked if many Indiana political leaders began their public careers as county prosecutors. Striking
contrasts emerge from a comparison of the public-office aspirants' beliefs and those of nonaspirants. Three out of every four politically interested prosecutors believed that Indiana political leaders began their
careers as county prosecutors. A similar pattern is observed in the case
of uncertain members. On the other hand, the majority of nonaspir-

TABLE VII

IMAGE OF PRIOR POLITICAL CAREER-PATTERN OF INDIANA POLITICAL LEADERS
HELD BY 66 INCUMBENT PROSECUTING ATTORNEYS OF INDIANA

"DO YOU THINK MANY INDIANA POLITICAL
LEADERS BEGAN THEIR PUBLIC CAREERS
AS COUNTY PROSECUTOR?"

| | N | YES % | DON'T KNOW % | No % | TOTAL % |
|---|---|---|---|---|---|
| Prosecutors with intention to seek other public office | 35 | 77 | 20 | 3 | 100 |
| Uncertain | 9 | 67 | 22 | 11 | 100 |
| No intention | 22 | 41 | 45 | 14 | 100 |
| All members | 66 | 64 | 30 | 6 | 100 |

ants for public office did not think the prosecutor's office was an initiating office for Hoosier politicians (14%) or did not know whether it
was or not (45%).

## The Office as an Instrument for Political Advancement

It has been shown that prosecutors with political ambitions tend
to view their office as a valuable aid to higher political and judicial at-
tainments. Does their expectation conform to historical fact? Since
Hoosier prosecuting attorneys are most likely to perceive the function
of their office in the context of their political careers in Indiana, it is
pertinent to ascertain how many of Indiana's political leaders who attain the office of Governor, U. S. Senator, or U. S. Representative did
indeed begin their public careers in the prosecutor's office, or held it
sometime prior to becoming Governor or Congressman.

In his study of the prior career-pattern of governors, Joseph A.
Schlesinger concerns himself with a given office as leading to the gover-

norship. In his own words, "the number of governors who have held a particular office indicates the general significance which the office has had in state politics." [12] Since there are no formal restrictions on the order in which a political leader holds a given position during his career, it is also interesting to know which office characteristically served as an immediate springboard,[13] or as an introduction to political life.

The office of county prosecutor was not a significant factor in the careers of those who became governor. From 1900 to 1963, the most important office in the gubernatorial career pattern of Indiana has been what Schlesinger terms the state legislative office.[14] Nearly half of all the Indiana Governors for the period from 1900 to 1963 served in the General Assembly at some time in their careers. Next in number, as far as experience is concerned, is the group which had held no public office (41%), followed by those who had held state-wide elective office (29%). As expected, most of the latter were Lieutenant Governors. Other categories did not rate significantly.

The office most frequently held first was that of state legislator, followed by law-enforcement positions. Three times as many Indiana Governors had legislative experience in their first public office as had law enforcement experience. No Indiana Governor during the period began his career in a state-wide elective office. Two most important terminal offices were state-wide elective and state legislative. While fewer than one-third of the ex-legislators stepped immediately into the gubernatorial office, all who had held a state-wide elective post went directly to the governorship. None of Indiana's Governors in the period studied held a law-enforcement position as the last office before the governorship. In Indiana, then, the state-wide elective post is characteristically an immediate prelude to the governorship, while the state legislature rates rather high in its overall importance as an entrée to the governor's office.

Only one Governor, Ed Jackson, who served from 1925 to 1929, came through the office of prosecuting attorney during the period studied. After a short period (4 years) of law practice, Jackson was elected prosecutor of Henry County; he served only one term in the office. He was then appointed county judge, and later elected to the same post. Prior to becoming governor, he was twice elected secretary of state, and on the latter occasion he held the office until he was elected governor.

These data seem to suggest that the office of prosecutor did not serve as a proximate springboard to the governorship in Indiana. Only one Governor out of seventeen—Ed Jackson—had been a county prosecutor, and he held this post at the very beginning of his public career. In fact, it was Jackson's first public office, elective or appointive, and he held it at the youthful age of twenty-eight. It is also well to remember that Jackson served as county prosecutor in the early 1900's. If these historical patterns repeat themselves, the possibility of an Indiana prosecutor becoming the governor of the state is very slim.[15]

How many of the U. S. Senators from Indiana came through the office of prosecuting attorney? Although both the state legislative (39%) and law-enforcement positions (39%) occupy a dominant place in the prior career pattern of U. S. Senators, less than half of those who held law-enforcement posts were county prosecutors. Of eighteen Senators, three had been prosecuting attorneys while five had held some other law-enforcement positions. Roughly the same pattern is observed when they are ranked in terms of the office in which they commenced their public life. The majority of Senators began their careers either in the General Assembly (27%) or in the law-enforcement offices (33%). Of those who began in law-enforcement positions, 17 percent were county prosecutors.[16]

As far as the distribution of Senators' last public offices is concerned, the highest percentage (28%) came from the state legislature. Of the Senators, 22 percent came directly from law-enforcement positions, while 16 percent were elected from the United States House of Representatives. It should be noted that none of the prosecuting attorneys who ultimately became United States Senators held that position as the end office just previous to that of Senator, in spite of the fact that the state legislative and law-enforcement offices are two major channels for immediate promotion to the United States Senate. For all of them prosecuting attorney was their first public office.[17]

Three U. S. Senators from Indiana who held the prosecuting attorneyship were James A. Hemenway, Frederick Van Nuys, and Samuel D. Jackson. Hemenway was only 26 years old when he was elected Prosecuting Attorney for the Second Judicial Circuit, an office which he held for two terms. He climbed the party ladder to become a member of the Republican Central Committee in 1890. Hemenway served as a Congressman from 1895 to 1905 and then moved to the United States Senate. A similar pattern is found in the case of Van Nuys, who served in the Senate from 1933 to 1944. Six years after his admission to the bar, he became the prosecutor of Madison County. After serving two terms as prosecuting attorney, he was elected to the Indiana Senate in 1912. While in the state senate, Van Nuys became President Pro Tem in 1915. In 1917 and 1918, he was chairman of the Democratic State Central Committee and U. S. Attorney for the District of Indiana; he was elected to the United States Senate in 1932. Samuel D. Jackson was 28 years old when he was elected county prosecutor of Allen County; he served two terms. He was defeated in his attempt for a congressional seat in 1928, but chaired the Democratic State Convention in 1936. Jackson was appointed Attorney General of Indiana in 1940 and held that office until appointed to the United States Senate in 1944.

It is of interest to note that all three of these Senators held some public office other than county prosecutor before becoming U. S. Senators, and for all of them the prosecutor's office served as an initiation. In no case was the prosecutor's office held after 1930. It is further to be observed that all of these men were party leaders. As noted in the

TABLE VIII

PATTERN OF OFFICE EXPERIENCE OF U. S. CONGRESSMEN FROM INDIANA
1900–1963

| TYPE OF OFFICE | THIS AS EXP. N | THIS AS THE FIRST OFFICE N | THIS AS THE END OFFICE N | THIS AS THE ONLY OFFICE N | INDEX OF FINALITY N |
|---|---|---|---|---|---|
| State Legislature | 22 | 12 | 13 | 8 | 59 |
| House | 16 | 9 | 8 | 4 | |
| Senate | 7 | 3 | 5 | 3 | |
| Law Enforcement | 46 | 36 | 37 | 26 | 80 |
| County Prosecutor | 26 | 19 | 14 | 8 | 54 |
| Local Attorneys | 14 | 9 | 3 | 2 | 22 |
| Judges | 10 | 1 | 9 | — | 90 |
| Others | 11 | 7 | 11 | 7 | |
| Administrative | 14 | 11 | 8 | 5 | 57 |
| Local Elective | 14 | 10 | 10 | 6 | 71 |
| State-Wide Elective | 1 | — | 1 | — | |
| Federal Elective | — | — | — | — | |
| No Public Office | 31 | 31 | 31 | 31 | |
| Others | 3 | 3 | 3 | 3 | |
| Total | | 103 | 103 | | |

case of governors, the prosecuting attorneyship did not serve as a doorway to the United States Senate, whereas other public posts and leadership in the party may have enhanced their chances for becoming U. S. Senators.

Table VIII summarizes the Indiana pattern of office recruitment of its U. S. Congressmen for the period between 1900 and 1963. From the point of view of experience, three dominant sources of congressional recruitment were the law enforcement, state legislative, and "no public office" categories. The most important of these was law enforcement. About 45 percent of the Indiana Congressmen from 1900 to 1963 had held some kind of law-enforcement office at one time in their public career. More than half of these (25%) had been prosecuting attorneys, while other local attorneys' posts and judgeships followed in popularity. Next in importance is the "no public office" category (30%). Ranking third is state legislative experience: 21 percent of the U. S. Congressmen had been in the Indiana General Assembly, most in the House. Other significant offices are administrative (13%) and local elective (13%). Only one Congressman had had state-wide elective experience, and none had held a federal elective position. In terms of experience, therefore, the prosecuting attorneyship is the most important single office in the recruitment of U. S. Congressmen from Indiana in the last sixty-three years.

In regard to the office with which these Congressmen began their public career, the most notable was again law enforcement. One in every three Indiana Congressmen began his public career in some kind of law-enforcement activity, whereas about one in every ten started as a state legislator. More Congressmen became involved in politics by way of the prosecuting attorneyship than by way of the state legislature. Slightly fewer Congressmen held administrative and local elective offices as their first public posts than sat in the General Assembly.

The most prominent end office is law enforcement, followed by the state legislative. Three times as many law-enforcement officials as state legislators stepped immediately into a congressional seat. In fact, slightly more county prosecutors were directly elected to Congress than state legislators—senators and representatives combined. Local elective offices and administrative positions rate third and fourth respectively.

In terms of an "index of finality," [18] the local attorneyship is the lowest ranking office, preceded by that of the county prosecutor. Only 22 percent of U. S. Congressmen from Indiana who had been local attorneys held that office immediately before entering Congress. For 54 percent of the Congressmen with prosecutor experience, the office of prosecuting attorney was the last previously held public office, in contrast to 57 percent of ex-administrators and 59 percent of ex-state legislators. With an index of 80, the law-enforcement category as a whole rates much higher than any other office group. The second highest ranking group is the local elective with an index of 71. In Indiana, the most important office leading to Congress seems to be that of judge, not that of prosecuting attorney, in spite of the latter's numerical superiority.

## The Office as an Initiative Experience

The office of prosecuting attorney in Indiana is more of an initiative office than a path to higher political positions. Not only were the Hoosier county prosecutors young and relatively inexperienced when they took office, but also those U. S. Congressmen from Indiana who had been prosecuting attorneys had held that office quite early in their public career. For 73 percent of the ex-prosecutor Congressmen, the office of county prosecutor was their first public post. In fact, the over-whelming majority of these Congressmen (96%) as well as of the in-cumbent prosecutors (91%) had never been elected to any public office prior to their election to the prosecuting attorneyship. The office served an important purpose in the career pattern of these Congress-men as their first public elective experience.

It is true that the majority of Congressmen who had been county prosecutors held that position as the end office. But the importance of this situation is considerably reduced by the fact that it took an aver-age interval of eight years before these prosecutors became Congress-men, in contrast to three years or less for ex-state legislators and five years or less for offices in the "other office" categories. Of the Congress-men with prosecutor experience as the end office, 43 percent had to wait ten years or more before they were elected to Congress, while this was the case for only 8 percent of the former legislators and for 23 per-cent of the other officeholders. On the other hand, 77 percent of the Congressmen who held the state legislative post as the end office and 65 percent of the ones who did not were elected Congressmen in less than five years, as compared with 34 percent of those who experienced the prosecuting attorneyship as the last office before Congress.

Two-thirds of the U. S. Congressmen from Indiana who had been county prosecutors at some time in their public career served in that office less than four years. Only two ex-prosecutor Congressmen served more than six years as prosecuting attorneys. They were Charles A. Halleck and Lincoln Dixon, each of whom began his public service as prosecutor at the age of 24, and left the office before reaching the age of 35. It should be added that one-fourth of the ex-prosecutor Con-gressmen served only one two-year term as prosecuting attorney. The office of county prosecutor, therefore, is at best transitional; it is for most Congressmen who have held it an initiative political experience.

## Characteristics of Ex-Prosecutor Congressmen

Table IX summarizes the career pattern of U. S. Congressmen from Indiana who have had experience as prosecuting attorneys. It is apparent that most of those Congressmen who have been county prose-cutors either came from or moved to other law-enforcement positions. The overwhelming majority (92.5%) of prosecuting attorneys who be-came U. S. Representatives either started as county prosecutors or came through appointive local attorneyships. From 1900 to 1963 less than 8 percent of the ex-prosecutor Congressmen arrived at the prosecutor's office without having any other law-enforcement experience. For the majority, the office of county prosecutor was the last public office held before becoming U. S. Representatives, while one-fourth of them came to Congress via some other law-enforcement post, primarily that of local judge. Only 19 percent of the Congressmen with prosecutor experience did not hold a law-enforcement position as the last office prior to Congress.

A partial explanation for this inter-office movement within the law-enforcement category is that these positions are functionally related. Another probable reason, which seems appropriate for Indiana, is

TABLE IX

CAREER PATTERN OF EX-PROSECUTOR U. S. CONGRESSMEN FROM INDIANA
1900–1963

| PATTERN LEADING TO THE OFFICE OF PROSECUTOR | | LAST PREVIOUS OFFICE BEFORE CONGRESSMAN | |
|---|---|---|---|
| County Prosecutor | 73 | County Prosecutor | 54 |
| Appointive Local Attorney— | | Judge | 19 |
| County Prosecutor | 12 | Other Law-Enforcement Offices | 8 |
| Others—Local Attorney— | | State Legislature | 12 |
| County Prosecutor | 7.5 | Others | 7 |
| Non Law-Enforcement Offices— | | | |
| County Prosecutor | 7.5 | | |
| Total | 100 | Total | 100 |

pointedly stated by Schlesinger: "Of greater importance . . . is the fact that the law enforcement offices themselves form a hierarchy, indicative of a unity of organization which goes beyond functions to include related bases of political support." [19] In the case of Indiana, the hierarchical setup is split-directional: The county prosecutorship is the middle part of the hierarchy: local appointive attorneyship—county prosecutor—local judgeship.

There are two basic career patterns in law enforcement. Those who start as local attorneys, such as city attorney, county attorney, and deputy prosecutors, tend to proceed to the office of county prosecutor, then go directly to Congress or to some elective office other than law enforcement, and finally go on to Congress. About one in five ex-prosecutor Congressmen followed this route. This career pattern seems quite appropriate for a future Congressman because service as a local attorney provides valuable experience in public office, while running for the office of county prosecutor furnishes the first public elective experience. Those who begin their careers in the office of prosecutor usually

TABLE X

DEMOCRATIC-REPUBLICAN RATIO OF EX-PROSECUTOR
CONGRESSMEN TO EX-LEGISLATOR CONGRESSMEN, 1900–1963

| PARTY | N | PROSECUTOR EXPERIENCE % | STATE LEGISLATIVE EXPERIENCE % |
|---|---|---|---|
| Democrats | 48 | 27 | 21 |
| Republicans | 55 | 24 | 22 |
| Total | 103 | 25 | 21 |

seek some other judicial office before being elected to Congress. The judicial post most often held is the local judgeship. The circuit court judge in Indiana is an elective office, which can thus provide experience in a related field with related bases of political support for politically interested prosecutors. This channel to Congress was used by one-fifth of the ex-prosecutor Congressmen. Even though the prosecuting attorneyship is in the middle of the hierarchy, it serves as an initiator for the elective public life. Very few (4%) climbed the career ladder in sequence—from the bottom to the top of the hierarchy as expressed in the local attorney–prosecutor–circuit judge pattern.

Table X concerns the Republican-Democratic ratio of ex-prosecutor Congressmen to ex-legislator Congressmen for the last 63 years. Slightly more Democrats held the prosecutor's office than did Republicans, whereas slightly more Republicans preferred the state legislature over the prosecutorship. Neither Republicans nor Democrats favored the one office significantly more than the other.

It has been noted that the prosecuting attorneyship in Indiana is basically an initiative experience for those interested in public office. Data in Table XI seem to support the supposition that the office of

TABLE XI

CHARACTERISTICS OF U. S. CONGRESSMEN FROM INDIANA, ACCORDING TO TYPE OF
OFFICE, 1900–1963

| TYPE OF OFFICE | N | AVERAGE YEARS OF PUBLIC CAREER BEFORE CONGRESS | AVERAGE YEARS OF SERVICE IN CONGRESS | TERMS OF SERVICE AS CONGRESSMEN 1–2 % | 3–4 % | 5+ % |
|---|---|---|---|---|---|---|
| County Prosecutor | 26 | 9 | 11 | 19 | 27 | 54 |
| State Legislature | 22 | 9 | 7 | 45 | 32 | 23 |
| Others | 60 | 3 | 8 | 38 | 30 | 32 |
| All Members | 103 | | | | | |

county prosecutor—at least in Indiana—is preferred historically by the successful politicians. While the average number of years in public posts prior to election to Congress was much greater for those Congressmen who had been prosecutors or legislators than for other Congressmen, ex-prosecutor Congressmen served longer periods in Congress than did those who did not have experience as prosecuting attorneys. This phenomenon is partially due to the fact that the prosecuting attorneyship is naturally the monopoly of lawyers and lawyers as a group tend to outlast other occupational categories in Congress. It is also due to the fact that in Indiana, where prosecuting attorneys are partisanly elected, the office of county prosecutor rates high in the career pattern of "professional" politicians, and as in other fields of human endeavor, an apprenticeship is a necessary prerequisite for a successful political leader.[20]

## Decline in Importance of the Prosecutor's Office

The increasing importance of law-enforcement offices—particularly that of public attorneys—has been observed by Schlesinger in his study of governors.[21] Would this trend be applicable to the prosecuting attorneyship in Indiana? Table XII shows data concerning incidence of former county prosecutors among Congressmen from Indiana between 1880 and 1960. It is salient that the prosecuting attorneyship in Indiana has declined in importance in this regard during this eighty-year period. Even though the law-enforcement offices—particularly that of county prosecutor—have been the most important in the state

TABLE XII

DECREASE IN IMPORTANCE OF COUNTY PROSECUTOR'S OFFICE
FOR INDIANA CONGRESSMEN, 1880–1960

| DECADE | CONGRESSMEN ELECTED N | PROSECUTOR EXPERIENCE % | PROSECUTOR AS THE LAST PREVIOUS OFFICE % |
|---|---|---|---|
| 1880–1889 | 69 | 38 | 13 |
| 1890–1899 | 66 | 41 | 14 |
| 1900–1909 | 66 | 41 | 18 |
| 1910–1919 | 66 | 30 | 18 |
| 1920–1929 | 65 | 29 | 20 |
| 1930–1939 | 61 | 27 | 21 |
| 1940–1949 | 57 | 25 | 15 |
| 1950–1960 | 55 | 27 | 20 |

pattern of congressional recruitment, Tables XII and XIII suggest that the importance of the prosecutor's office will continue to decrease. This decline has not been related in any way to the rise of the state legislative office, traditionally the second most important for promotion to Congress.

Findings in Table XIII reinforce the observation concerning the declining role of the prosecutor's office in the recruitment pattern of U. S. Congressmen from Indiana. Between 1880 and 1899, one-third of the new Congressmen had been prosecuting attorneys, whereas only 12 percent of the new Congressmen elected in the last two decades had

TABLE XIII

DECLINE IN IMPORTANCE OF PROSECUTOR'S OFFICE FOR
INDIANA CONGRESSMEN, 1880–1960

| DECADE | NEW FACES AMONG CONGRESSMEN ELECTED N | PROSECUTOR EXPERIENCE % | PROSECUTOR AS THE LAST PREVIOUS OFFICE % |
|---|---|---|---|
| 1880–1899 | 57 | 33 | 19 |
| 1900–1919 | 34 | 26 | 15 |
| 1920–1939 | 29 | 24 | 17 |
| 1940–1960 | 25 | 12 | 8 |

held the prosecuting attorneyship. From 1960 to 1963, three new men were added to the Indiana Congressional delegation, but none of them had been a county prosecutor.[22]

## Summary and Conclusion

This chapter has reviewed the characteristics of the office of county prosecutor in Indiana. Data presented in the preceding discussion may be summarized as follows:

1. Indiana prosecutors are younger at their entry into the office than lawyers in the Indiana General Assembly and much younger than state legislators in general. The overwhelming majority of politically successful prosecutors—in terms of obtaining the office of Governor, U. S. Senator, or U. S. Representative—left the office of county prosecutor before their fortieth birthday.

2. Prosecuting attorneys in Indiana are less experienced in terms of years in practice than lawyer-legislators in the General Assembly, and much less experienced than the general lawyer population of Indiana.

3. The majority of Hoosier prosecutors are politically ambitious, as measured by the "future office interest" test. As expected, younger prosecutors are more aspiring politically than are older members. More lawyer-legislators come from politically oriented families than do prosecuting attorneys, while prosecutors and legislators in general have a similar political background.

4. The politically minded prosecutors tend to rate their office more favorably as an instrument of political advancement than do the non-aspirants to public office.

5. The prosecuting attorneyship has not been of significance in the recruitment pattern of Indiana Governors and U. S. Senators from Indiana.

6. In terms of experience, the prosecutor's office has been the most important single office in the career pattern of U. S. Congressmen from Indiana in the last six decades. The prosecuting attorneyship in Indiana is more characteristically an initiation office for a political career, rather than an immediate channel to higher political preferment. In the process of career ladder-climbing, prosecutors tend to move within the law-enforcement category.

7. In spite of the fact that the prosecuting attorneyship is still an important office in the career pattern of U. S. Congressmen from Indiana, its importance has been decreasing in the last eighty years.

These findings support the general notion that county prosecutors are young and inexperienced and that they are politically ambitious and tend to view their office as a means of political advancement. The findings also suggest, however, that the traditional belief in the politicized nature of the office must be considerably qualified. The prosecuting attorneyship has not been of significance in the gubernatorial career pattern, nor has it been of cardinal value in the promotion pattern of U. S. Senators from Indiana. It has been significant only in the career pattern leading to the U. S. House of Representatives, and even in that instance has had a decreasing importance.

## 10 / Party Leadership and County Candidate Selection

### Thomas M. Watts

THIS CHAPTER IS BASED UPON AN EXPLORATORY FIELD STUDY OF POLITICAL recruitment within the state party system of Indiana, a system having strong formal organizations with closely associated informal leadership cliques. The purpose of the chapter is to identify those who are influential in the selection of county candidates and in the candidates' success in winning nominations, and to trace communication and interaction between these influentials and the aspirants for office.

Seligman distinguishes two stages in the nomination process: certification, which includes the social screening and political channeling that results in eligibility for candidacy; and selection, which includes the actual choice of candidates to represent parties in the general election.[1] Selection in turn has two stages, instigation, which concerns the decision one makes to become a candidate, and reinforcement, which concerns the support a candidate receives that contributes to his success in winning the primary election. Although certification is treated in passing, it is the selection process that is primarily described here. Data for this analysis are the result of a case study of a single Indiana county (Howard) and of a more limited study of fifteen other Indiana counties.[2] These data are largely leader and candidate perceptions of the nomination process and reflect lines of apparent influence derived from their reports of contacts during the pre-primary period in the spring of 1962.[3]

### Research Design

The research design for Howard County was based upon an adaptation of a "power attribution model" which sought to avoid some of the criticisms that have been directed toward studies which attribute influence to certain persons without adequately testing their involvement with the outcome of issues, in this case, nominations.[4] Underlying this approach was the assumption that there are certain identifiable groups and individuals which exercise a great deal of political power in communities.

To guide research, three broad categories were provisionally designated as potential contributors to the decisions of which persons will seek office: (1) party leadership (formal and informal), (2) nonparty groups, and (3) the candidates themselves (whose personal desires and initiatives are likely to be involved in varying degrees, with some actively and others reluctantly seeking office). Members of these categories were thought to be instrumental in varying degrees at different stages in the nominating process.

For data on the role of party leadership in candidate selection, interviews were conducted with nineteen first-level and second-level Howard County leaders; most of these were first-level leaders. These included the formally elected chairman for each party and those nonformal leaders identified by reputation.[5] In addition, thirty-one candidates for Howard County elective office were interviewed.[6] To these data were added responses from twenty-seven Republican and Democratic county chairmen in the other selected counties.[7]

Candidates were asked questions concerning the way they were recruited and contacts they made, and leaders were queried about their roles in recruiting candidates. The county chairmen supplied information on leadership groups in their respective counties as well as on their own recruitment activities.

## The Aspirants

The social screening and political channeling by which candidates become eligible for office in Howard County result in a "typical" county candidate who is approximately 47 years of age, a long-time resident of his county, probably not a veteran, and probably an active Protestant church member (if he is a Catholic, he is a Democrat). If he is a Democrat he is likely to belong to several organizations. Unless he is running for judge or prosecutor, he comes from the middle or lower status levels of society, somewhat comparable to the relative prestige of his office.[8] If he is a Democrat, he has a broker-type occupation. This is less likely to be the case if he is a Republican.[9]

His parents probably have been active politically, and he has been a member of his party since his first vote, or before, particularly if he is a Democrat. He first became involved in politics much later, however, at 34, but only if he is a Democrat has he been so highly involved as to hold party office, and if his party has been highly successful in recent years (as with Howard County Democrats) he is likely to have run for office before.

Presumably, there are other members of any community to whom much of this profile might apply. Under what circumstances are we likely to find some of these individuals actually facing the voters and what determines how many and with what likelihood of success?

## Inter-Party Competition and Candidate Selection

There is a substantial body of literature which suggests that the effect of party competition and organization strength will have a bearing on the candidate selection process. For example, V. O. Key has written that the competition for a particular office within a party will increase with the likelihood that the party's nominee will win office in the general election.[10] In jurisdictions leaning strongly to one party or the other, contests for the lesser party are relatively unknown, and the problem is not one of settling rivalries among would-be candidates, but of finding enough candidates to present a complete slate.[11]

In his *American State Politics,* Key analyzes data from Missouri and Ohio legislative districts which indicate that in the safe districts, primaries in which incumbents seek renomination are less likely to involve competition than those in which no incumbent is running.[12]

The extent to which such propositions are supported in Indiana is important to a description of the selection process. Fortunately, some Indiana data is available. Charles S. Hyneman, in an early study, speculates on causes for voluntary retirement of Indiana legislators, and suggests a relationship between fear of defeat and tendency to seek re-election on the part of incumbents, although by his own pronouncement, his data provide meager evidence for the hypothesis.[13] In a study of Indiana primary elections from 1926 to 1954 for Prosecuting Attorney, Indiana House, and Indiana Senate candidates, Standing and Robinson find support for the proposition that more candidates enter the primary of the dominant party (although the combined total number of contestants does not vary with the competitiveness of the general election).[14] More data are on file in the Government Department at Indiana University which have not yet been analyzed to test similar propositions.

Key offers other possible explanations for an uncontested primary in addition to small likelihood of success. For example, it may reflect an endorsed slate of candidates by the party's organizational structure, and if the structure is united and well financed, it may be futile to challenge its slate in the primary.[15] On the other hand, serious contests within the primary may also reflect a fractionalization of the leadership echelons of the party.[16]

Seligman's Oregon study was structured around some of the questions suggested by Key—such as whether the method whereby candidates enter primary contests will vary with the degree of competition among parties.[17] He found that in areas safe for the majority party, majority party officials were least active in instigating or supporting candidates, that the minority party had to conscript candidates for the primary, and that there was little interest group intervention. In more competitive districts, the candidacy market appeared to be wide open with little evidence of centralized control.

Probably the most complete set of hypotheses relating the nature of the party system to candidate selection are suggested by William Crotty in his study of party organization in North Carolina. Securing data through mail questionnaires to county chairmen in 1962–63, he found evidence in support of propositions discussed above along with a number of others closely related. For example, Crotty found that the better organized a county party is the more likely it is to draft candidates for office.[18]

This chapter will examine the following hypothesis, which is taken from the literature cited above.

1. The competition for a particular office within a party will increase with the likelihood that the party's nominee will win office in the general election.
   a. In jurisdictions leaning strongly to one party or the other, contests for the lesser party are relatively unknown and the problem is not one of settling rivalries among would-be candidates, but of finding enough candidates to present a complete slate.
   b. In safe districts, primaries in which incumbents seek renomination are less likely to involve competition than those in which no incumbent is running.
2. There is a relationship between fear of defeat and tendency to seek re-election on the part of incumbents.
3. More candidates enter the primary of the dominant party (although the combined total number of contestants does not vary with the competitiveness of the general election).
4. An uncontested primary may reflect an endorsed slate of candidates by the party's organizational structure.
   a. If the structure is united and well financed, it may be futile to challenge its slate in the primary.
   b. Serious contests within the primary may reflect a fractionalization of the leadership echelons of the party.

5. The method by which candidates enter primary contests will vary with the degree of competition among parties.
   a. In areas safe for the majority party, majority party officials will be least active in instigating or supporting candidates, the minority party will conscript candidates for the primary, and there will be little interest group intervention.
   b. In competitive districts the candidacy market will be wide open with little evidence of centralized control.

Control for competitiveness was introduced for the sixteen counties in the present study. Counties were classified according to the procedure outlined by J. Schlesinger.[19] This scheme was applied for the office of state representative with respect to division of party control over time and for the rapidity with which parties alternate in their control of an office. In Howard County, the dominant party (Democratic) had won 53 percent of the time, well within the 65 percent posed by the test. A change had occurred in 37 percent of the elections, only slightly under the standards suggested. This classification was supported by perceptions of the candidates as to the degree of party competition in their county. Thus, the Democratic party was found to be dominant in Howard County with a high degree of competition prevailing. Of the remaining fifteen counties, four were found to be competitive (two Republican and two Democratic) and eleven were found to be one-party counties (eight Republican and three Democratic).

The degree of competition in the primaries is analyzed for a total of eighty-eight county offices which were to be filled for each party (see Table I). Of these, forty-two were in the eight one-party, Republican counties. All offices in these counties which were not filled at the primary were found to be in the weaker party, the Democratic party. This supports statement 1a of the hypothesis.

In these one-party, Republican counties, there were also more contests for offices in the dominant party: The Republicans had thirty-three contests; the Democrats, twenty-one. This supports statements 1 and 3 of the hypothesis. We would expect it to follow that the number of contestants would also be greater in the dominant party. The Republicans had 117 aspirants for office while the Democrats had only eighty-six. This difference apparently is not only a result of more contests in the Republican primaries but also a reflection of more candidates for each contested Republican office, since twenty-one of the thirty-three Republican contests had at least three candidates, while only eleven of the twenty-one Democratic contests had that many entries.

That there was more competition for offices in these one-party, Republican counties in the Republican primaries than in the Democratic

## TABLE I

PRIMARY COMPETITION IN 16 SELECTED INDIANA COUNTIES

| | ONE-PARTY, REPUBLICAN (n = 8) | | ONE-PARTY, DEMOCRATIC (n = 3) | | COMPETITIVE (n = 5) | |
|---|---|---|---|---|---|---|
| | REPUB-LICAN | DEMO-CRATIC | REPUB-LICAN | DEMO-CRATIC | REPUB-LICAN | DEMO-CRATIC |
| Number of offices to be filled | 42 | 42 | 19 | 19 | 27 | 27 |
| Number of vacancies after the primary | 0 | 5 | 1 | 0 | 2 | 0 |
| Number of incumbents seeking renomination | 15 | 11 | 0 | 12 | 5 | 12 |
| Number of incumbents with no opposition | 7 | 2 | 0 | 7 | 2 | 7 |
| Number of incumbents winning nomination | 14 | 8 | 0 | 9 | 5 | 12 |
| Total number of contests | 33 | 21 | 9 | 12 | 20 | 17 |
| Total number of candidates | 117 | 86 | 37 | 42 | 70 | 61 |
| Number of offices contested by two or more candidates:   2 cand. | 12 | 10 | 3 | 5 | 8 | 7 |
| 3 cand. | 11 | 6 | 3 | 6 | 7 | 5 |
| 4 cand. | 5 | 2 | 3 | | 3 | 3 |
| 5 cand. | 3 | 2 | | | | 2 |
| 6 cand. | | | | | | |
| 7 cand. | 2 | | | 1 | 2 | |
| 8 cand. | | | | | | |
| 9 cand. | | 1 | | | | |
| 10 cand. | | | | | | |
| Number of "vigorous" contests | 29 | 13 | 6 | 5 | 14 | 9 |
| Number of offices neither contested nor with incumbents | 2 | 19 | 9 | 0 | 5 | 3 |

primaries does not necessarily mean that there was in all cases "little" competition within the minority party. We find for example that nine of the eleven Democratic incumbents had opposition as compared with eight of the fifteen Republican incumbents who were opposed.

Eight of the eleven Democratic incumbents managed to win renomination despite their opposition. That they had competition might be explained by the fact that there had been very recent Democratic successes which were not reflected when the counties were classified according to competitiveness. These offices had been last before the voters in 1958, a big Democratic year in Indiana, and considerable success in that year followed by some success in 1960 gave the Democrats, the party which seldom wins in these Republican counties, a "taste of blood," as one chairman put it, stimulating party activity in 1962. There may be little evidence that fear of defeat discourages incumbents, but there does seem to be some suggestion that the smell of victory encourages their opposition. Further, as the weaker party in these counties, the Democrats, having little hope of success, may have been submitting less than the best of their potential candidates to the voters. Once it was demonstrated that Democrats could win, the party could have been concerned with improving the caliber of its office-holders. Whatever the explanation, there apparently are situations in which there is little support for statement 1b of the hypothesis, that incumbents are less likely to be in contests.

Considerably more support for statement 1b of the hypothesis was found in counties heavily dominated by the Democratic party, although the number of counties, three, is small since seven of the twelve Democratic incumbents had no opposition. There were no Republican incumbents. Republicans did have a relatively high number of contested offices in these counties, however: Nine contested offices in the Republican party were reported as compared with twelve in the Democratic party. A revitalization of the Republican party in one county was partially responsible. A citizens' group set out to throw off the old guard, and each faction had candidates for all offices. This supports statement 4b of the hypothesis. In a second county, internal troubles in the Democratic party gave Republicans new hope and stimulated primary activity, according to the chairmen.

The counties classified as competitive reflected party rivalries by the nearly equal number of contests in each party and by the nearly equal number of contestants. There were twenty Republican contests and seventeen Democratic contests. As compared with sixty-one Democratic candidates, seventy Republican candidates sought office. Again, the 1958 Democratic landslide may explain the greater number of Democratic incumbents (twelve as compared to five for the Republicans), but since success is not such a new experience for Democrats in these competitive situations, it may only have been that stronger candidates may have been seeking renomination. That only five of the twelve were challenged and all were renominated supports the latter conjecture.

Not only the number of the contests were greater in the dominant party, but also the vigor of the contests. Of course, the number of contestants for each office has some bearing upon the vigor of the contests, but this is insufficient as a measure. Other data considered were these: newspaper assessments of how spirited the contests were, county chairmen's accounts of the competition in these primaries, and the 1962 primary voting statistics. If no contradictory information was available from newspapers or county chairmen and the winner in a two-candidate race received less than 60 percent of the vote, the contest was judged vigorous. If more than two candidates were running, the line was drawn at 50 percent. The criteria were applied identically to both parties, resulting in observations that there were, in one-party, Republican counties, twenty-nine vigorous Republican contests while only thirteen such Democratic contests. This finding supports the hypothesis. That Republicans had six vigorous contests in one-party, Democratic counties and Democrats had five might again be explained by the Republican revitalization and the Democratic factionalism noted above; thus, this does not dispute the hypothesis.

Analysis of these data suggests several further aspects of the instigation stage of candidate selection in these counties. For instance, in the one-party, Republican counties, only two of the forty-two offices in the Republican primaries were not interesting enough to draw more than one Republican candidate or else were held by the Democrats. The other forty offices were either contested or held by uncontested Republican incumbents. The Democrats, as the minor party, found nineteen of forty-two offices not attractive enough to draw more than one candidate, and these lone candidates may well have been drafted. In the one-party, Democratic counties, however, the Democratic party had no offices go uncontested (nineteen had nineteen incumbents or contests), whereas the Republicans may have drafted nine of eighteen. Most offices were attractive in competitive counties: There were but five of the twenty-seven in the Republican primary which were not, and for the Democrats only three.

These possibilities for party instigations in one-party situations do not permit the conclusion that some candidates were in fact drafted, however. The party's role in instigation as well as in reinforcement must next be examined.

## Party Organization and Candidate Selection

The interviews with the twenty-seven county chairmen provide evidence that, in Indiana, major party decisions at the county level are generally made by informal party leadership groups which meet occasionally. These chairmen were asked to report on whether or not the groups in their counties had met during the six months preceding the primary elections, whether nominations were specifically talked about, and whether decisions were made to try to recruit candidates for county offices.

Responses were difficult to aggregate but generally suggest that groups and chairmen in both parties were somewhat active in recruiting in competitive counties, possibly contrasting with Seligman's Oregon findings. Democratic groups and chairmen were more active than Republicans where Republicans were dominant; and Democrats, where they were dominant, did not as groups find it necessary to recruit at all.

It would appear that the degree of competition between parties has some bearing upon the actions of this informal leadership structure, but other factors must be present since there were party groups which did actively recruit despite their party's dominance and there were those which failed to recruit even when it should have been unlikely that candidates would file on their own.

Generally, however, these interviews tend to support one part of statement 5a of the hypothesis—in counties dominated by one party, the minority party candidates will be selected to run principally by the party hierarchy, which is represented by the county chairman who may be assisted by his informal advisors. Another part of statement 5a, that the majority party candidates are seldom selected by the party hierarchy, is also supported by these responses.

Not so clear is what happens in more competitive situations. Only where one party is relatively weaker, as in the case of the Republican party in Howard County, were leaders clearly ready to act, but often good prospects for both parties made their interventions unnecessary, except with lesser offices of either low prestige or of interest primarily to a small segment of the county's population, such as a township. Frequently chairmen remarked that where candidates are confident of winning and where they are satisfied with the organizations, there are very few recruitment problems; there may be so many good candidates that no matter how strong a chairman and his organization may be, they will want to stay out of the contests since they can be certain that a good man will win. (Some also felt that recently increased salaries for county offices had made it easier to get candidates.) These findings support statement 5b of the hypothesis.

The plight of the weak organization in a county dominated by the other party is quite different. In such a situation, quality candidates are very hard to find. Sometimes the weak chairman will wait until the deadline for filing and will then beg people to allow their names to be put up to fill the ticket. Generally there is only one man runnning for office. If things improve, it is because new spirit has been injected into an organization with a resulting increased confidence in the prospects for that party. These findings support part of statement 5a of the hypothesis.

The willingness of chairmen and their support groups to initially approach potential candidates is not matched by a willingness to support openly their preferences. Although election laws in Indiana do not prohibit party organizations from openly supporting candidates in a primary,[20] many counties have a tradition of allowing the primaries to be wide-open affairs. Often only the incumbents are given protection by the organizations. Sometimes they are not.[21] When candidates are given encouragement at the support stage, they are more likely to be candidates who were recruited initially and to whom an obligation is felt. This support is given privately and covertly.

Table II reveals that six of the seven Democratic chairmen privately supported 1962 candidates when Democrats were the minority party

### TABLE II

ROLE OF COUNTY CHAIRMEN IN SLATING OR PUBLICLY SUPPORTING 1962 PRIMARY CANDIDATES, 28 ORGANIZATIONS IN SELECTED INDIANA COUNTIES

|  | COMPETITIVE | | ONE-PARTY, REPUBLICAN | | ONE-PARTY, DEMOCRATIC | |
|---|---|---|---|---|---|---|
|  | REPUBLICAN (n = 4) | DEMOCRATIC (n = 4) | REPUBLICAN (n = 7) | DEMOCRATIC (n = 7) | REPUBLICAN (n = 3) | DEMOCRATIC (n = 3) |
| Public support | 1 | 2 | 2 | 0 | 0 | 2 |
| Private support | 2 | 1 | 1 | 6 | 3 | 1 |
| Neutral | 1 | 1 | 4 | 1 | 0 | 0 |

and that all three Republican chairmen in one-party, Democratic situations did the same.[22] In the dominant party in one-party situations, and in both parties in competitive situations the few cases of public support by chairmen might reflect strong organizations where there is also a history of factionalism, requiring the organization to defend itself from attacks within by going to the public for support.

Regardless of whether support was public or private and whether the chairmen remained neutral, candidates preferred by chairmen won. Only one of twenty-seven chairmen reported not getting his preference with as many as two major candidates. Six others missed on one each and the other twenty-one had all of their favorites nominated. There seems little question that it is generally futile to oppose the organization's desires; this supports statement 4a of the hypothesis.

### The Case Study

To what extent are these generalizations based upon newspaper records and upon reports from chairmen supported by intensive case examination? The Howard County experience provides a basis for further testing and fuller descriptions.

Before detailed questions about persons and events were put to candidates, each was asked to summarize briefly his reasons for running. Although responses varied widely, many reported that the idea grew gradually over a period of several years.

When an aspirant makes up his mind slowly, he is not always thinking about some specific office, but may settle on one according to how open it may be at a particular time and how much competition he anticipates. There will be angling for information during the early weeks, shortly before and after the opening date for filing, with potential candidates making discreet inquiries about the intentions of incumbents and other rumored aspirants. Sometimes statements such as this are made privately: "If so-and-so files, then I won't." Of course, the speaker may well file anyway. None of the candidates reported a sudden decision to file on his own; if he was a self-starter, he probably made his decision slowly.

Surprisingly, none of these candidates reported a desire to serve the public as the reason for his candidacy. A few expressed dissatisfaction at the ways some particular incumbent had been performing his job, with a desire to straighten things out. But for the most part, the slow deciders hinted at a better salary or an improved personal position. One, a factory worker, admitted that his salary had greatly increased while he was in office. A farmer had been the victim of an auto accident a year or so before the primary and was looking for something not quite so physically demanding than farming. Two of the Democratic incumbents admitted that they were nudged into running again by others (one was amenable and one reluctant), while the third filed again as a matter of course. One candidate admitted that he acted as a decoy in filing for office. He filed his candidacy because he thought his part of the county should be represented and thought he could stimulate someone stronger to file against him. He had little hope of being nominated.

Candidates were also asked questions about the groups most likely to help them in winning the nominations. Ranks were computed for a range of reference group alternatives. These were compared for successful and unsuccessful Republicans and Democrats, and most respondents in all four categories were in agreement that the support groups contributing the most would be business or professional groups with whom they had connections followed closely by persons prominent in politics with whom they had personal friendships.[23] If these are the connections perceived by the candidates as the two factors which would likely contribute most to their success, then it seems probable that the candidates had actual associations within these two areas while deciding to file and later during their campaigns. To explore further, candidates were asked for detailed information about their contacts up to primary day and as we shall see below, their responses point to the political contacts as being predominent.

*The Instigation Stage.* It is difficult to fit each candidate into a neat category according to whether he was a self-starter, was conscripted by a desperate organization, or was co-opted because he had unusual qualities or because he represented knowingly some interest groups, for he may be any combination of these types.

Those persons who do not file entirely on their own initiative (and those who do are rare) either originate the idea themselves and approach others for a reaction or someone comes to them to suggest that they run. Some twenty-three of the thirty-one Howard County candidates were initially approached by others.[24] The nature and extent of these contacts are displayed in Tables III, IV, V and VI.

Of all candidates for both parties, only the successful Democratic incumbent candidates for sheriff and clerk reported no contacts at the instigation stage. There were no other candidates who filed without talking it over with at least two other persons they felt to be important. All but two Republicans, both losers, were approached by one or more other persons before they filed. All but six Democrats had the same experience (and, except for the incumbent sheriff and clerk, these also lost) . Clearly, not only did nearly all candidates have some sort of contact with persons who were involved in their decisions to run, but nearly all winners reported persons coming to them, either to make the initial suggestion or to attempt in some way to influence the decision.

Another striking aspect of these reports is the preponderance of party-connected persons who were in contact with candidates at the instigation stage. Compare this with the very small numbers who seemed to be acting essentially as members of interest groups.[25] Also of note is the very small number of "friends, neighbors, and fellow workers" who were in these capacities contributors to the candidates' decisions to file. Only one Democratic candidate (unsuccessful) reported any such contacts, although five Republicans did (two successful, three unsuccessful) .

More surprising is the number of active members of the opposite party who were noted as contacts at the instigation stage. It would not be too startling to find a few party leaders offering to support an announced and filed candidate of the opposite party in the general election, especially if he should happen to be a friend or associate, but to

## TABLE III

PERSONS WHO SOUGHT OUT HOWARD COUNTY DEMOCRATIC CANDIDATES
BEFORE THEY FILED

| | | Judge | | Prose-cutor | Clerk | Recorder | | | | Sheriff | | | As-sessor | | | Commissioner Third District | | | First District |
|---|---|---|---|---|---|---|---|---|---|---|---|---|---|---|---|---|---|---|---|
| | | 1 | 2 | 1 | 1 | 1 | 2 | 3 | 4 | 1 | 2 | 3 | 1 | 2 | 3 | 1 | 2 | 3 | 1 |
| First-level influentials | I | | | | | | | | | | | | | | | 2 | | | |
| | W | | | 2 | | | | | | | | | | | | | | | |
| | N | | | | | | 1 | | | | | | | | | | | | |
| Second-level influentials | I | | | | | | | | | | | | | | | | | 1 | |
| | E | | | | | | | | | | | | 3 | | 1 | | | | |
| | W | | | 2 | | | | | | | | | 1 | | | | | | |
| | D | | | | | | | | | | | | | | | 1 | | | |
| Other party groups, candidates, and committeemen | I | | | | | 1 | | | | | | | 2 | | | | | 1 | |
| | S | | | | | | | | | | 1 | 1 | | | | 1 | | 2 | |
| | N | | | | | | 1 | | | | | | | | | | | | |
| | D | | | | | | | | | | | | | | 1 | | | | |
| Interest groups Lawyers | S | 1 | | | | | | | | | | | | | | | | | |
| Lawyers | E | 3 | | | | | | | | | | | | | | | | | |
| Real Estate | E | | | | | | | | | | | | | | 1 | | | | |
| Republicans First-level influentials | E | | | | | | | | | | | | | | | 3 | 1 | | |
| Friends, neighbors, and fellow employees | E | | | | | | | | | | | | | | 2 | | | | |
| Total contacts | | 4 | 0 | 4 | 0 | 1 | 2 | 0 | 0 | 0 | 1 | 1 | 6 | 0 | 5 | 7 | 1 | 4 | 0 |

Key: I = Initial Suggestion  
     S = Strong Encouragement  
     E = Encouragement  
     W = Weak Encouragement  
     N = Noncommittal  
     D = Discouragement

Note: Candidates are arranged in order of votes received, the successful candidate being number 1.

find party leaders actively recruiting candidates for the other party is something else. Yet ten Republicans and eleven Democrats were reported engaged in such activity.[26] There are these possible explanations: (1) Where both parties exercise control of some offices, working relationships may develop among the officeholders in both parties which are smooth and which they do not want to see upset; (2) some leaders are dissatisfied with all potential candidates for an office in their own party and would like to have someone they could support; (3) factional partisans may fear that their candidates will lose and

## TABLE IV

### PERSONS SOUGHT OUT BY HOWARD COUNTY DEMOCRATIC CANDIDATES BEFORE THEY FILED

| | | Judge | | Prose-cutor | Clerk | Re-corder | | | | Sheriff | | | As-sessor | | | Commissioner Third District | | | First District |
|---|---|---|---|---|---|---|---|---|---|---|---|---|---|---|---|---|---|---|---|
| | | 1 | 2 | 1 | 1 | 1 | 2 | 3 | 4 | 1 | 2 | 3 | 1 | 2 | 3 | 1 | 2 | 3 | 1 |
| First-level influentials | E | 3 | | | | | 1 | 1 | | | 2 | | 5 | | | | | | |
| | W | | | | | | 1 | | | | | | | | | | | | |
| | N | | | | | | 1 | 1 | | | | | | | | | | | |
| | D | | | | | | | | | | | 1 | | | | | | | |
| Second-level influentials | E | 1 | 1 | | | | | | | | 2 | | 1 | | | | 1 | | |
| | D | | | | | | | | | | 2 | | | | | | | | |
| Other party groups, candidates and committeemen | S | | | | | | | 1 | | | | | 1 | | | | | | |
| | E | 3 | | | | | | | 2 | | 1 | | 6 | 5 | 1 | | 2 | | |
| Interest groups Abstract and real estate | E | | | | | 1 | | | | | | | 3 | | | | | | |
| | W | | | | | 1 | | | | | | | | | | | | | |
| AFL–CIO | E | | | | | | 1 | | | | | | 1 | | | | | | |
| Finance and business | E | | | | | | | | | | | | 2 | | | | | | |
| Trucking | E | | | | | | | | | | | | | | | | 1 | | |
| Voter blocs Negro | E | | | | | | | | | | | | 2 | | | | | | |
| Republicans First-level influentials | E | | | | | | | 1 | | | | | 1 | | | | | | |
| Second-level influentials | E | | | | | | | | | | | | 1 | | | | | | |
| Others | E | | | | | | | | | | | | 3 | | | | | | |
| Total contacts | | 4 | 4 | 0 | 0 | 2 | 4 | 4 | 2 | 0 | 7 | 1 | 20 | 6 | 6 | 0 | 4 | 0 | 0 |
| Total of Tables III and IV | | 8 | 4 | 4 | 0 | 3 | 6 | 4 | 2 | 0 | 8 | 2 | 26 | 6 | 11 | 7 | 5 | 4 | 0 |

Key: I  = Initial Suggestion      N = Noncommittal      NOTE: Candidates are arranged in
S  = Strong Encouragement      D = Discouragement      order of votes received, the success-
E  = Encouragement      ful candidate being number 1.
W  = Weak Encouragement

may be unwilling to support a candidate of another faction in their own party and will therefore hedge this possibility; or (4) each party interferes with the other in hopes that weaker candidates will be nominated, making the job at the general election easier. In Howard County, there was evidence that the first of these was the most significant. There was some evidence for the second and third but there were

## TABLE V

PERSONS WHO SOUGHT OUT HOWARD COUNTY REPUBLICAN CANDIDATES
BEFORE THEY FILED

| | | JUDGE | PROSECUTOR | RECORDER | | | SHERIFF | | | | ASSESSOR | | | COMMISSIONER |
|---|---|---|---|---|---|---|---|---|---|---|---|---|---|---|
| | | 1 | 1 | 1 | 2 | 3 | 1 | 2 | 3 | 4 | 1 | 2 | 3 | 1 |
| First-level influentials | I | | | | | | | | | | | 2 | | |
| | S | 5 | | | | | | | | | | 2 | | |
| | E | | | | | | | | 2 | | | | 1 | |
| Second-level influentials | I | | 1 | | | | | | | | | | | |
| | S | 2 | | | | | 1 | | | | 1 | | | 1 |
| Other party groups, candidates and committeemen | I | | | | | | | | | | | | | |
| | S | 1 | | | | | | | | | | | | |
| | E | | | | | | | 2 | | | | | | 3 |
| Interest Groups | | | | | | | | | | | | | | |
| Attorneys | S | 3 | | | | | | | | | | | | |
| Law | S | | | | | | 1 | | | | | | | |
|  enforcement | I | | | | | | 1 | | | | | | | |
| Real estate | S | | | | | | | | | | 1 | | | |
| Democrats | | | | | | | | | | | | | | |
| First-level influentials | I | | | | | | | | | | 1 | | | |
| Second-level influentials | E | 2 | | | | | 1 | | 1 | | | | | |
| | D | | | | | | | | 1 | | | | | |
| Others | I | | | 1 | | | 1 | | | | | | | 1 |
| | E | | | | | | | | 2 | | | | | |
| Friends, neighbors or fellow employees | S | | 2 | | | | 1 | 1 | | | | | | |
| | E | | | | | | | 2 | | | | | | |
| | I | | | | | 1 | 1 | | | | | | | |
| Total contacts | | 13 | 3 | 1 | 0 | 1 | 5 | 2 | 3 | 8 | 6 | 1 | 1 | 5 |

Key: I  = Initial Suggestion     NOTE: Candidates are arranged in order of votes
   S  = Strong Encouragement   received, the successful candidate being num-
   E  = Encouragement       ber 1.
   W = Weak Encouragement
   N  = Noncommittal
   D  = Discouragement

no reports from influentials or from candidates that there were attempts to weaken the other party.

Other interesting aspects of instigation are revealed from summary totals in Table VII. For example, involvement by first-level party influentials in recruiting candidates for the primary is proportionately higher for Republicans than Democrats. Investigation turned up reports of factionalism in the Democratic party and a comparative lack of cohesiveness within the total leadership of the party which might well explain this. It is also interesting to note that Democrats pursued

## TABLE VI

### Persons Sought Out by Howard County Republican Candidates Before They Filed

| | | Judge | Prosecutor | Recorder | | | Sheriff | | | | Assessor | | | Commissioner |
|---|---|---|---|---|---|---|---|---|---|---|---|---|---|---|
| | | 1 | 1 | 1 | 2 | 3 | 1 | 2 | 3 | 4 | 1 | 2 | 3 | 1 |
| First-level influentials | S | 2 | 1 | | | | | | | | | | | |
| | E | | | 2 | | | | | | | | | | 4 |
| | W | | | | 2 | 1 | 2 | | | | 2 | | | |
| | N | | | | | | | | | | | | 2 | |
| Second-level influentials | E | | | 1 | | | | | | | 1 | | | 1 |
| | D | | | | | | | 1 | | | | | | |
| Other party groups, candidates and committeemen | E | | | | | | | | 1 | | 1 | 1 | | |
| | W | | | | 2 | | | | | | | | | |
| | D | | | | | | | 1 | | | | | | |
| Interest groups Lawyers | E | 1 | | | | | | | | | | | | |
| Democrats First-level influential | E | | | | | | | | | | 2 | | | |
| Friends, neighbors and fellow employees | E | | | | 1 | | | | | | | | | |
| Total contacts | | 3 | 1 | 3 | 4 | 2 | 0 | 4 | 0 | 1 | 3 | 3 | 3 | 5 |
| Total of Tables V and VI | | 16 | 4 | 4 | 4 | 3 | 5 | 6 | 3 | 9 | 9 | 4 | 4 | 10 |

Key: I = Initial Suggestion
S = Strong Encouragement
E = Encouragement
W = Weak Encouragement
N = Noncommittal
D = Discouragement

Note: Candidates are arranged in order of votes received, the successful one being number 1.

interest groups for support (there were twelve such contacts) while there was only one Republican contact with interest groups. The overall small amount of interest group contact is supported by the general perceptions of both leaders and candidates which attribute low influence to such groups in primaries. The fact that some Democrats did seek interest group support is consistent with the further findings that, in Howard County, the Democratic candidates were more professional in their approach to politics and thus may have had a better sense of what groups might aid their cause. (Democrats had a longer record of political involvement than did Republicans.) That the Republicans tended to be amateurs is further supported by the comparatively large number of friends, neighbors, and fellow workers who approached these aspirants, although only one of the eight was reported by a winner.

TABLE VII

Totals for All Offices by Influence Category of Contacts Made by
Howard County Candidates at the Instigation Stage

| | REPUBLICANS (n = 13) | | DEMOCRATS (n = 18) | |
|---|---|---|---|---|
| | No. of Contacts from Others | No. of Contacts to Others | No. of Contacts from Others | No. of Contacts to Others |
| Party connected: | 24 | 28 | 25 | 46 |
| First-level influentials | (12) | (18) | ( 5) | (16) |
| Second-level influentials | ( 6) | ( 4) | ( 9) | ( 8) |
| Party groups, candidates, and committeemen | ( 6) | ( 6) | (11) | (22) |
| All interest groups and voter blocs | 6 | 1 | 5 | 12 |
| Opposite party | 11 | 2 | 4 | 6 |
| Friends, neighbors, fellow employees | 8 | 1 | 2 | 0 |
| Total | 49 | 32 | 36 | 64 |

*The Reinforcement Stage.* Once an aspirant has filed his candidacy
and his intentions become known, a new set of interpersonal relationships takes place. Certain persons seek out candidates and offer them
varying degrees of encouragement and, occasionally, discouragement.
Candidates also seek out certain persons to directly or indirectly solicit
their support. It was beyond the scope of this study to account for all
of the variables which may contribute to a candidate's success although
a number of these were suggested by the data, that is, incumbency, political experience, activity within the party, and memberships in organizations. It was a central concern, however, to identify those groups
and individuals who exerted their influence on behalf of the candidates and, insofar as possible, to ascertain the effectiveness of these influence attempts.

Tables VIII, IX, X, and XI report the responses of Howard County
candidates concerning the persons and groups they were in contact
with after their filings. As in other tables, candidates are listed in the
order of votes received. For the Democrats, five winners reported that
someone approached them about their candidacies. The two unopposed candidates (Commissioner from the First District and Clerk of
the Circuit Court) reported no contacts as might be expected. The
only winning contestant who reported no contacts was the County
Commissioner from the Third District, an incumbent. His principal
opponent had many callers, however; the investigation revealed that
the opponent was a major hope for a Democratic out-faction, and no

## TABLE VIII

### Persons Who Sought Out Howard County Democratic Candidates After They Filed

| | Judge | | Prose-cutor | Recorder | | | | Sheriff | | | As-sessor | | | Commissioner Third District | | | Commissioner First District | Clerk |
|---|---|---|---|---|---|---|---|---|---|---|---|---|---|---|---|---|---|---|
| | 1 | 2 | 1 | 1 | 2 | 3 | 4 | 1 | 2 | 3 | 1 | 2 | 3 | 1 | 2 | 3 | 1 | 1 |
| First-level influentials   E | | | | 1 | | | | 1 | 1 | | 1 | | | | | | | |
| Second-level influentials   S | 4 | | | | | | | | | 1 | | | | | 1 | | | |
|   E | | | | 1 | | | | 3 | 1 | | | | | | 1 | | | |
|   D | | | | | | | | | 3 | | | | | | | | | |
|   W | | | | | | | | | | | 1 | | | | | | | |
| Other party groups, candidates, and committeemen   S | 2 | | 1 | | | | | | | 1 | | | | | | | | |
|   E | | | | | | | | 1 | 3 | | | 2 | 1 | | 3 | | | |
|   D | | | | | | | | | | | | | 1 | | 1 | | | |
| Interest groups: Finance   E | | | | 2 | | | | | | | | | | | 1 | | | |
| Real estate   E | | | | 1 | | | | | | | | | | | | | | |
| Contractor   E | | | | | | | | | | | | | | | 1 | | | |
| Republicans First-level influentials   E | | | | | | | | 2 | | | | | | | 1 | | | |
| Second-level influentials | | | | | | | | | | | | | | | | | | |
| Other   E | | | | 5 | | | | | | | | | | | | | | |
| Total contacts | 6 | 0 | 1 | 10 | 0 | 0 | 0 | 7 | 8 | 2 | 2 | 2 | 2 | 0 | 9 | 0 | 0 | 0 |

Key: I = Initial Suggestion
S = Strong Encouragement
E = Encouragement
W = Weak Encouragement
N = Noncommittal
D = Discouragement

Note: Candidates are arranged in order of votes received, the successful one being number 1.

doubt much encouragement was sent his way, while the in-faction sup-porting the winner felt this unnecessary. For the Republicans, all con-test winners reported contacts at this stage, although two unopposed and two losing candidates did not.

The contacts do not indicate a clear pattern to differentiate winning and losing candidates who were themselves looking for help after they had filed. Apparently, by then they were calling on voters and must have known where they stood with the influentials to which they had access. The Democratic Prosecutor went to work after he encountered unexpected opposition from outside the county and the low man in the four-man race for recorder reported sudden activity. Most felt, however, that much of their influential support was arranged for while

## TABLE IX

PERSONS SOUGHT OUT BY HOWARD COUNTY DEMOCRATIC CANDIDATES
AFTER THEY FILED

| | | Judge | | Prose-cutor | Recorder | | | | Sheriff | | | As-sessor | | | Commissioner Third District | | | Commissioner First District | Clerk |
|---|---|---|---|---|---|---|---|---|---|---|---|---|---|---|---|---|---|---|---|
| | | 1 | 2 | 1 | 1 | 2 | 3 | 4 | 1 | 2 | 3 | 1 | 2 | 3 | 1 | 2 | 3 | 1 | 1 |
| First-level influentials | S | | | | 1 | | | | 1 | | | | | | | | | | |
| Second-level influentials | S | | | 2 | 1 | | | | | | | | | | 1 | | | | |
| | E | | | | | | | 1 | | | | | | | | | | | |
| | W | | | 2 | | | | | | 2 | | | | | | | | | |
| | D | | | | | | | | | | 1 | | | | | | | | |
| Other party groups, candidates and committeemen | S | | | 2 | 2 | | | 4 | | | | | | | | | | | |
| | E | | | 3 | | | 2 | 2 | | | | | | | | | | | |
| | W | | | 2 | | | | 1 | | | | | | | | | | | |
| | D | | | | | | | | | | | | | | | | 1 | | |
| Friends, neighbors, and fellow employees | E | | | | | | | 1 | | | | | | | | | | | |
| Republicans First-level influential | E | | | | | | | | 2 | | | | 1 | | | | | | |
| | W | | | | | | | | | 1 | | | | | | | | | |
| Interest groups Labor unions | S | | | | | | | | | | 2 | | | | | | | | |
| Total contacts | | 0 | 0 | 11 | 4 | 0 | 2 | 9 | 3 | 3 | 3 | 0 | 1 | 0 | 1 | 0 | 1 | 0 | 0 |
| Total Table VIII and IX | | 6 | 0 | 12 | 14 | 0 | 2 | 9 | 10 | 11 | 5 | 2 | 3 | 2 | 1 | 9 | 1 | 0 | 0 |

Key: I = Initial Suggestion    NOTE: Candidates are arranged in order of votes
S = Strong Encouragement    received, the successful one being number 1.
E = Encouragement
W = Weak Encouragement
N = Noncommittal
D = Discouragement

they were deciding, as did the winning Democratic Assessor who went to see twenty people before she filed and none after. Republicans were even less active after their filings.

The summary totals for all offices, for both parties, reported in Table XII support these impressions. For the Republicans, the total number of contacts after filing was greatly reduced (from 81 to 45), suggesting that the heaviest recruitment activity took place before filing, at the instigation stage, and that there was less tendency to interfere once Republican aspirants had been persuaded to become candi-

## TABLE X

### Persons Who Sought Out Howard County Republican Candidates After They Filed

| | | Judge | Prosecutor | Recorder | | | Sheriff | | | | Assessor | | | Commissioner |
|---|---|---|---|---|---|---|---|---|---|---|---|---|---|---|
| | | I | I | 1 | 2 | 3 | 1 | 2 | 3 | 4 | 1 | 2 | 3 | I |
| First-level influentials | S | | 3 | | | | | | | | | | | |
| | E | | | 1 | | | | | | | 1 | 1 | | |
| | W | | | 1 | | | | | | | | | | |
| Other party groups, candidates, and committeemen | S | | | | | | 3 | | | | | | | |
| | E | | | 1 | 1 | | | | | | 2 | | | |
| Interest Groups | | | | | | | | | | | | | | |
| Finance | S | | | 1 | | | 1 | | | | | | | |
| Utilities | E | | | | | | 3 | | | | | | | |
| Local business | E | | | | | 2 | | | | | | | | |
| Real estate | S | | | | | | | | | | 1 | | | |
| Democrats | | | | | | | | | | | | | | |
| Second-level influentials | E | | | 1 | | | | | | | | | | |
| Others | E | | | | | | | | | | | 1 | | |
| Friends, neighbors, and fellow employees | E | | | | | | | | 3 | | | | 3 | |
| Total contacts | | 0 | 3 | 5 | 1 | 2 | 7 | 0 | 3 | 0 | 5 | 1 | 3 | 0 |

Key: I = Initial Suggestion  
S = Strong Encouragement  
E = Encouragement  
W = Weak Encouragement  
N = Noncommittal  
D = Discouragement

Note: Candidates are arranged in order of votes received, the successful one being number 1.

dates. These candidates also must have felt that party people were, at least on the surface, trying to remain neutral, for they themselves initiated even fewer contacts—practically none outside the party. Interest groups, friends, neighbors, and fellow workers were still seeking out candidates.

There was also a drop in activity for the Democrats, but not nearly as marked. The number of persons connected with politics who contacted candidates actually increased after the candidate filed, as factions sought to maneuver behind their candidates (particularly the partisans below the first level). These totals also indicate a substantial number of reinforcement stage contacts initiated by the Democratic candidates toward second-level and third-level party groups, but practically none toward interest groups.

The total amount of interaction between candidates and supportive groups for each party was proportionately about the same. There were

187 contacts recorded for Democrats and 126 for Republicans, with eighteen Democratic candidates and thirteen Republicans.

From the discussion above, it is apparent that party leadership made most of the direct recruitment contacts. For Republicans this was first-

### TABLE XI

#### PERSONS SOUGHT OUT BY HOWARD COUNTY REPUBLICAN CANDIDATES AFTER THEY FILED

| | | JUDGE | PROSECUTOR | RECORDER | | | SHERIFF | | | | ASSESSOR | | | COMMISSIONER |
|---|---|---|---|---|---|---|---|---|---|---|---|---|---|---|
| | | I | I | 1 | 2 | 3 | 1 | 2 | 3 | 4 | 1 | 2 | 3 | I |
| First-level influentials | S | | | | | | | | | | 1 | | | |
| | E | | 1 | | | | | 1 | | | | 2 | | |
| Second-level influentials | S | | | | | | | 1 | | | 1 | | | |
| | W | | | | | | | | | | | | 1 | |
| Other party groups, candidates and committeemen | S | | | | | | | 1 | | | | | | |
| | E | | | | | | | | 3 | | | | | |
| Interest groups Law enforcement | S | | | | | | | | 1 | | | | | |
| Voter blocs: Amish | S | | | | | | | | | 1 | | | | |
| Friends, neighbors and fellow employees | S | | | | | | | | | 1 | | | | |
| Total contacts | | 0 | 1 | 0 | 0 | 0 | 0 | 3 | 4 | 2 | 2 | 2 | 1 | 0 |
| Total of Tables X and XI | | 0 | 4 | 5 | 1 | 2 | 7 | 3 | 7 | 2 | 7 | 3 | 4 | 0 |

Key: I  = Initial Suggestion
    S  = Strong Encouragement
    E  = Encouragement
    W = Weak Encouragement
    N  = Noncommittal
    D  = Discouragement

NOTE: Candidates are arranged in order of votes received, the successful one being number 1.

level leadership; for Democrats, second-level and third-level, involving some committeemen who were not often found in decision-making circles. Whether these contacts were provided for by design or came about because various leaders acted in recruiting on their own initiative is not answered from the data secured from candidates. More can be said about how this was done, however, since many of the leaders were also interviewed and were asked several questions about their involvement during the time span of the study.

For the Republican party, the weaker party, all of the ten first-level leaders interviewed reported attending, during the filing period, at least one and as many as four meetings where nominations were dis-

cussed.[27] All offices were considered at these meetings, although decisions were not made on all of them. For most offices, there was general
agreement on which persons the group would solicit and support and
contacts at the instigation stage were made as a result of these meetings.
For example, the leaders agreed in their reports that the following
offices had been filled directly by group efforts: superior court judge,
prosecutor, and assessor. Two of these turned out to be unopposed and

TABLE XII

Total of Contacts Made by Howard County Candidates at the Support
Stage for All Offices by Influence Category

| | REPUBLICANS (n = 13) | | DEMOCRATS (n = 18) | |
|---|---|---|---|---|
| | No. of Contacts from Others | No. of Contacts to Others | No. of Contacts from Others | No. of Contacts to Others |
| Party connected | 14 | 12 | 36 | 31 |
| First-level influentials | ( 7) | ( 5) | ( 4) | ( 2) |
| Second-level influentials | ( 0) | ( 3) | (16) | (10) |
| Party groups, candidates, and committeemen | ( 7) | ( 4) | (16) | (19) |
| All interest groups and voter blocs | 8 | 2 | 5 | 2 |
| Opposite party | 2 | 0 | 8 | 4 |
| Friends, neighbors, and fellow employees | 6 | 1 | 0 | 1 |
| Total | 30 | 15 | 49 | 38 |
| Total of Tables VII and XII | 81 + 45 = 126 | | 100 + 87 = 187 | |

the third, although contested, was the winner. They also discussed the
office of recorder but took no group action. However, one member, on
his own, when approached by the man who subsequently was nominated for this office, talked him out of running for assessor and into
running for recorder instead. Affirmative action was also taken on several offices at higher levels which were not examined in this study.
Some prospects were contacted who refused to run—names of four were
mentioned, and one active member of the group claimed that he was
able to discourage still another man from running for assessor.

For the dominant but fractionated Democratic party, all leader reports indicated that no meetings were held on nominations either during or after filing time. To be sure, there were meetings of the various
factions, but they were to discuss control of the organization, not nominations. Apparently, there were enough potential candidates that or-

ganized recruitment was not deemed necessary. No doubt this was also partly due to the fact that several incumbents were running and, although there is no informal understanding that incumbents are entitled to a second term, the campaign edge which they hold makes opposition difficult.

Republican leaders, when asked to assess their influence as individuals, spoke modestly about their personal degree of involvement. None perceived themselves as being widely influential but referred to one, two, or perhaps three offices in which they were particularly interested or where they had been assigned to make a contact. However, they were generally more confident about their contribution at the instigation stage than about their influence in helping their favorites to win. Democratic first-level leadership was even more modest as well.

In total, the foregoing reports of contacts and meetings are indicative of substantial first-level party leadership involvement in the Republican party at the instigation stage and of lower-level leadership activity in the Democratic party, with its less cohesive leadership structure.

It has been more difficult to identify those instrumental in the success of primary candidates. This may be partly due to the likelihood that there are a number of possible contributing factors at this stage and only a few are considered here inasmuch as the purpose was to identify persons and groups rather than to assess a candidate's previous record or evaluate the attractiveness of his name to voters. The nature of the contacts which candidates had prior to the primary election do, nonetheless, furnish important clues even though the top leaders were not particularly disposed to assess the amount of their own influence over the success of those who won nominations. Some additional evidence pointing to the importance of their role was obtained when lists of candidates were submitted to leaders and they were asked to indicate any candidates whom they particularly or strongly favored or opposed.[28]

Of Republican first-level leaders reporting strong concerns, successful candidates were mentioned twenty-five times, unsuccessful candidates, five times. Three instances of strong opposition were directed toward candidates who lost. There was evidence that first-level Democrats were interested in the outcome of Republican contests, but only one of the six so stating was in support of a winner. There were also Republicans who expressed interest in six Democratic contests, supporting three winners and three losers, and one other Republican unsuccessfully opposed a Democratic winner. It would appear that leader influence across party lines is also not as effective at the reinforcement stage as it may have been at instigation since only four of thirteen cross-party desires were fulfilled by the primary outcome.

Top Democratic leadership strongly favored winners seventeen times and losers eight times, not quite as convincing a relationship as with the Republicans, suggesting reduced effectiveness accompanying the factionalism and lower cohesion in Democratic leadership ranks.

Finally, by cross-checking the reports of candidates with reports from the leaders, it was possible to trace the extent to which each leader was involved in the total nominating process by verifying the nature of the contacts made, and by comparing the kinds of contacts made with the success of each candidate involved.

## Conclusion

What further insights does the Howard County study add to the hypothesis tested by multiple county analysis? Several points should be re-emphasized:

1. In competitive situations, the degree to which the candidacy market is wide open and the degree of centralized control seems dependent upon the relative electoral strengths of the two parties. The dominant party is less apt to recruit formally as a party, opening the way for lower-level party functionaries to make their own independent recruitment contacts. The weaker party, on the other hand, may function very much as if it were in a one-party situation. The difference lies largely in the number of potential candidates willing to make the race, but the party leadership is much concerned about which ones of this number actually do make it.

2. Winners of nomination races are not very likely to be self-starters. The aspirant who makes his initial bid for office independent of necessary support groups at the instigation stage is probably in trouble. Most county candidates, if not incumbents, are either desperately conscripted or else co-opted because of special qualities. If interest group representation is involved, it is not promoted by the interest groups proper.

3. In terms of the broad categories originally designated as potential contributors to the decisions of which persons seek office, the most significant category is party leadership.

Discovery that a small group of party-connected persons appears to be the most heavily involved in political recruitment at the county level is perhaps not too surprising considering that, other than when they vote, it is unlikely that large numbers of people are directly involved in the outcome of very many political issues. However, nominations may be somewhat of an exception in the sense that they may call forth efforts of comparatively large numbers of persons, each interested in who will run for particular offices. To be sure, it is a small percentage of a community's population, but it is a part which takes its place in decision-making. In Howard County this group numbered 138 persons who participated directly in selecting Democratic candidates and 99 who participated in Republican recruitment. But most of these persons participated to a limited extent, concerning themselves with one, possibly two, candidates. Primarily it was the small groups of party leaders, both formal and informal, whose involvement was extensive and whose efforts appeared effectively placed.

The research reported in this chapter has touched several aspects of the recruitment process. No attempt was made to set forth a comprehensive theory or model of recruitment although such efforts need increasingly to be encouraged.[29] Despite its lack of inclusiveness however, this study, by using Seligman's categories, does suggest gaps in our knowledge and thereby directions for studies which, when researched, can contribute to fuller understanding of the ways leaders perform in their roles as decision-makers within various political systems.

In arguing for further research, it is tempting to first suggest that more be done in areas left largely untouched in studies such as this. And indeed, it is in the certification stage where our knowledge may be weakest for we have yet much to learn of how personality characteristics, attitudes, and values of people relate to their involvement in political affairs, although considerable work has been done with respect to the social backgrounds of various political elites. The concern of the present study has been primarily within the context of the selection stage, however, and it is within this context that selected questions and next steps may be posed.

In examining broadly the relationships between the electoral system as reflected by inter-party competition, the data presented here largely reinforce previous studies but add little in the way of new insights despite the suggestion that vigor of contests, as well as number of contests, should be made part of hypotheses where competitiveness is treated as an explanatory variable. But such hypotheses probably have relatively little more to contribute to the development of recruitment theory. Rather, it is the dynamics within each party to which the findings of this exploration point as being fruitful for more careful inquiry. True, we still do not know much about the relations of governmental and electoral systems to party nor do we know much about the impact of voters' attitudes on party—but it is the informal groups and individuals within the party that emerge here as foci for further study. For it was instigation rather than reinforcement that called forth the greatest nomination activity in Howard County, and it was the informal elites within the party that appeared to dominate at that stage. Who then are the informal party elites in other states and at other levels of government? Can they be efficiently identified? How did they rise to positions of influence within their party structure? How do they differ from those who stand for elective office? What resources do the elites have at their disposal which give them influence in nominations? When the party elites take a direct and active part in recruitment, how do they identify aspirants for office who have survived the screening process that makes them eligible? What attitudes do the candidates develop toward such party elites? How do these attitudes affect the behavior of nominees once they have achieved office?

For answers to such questions, what is needed then is (1) replication of studies such as this to both refine techniques for identifying elites and for verifying the prominence of their roles in the instigation of candidacies, (2) more careful attention in candidate interviews to the perceptions and attitudes about elites and the obligations they feel toward these elites, and (3) comparison of such perceptions and attitudes with those of leaders who attain offices. The last, most important, and most challenging step is, of course, to develop ways of relating the decision-making activities of leaders to attitudes stemming from the way they were selected and of comparing such attitudes with other variables entering the decision-making process, thus pointing to the integration of recruitment theory into broader theory of the polity.

# 11 / Control in the Party Convention Nominating System: the Case of Indiana

*David Calhoun Leege*

THE DUAL QUESTIONS "WHO SHOULD GOVERN" AND "WHO DOES GOVERN" are central to political inquiry. Answers to these questions have been based on (1) formal structural arrangements within a polity, for example, laws governing popular participation, election of public officials, relations between functional and geographical governing units and (2) political cultures, that is, informal norms, customs, folkways, or practices which either prescribe or make probable certain styles of political behavior.

In a formal structural way, the question of who ought to govern has been decided in most Western democracies, presumably, by popular elections. Elections are contested by people working more or less in concert to control the personnel and policies of government, that is, by political parties. The party or candidate attracting a majority or plurality in the polling places governs. But the selection of candidates has rested with the parties and their identifiers. When we ask who are not only the legitimate but also the effective governors of a polity, among other places, we are forced to move behind the election to the nominating process. We must examine the nature of the control structure within the party. As Schattschneider has argued: ". . . he who can make the nomination is the owner of the party." [1]

Controversy over nominating techniques in the United States has centered primarily on structural arrangements. The legislative caucus, the party convention, the direct primary—each replaced its predecessor with what was thought to be a "more democratic" control structure. Yet, control is a behavioral pattern that is sometimes affected by structural change, but often persists despite new arrangements. Advocates of the direct primary argued differently. For them, structure was independent; behavior, dependent. If selfish, self-perpetuating elites controlled the party nominating convention, a structural change to the direct primary system would render this type of control impossible;

widespread popular sharing in control would result.[2] As Key points out, however, even the most ardent advocates of structural change were dealing with a political cultural question:

> Whether the indictments of the convention system were correct in all particulars, the primary advocates had hold of a fundamental problem in popular government. The process of popular government tends to be a sequence of clashes to check the accretion of privilege in the hands of those who manage to grasp public power. In the circumstances of the time the enemies of privilege had to try to bust the political machines, as well as the trusts, and the attack against the machines became in part an attack against the convention system, an instrument for the monopolization of political power, given the nature of the party system at the time.[3]

Experience with the direct primary has indicated that behavior—in this case, informal control structures—can readily adapt to and even take advantage of new structural arrangements.

This chapter seeks to examine a nominating technique through an explicitly political cultural approach. It uses a configurational approach, relating norms and behaviors within a political system to structure. It attempts to delineate associations, not to impute causality. It will later argue for a comparative state politics focusing on political cultures as well as on structures.

Specifically, the chapter is a case study of the Indiana Democratic Party's four state nominating conventions assembled in 1956, 1958, 1960 and 1962. Indiana is one of four states—the others are New York, Connecticut, and Delaware—continuing to utilize the nominating convention for all statewide elective offices. Power, defined as control over outcomes, is the central focus. For the purposes of this study, other questions stemming from a model of democracy including popular sovereignty, political equality, majority rule, and responsiveness are secondary. The approach is that of community power studies, which focus on a set of crucial decisions; in this case, the central question is, Who controls decisions about whom the party will nominate? This approach is particularly well-suited to nominations for state-wide elective offices in Indiana, since its elected officials may exert extensive appointive, policy-making, and party influences lacking in many other states.[4]

This chapter deals with control over outcomes at two crucial points: (1) the recruitment and selection of delegates through the primary election process, and (2) the nominating decisions made or verified on the convention floor. It will also examine efficacy and alienation, important aspects of a democratic political culture, among the direct participants in the Indiana convention system. It will conclude with a discussion of research strategies for explaining political system variation by relating norms, behaviors, and structures.

Earlier convention critics argued that bosses controlled conventions. By doing away with the convention system, boss control would be minimized. After examining the norms and behaviors of various types of participants in Indiana Democratic conventions, this study finds that control rests, not with bosses, but is at least as widespread as the delegates themselves.

## Control at the Primary Stage

Since delegates to the Indiana state conventions are popularly elected in party primaries, since the county delegation is the principal organizational unit in the convention, and since the county chairman is likely to be the *de facto,* if not *de jure,* leader of his delegation, questions of convention control must first focus on (1) the manner of recruiting and selecting delegates and (2) the relationship of the county chairman or other potential controllers to this process.

Nineteenth- and early twentieth-century critics of the convention system argued that conventions were overwhelmingly constituted by delegates ill-suited to public-spirited deliberation. Many were unsavory characters, politically or financially beholden to party bosses; others were easily stampeded by crowd psychology.[5] In short, control over conventions was not difficult because of the personal characteristics of the delegates.

Delegates to Indiana Democratic conventions, by customary standards of evaluation, are drawn from an elite stratum both in terms of political experience and social backgrounds.[6] Nearly 80 percent of them have had previous experience in elective public office, appointive office, or in a party office; many have held all three. Rural delegates were significantly more likely to have been elected to public office, while urban delegates tended slightly, but not significantly, to have held patronage appointments. Most of the delegates present evidence of some degree of economic independence. Depending on the convention year, 15 to 25 percent of the delegates were employees of private businesses or corporations; 20 to 29 percent were government employees, for the most part, elected officials; 10 percent were housewives; and 36 to 55 percent were self-employed. Fully 50 percent of the delegates were in business and professional occupations, in contrast with 17 percent of the Indiana labor force thus employed. The remaining 50 percent were farmers, blue- and white-collar employees, and housewives. Over eight out of every ten delegates were male, while nearly three-fourths of them were in the prime political age range of 33 to 56 years. In contrast with the Indiana population, where the modal class had completed high school and the median class had slightly over a grammar school education, Democratic convention delegates present a multimodal distribution peaking at completion of high school, completion of college, and receipt of graduate degrees; the median education level of the delegates includes some college work. Delegates are also deeply enmeshed in a network of voluntary organizations. While the majority of Americans do not belong to a single organization,[7] most delegates belong to at least two or three different types of associations; church, service, professional, and veterans groups predominate. Delegates are active members as indicated by the 41 percent of them who reported holding office within at least one of these organizations. Such evidence contrasts vividly with descriptions of the social and political backgrounds of convention delegates offered by convention critics during the Progressive era.

Democratic theory, while concerned with the qualities of popular representatives, is more expressly addressed to the condition of competition. Schumpeter identified the "competitive struggle for the people's vote" as crucial to the democratic method.[8] The implication is that competition among alternatives provides the voter with safeguards from control by selfish, self-perpetuating elites. Whether individuals are well- or ill-suited to their obligations is a decision voters must make among competing aspirants for delegate seats. In effect, democratic theorists direct us beyond the characteristics of delegates to the condition of competition in the selection process.

An earlier study of competition for Indiana convention delegate seats indicated that, on the average, only 12 percent of the seats were contested.[9] Although the measure of competition is not strictly comparable, a later study indicates that competition had increased considerably in the late 1940's and early 1950's and that contests over delegate seats were more likely in urban counties than in rural ones.[10] Ironically, many of the convention system's detractors saw the only prospect for democratic government through the convention system in the public-spirited, independent, thoughtful individuals sent by rural areas; urban delegates were uniformly presumed subject to boss control.[11]

The data on present Indiana conventions, however, indicate that with few exceptions opportunities for voter choice among competing delegate aspirants are more likely in urban areas than in rural ones. Additionally, competition has increased in many counties to the point where voters are confronted with choices between two or more individuals or even rival slates within a sizable proportion of the delegate districts. Table I illustrates these observations by presenting an index of competition along with selected county characteristics.

Although each county's degree of competitiveness results from a

TABLE I

INDEX OF COMPETITIVENESS FOR DEMOCRATIC CONVENTION DELEGATE SEATS
15 INDIANA COUNTIES INCLUDED IN SAMPLE [a]

| COUNTY | URBAN-RURAL CLASS [b] | % URBAN | DEMO. STRENGTH [c] | AVE. NO. CON. DEL. | COMPETITIVENESS 1956 | 1958 | 1960 | 1962 |
|---|---|---|---|---|---|---|---|---|
| Lake | 1 | 93.6 | 6 | 252 | 1.63 * | 1.47 * | 1.56 | 1.29 * |
| Marion | 1 | 91.2 | 1 | 274 | 1.71 | 1.46 | 1.33 | 1.26 |
| Vanderburgh | 1 | 86.6 | 4 | 86 | 1.91 | 2.13 | 2.94 | 1.31 |
| Howard | 2 | 67.9 | 2 | 35 | 1.53 | 1.62 | 2.11 | 1.87 |
| Elkhart | 2 | 54.2 | 0 | 40 | 1.62 | 1.51 | 1.60 | 2.00 |
| Knox | 3 | 52.8 | 4 | 27 | 1.11 | 1.27 | 1.24 | 1.00 |
| Henry | 3 | 41.6 | 1 | 23 | 1.42 | 1.27 | 2.15 | 1.42 |
| Dearborn | 4 | 41.8 | 5 | 16 | 1.00 | 1.13 | 1.29 | 1.11 |
| Hendricks | 4 | 32.3 | 0 | 15 | 1.08 | 1.00 * | 1.29 | 1.28 |
| Noble | 5 | 33.2 | 0 | 13 | 1.18 | 1.00 * | 1.00 | 1.07 |
| Vermillion | 5 | 33.0 | 6 | 14 | 1.71 | 1.71 | 3.14 | 1.50 |
| Martin | 5 | 26.9 | 6 | 7 | 1.18 | 1.14 | 1.71 | 1.43 |
| Jennings | 5 | 23.5 | 2 | 9 | 1.25 | 1.00 | 1.00 | 1.00 |
| Starke | 5 | 19.3 | 3 | 9 | 1.00 | 1.11 | 1.00 | 1.00 |
| Harrison | 5 | 14.1 | 5 | 12 | 1.42 | 1.00 | 1.00 | 1.00 |

[a] The index of competitiveness is found by calculating the ratio between the number of candidates filing for delegate seats and the number of seats apportioned to the county. Munger argues that the minimum ratio is 1.00; since all vacancies are eventually filled by appointment of the county chairman, it matters little whether a single candidate files for each seat or it is left vacant to be assigned at a later date. Because various apportionment criteria are used by the counties, this index is more useful than a simple percentage of seats contested; it more clearly reflects level of interest in the county. The index is drawn from Frank J. Munger, "Two-Party Politics in Indiana" (1955).

[b] The urban-rural class measure includes not only population density but also location in relation to a central city. All type 1 counties are Standard Metropolitan Statistical Areas; type 2 includes all counties with single or twin cities containing 25,000–50,000 inhabitants and over 50% of the county's population; type 3 is reserved for counties with a single city of 10,000–25,000 and no other urban place of greater than 5,000; type 4 counties are neighboring satellites of SMSA counties; and type 5 counties neither contain a town of 10,000 or more inhabitants nor are satellites of SMSA counties.

[c] Democratic strength here refers to the number of elections in the past six election years carried by the Democratic party in each county. It is based on voting for secretary of state, the legally defined party office in Indiana. Lake County's 6, for example, indicates that the party carried all six elections.

* Asterisks indicate seats unfilled by primary election; in Lake County the vacancies were 9 in 1956, 13 in 1958, and 35 in 1962; Hendricks County had 7 vacancies in 1958 and Noble had 1 in 1960; only the Lake County (1962, 10%) and Hendricks County (1958, 44%) vacancies accounted for a sizable proportion of their total delegations.

unique constellation of factors, not the least of which are local factional struggles for control of the county party apparatus that spill into delegate races, several general patterns are suggested by some, if not all, of the sample counties:

(1) Competition is greater in gubernatorial convention years (1956, 1960) than in biennial-election years where U. S. Senators or secretary of state nominees lead the ticket.

(2) Competition is greater in urban counties than rural counties; no competition whatsoever is a characteristic primarily of rural counties.

(3) Rural counties in economically depressed areas with strong Democratic voting traditions (e.g., Vermillion, Martin) experience greater competition than other rural counties.

(4) Urban, moderately urban, and urban-fringe counties where organized labor has attempted to mobilize politically, experience greater competition than most other counties.

(5) Urban and moderately urban counties where two-party competition is strong display patterns of competitiveness within the Democratic party which reflect (or perhaps precipitate) the waxing and waning of party fortunes in the general election.

The most striking pattern, of course, is the urban-rural difference in competitiveness. When counties are further examined by urban and rural delegate districts within the county (urban is here defined as a delegate district located primarily within an incorporated place of 2,500 or more residents), similar differences in competition appear; in only five of thirty-two instances where urban-rural within-county comparisons could be made did the rural districts experience competition equal to or greater than urban districts.

When competition did take place in rural areas, according to county chairmen, it was different in kind from that of urban areas. Rural chairmen attributed delegate seat contests to "disgruntled" party workers, "bad eggs," or "outsiders." In the urban counties, however, chairmen attributed competition to organized opposition, that is, to the efforts of rival factions. In short, urban competition was the type that could confront party identifiers with more highly visible alternatives.[12]

Both attempted and actual control over the composition of their delegations is more characteristic of rural chairmen than urban chairmen. Rural chairmen generally reported expending considerable effort to achieve a consensus on who should file for delegate seats within each district; those not chosen by the county chairman or his screening committee were discouraged from filing for seats; many rural chairmen pointed with pride to the lack of competition as evidence of their ability "to select the right man." Choice was not left to the voters. In urban areas, most chairmen indicated an attempt to recruit large proportions of their delegations, but the recruitment was generally undertaken by the decentralized precinct-level organization. If the chairman did not like the committeeman's selection, he had little ability to circumvent it short of direct appeals to voters; the precinct committeeman could still indicate his own slating preference to voters. And, the county chairman's own tenure in office was dependent on the support of a majority of his committeemen. To be sure, chairmen could withdraw certain types of services—jobs, contracts, entrée—from recalcitrant committeemen; virtually all urban chairmen, however, felt it more important to maintain harmony in the precinct-level organization than to punish individuals for their delegate preferences. Most argued that the activities of committeemen in local affairs were far more important than their selection of delegates to nominate statewide officials. Thus, insofar as the official leadership of the party is related to delegate selection, the control structure in urban counties is far more decentralized and less effective than the control structure in rural counties. Competition figures simply attest differing norms and behavior.[13]

One might argue that competition is an artifact of apportionment and that districting patterns can greatly contribute to the county chairman's control.[14] In Indiana, however, the 400 votes = 1 delegate seat ratio is applied every biennium. Once notified of the number of seats a county is allowed, the county board of election commissioners must draw district lines. All but one county in the sample apportioned units roughly equal to party vote. Counties utilized single- or multiple-member districts coinciding with existing precinct, ward, township, or county councilmanic boundaries. Only one of the five most urban counties relied on single-member districts; on the other hand, all but two of the remaining ten less urban and rural districts relied on a combination of single-member districts for sparsely settled areas and multiple-member districts for heavily populated areas. In no instance, however, was there any evidence indicating that chairmen had manipulated boundaries to control the selection of delegates; apportionment criteria remained the same within each county throughout all four convention years.

A modest relationship does appear between districting patterns and competition. Multi-member districts, whether urban or rural, experience slightly greater competition than single-member districts. Utilizing Pearsonian r as a measure of association, the correlation between percent multiple-member districts and percent competitive districts is .14 for rural counties (N = 26) and .27 for urban counties (N = 16). Thus, both urbanness and districting patterns affect leadership control. If single-member districts are utilized, competition tends to decrease; yet, it is more difficult for the county chairman or his entourage to control the selection of nominees in every decentralized single-member district. Some people remain popular in their own neighborhoods despite the organization's external effort to oust them. If multiple-member districts are utilized, competition tends to increase; with more names appearing on the ballot, it becomes necessary for the county organization to distribute slates and hope that voters will follow their advice. In either instance, constraints are placed on the leaders' ability to control outcomes.

A special case of the use of multiple-member districts is found in candidate substitution in favor of people with last names at the beginning of the alphabet and the replacement of these people, thus elected, with proxies. Leaders can manipulate multiple-member districts, long ballots, and voter fatigue and apathy by filing only names of individuals that are high in the alphabet, for example, A, B, or C; these names appear first on the ballot, and if the voter is instructed to choose, for example, eight delegates, he may simply select the first eight names.[15] Once elected, these individuals are then given a reward in return for their convention proxy votes, and these proxies are reassigned to individuals selected by the leaders. This practice was found in isolated but insignificant instances in two urban counties, but was the common practice in a third. In the last case, however, both the in-faction and the out-faction of the party recruited slates with names in most instances no lower in the alphabet than "Be"; yet although these rival slates were interspersed alphabetically, the consistent success of one faction indicates that position on the ballot alone does not guarantee electoral success. Nevertheless, the leadership of the winning side can exert considerable control in the selection of proxies. Contrary to rumors, evidence indicates that the abuse of voting choice by using substitute candidates to gain ballot-position advantage is of little significance in the Indiana Democratic primaries.

Even when popularly elected delegates are recruited by the organization leadership, the conditions of recruitment seldom stipulate that the delegates must support a particular candidate for state-wide office. In fact, county chairmen are very cautious about this type of control before the primary election. All but one chairman stressed absolute noncommitment to state-level candidates prior to this time. In fact, the argument that the potential delegate not commit himself to any candidate is generally underscored by chairmen in their recruitment conversations. This laissez-faire practice is reflected in the delegates' own statements; of the thirty-two who had reported being asked by their chairmen to run for a delegate seat, only three reported an attempt by the recruiter to generate support for a specific state-level candidate. To generate support for a specific state-level candidate might well incite potential controllers from outside the county to recruit candidates for the county's delegate seats. Although aspirants for state-wide offices may write letters to former delegates urging them to file again and soliciting their support, they are hesitant to launch full-scale recruitment efforts either personally or through their entourage in counties outside their own. Their caution is well grounded. Of the eight chairmen who suspected this had happened in their counties, five voiced strong opposition to the practice. Said one: "It always goes against the grain—like a mobster muscling in on your territory. We'll always beat 'em down if they try it." Seven of the twelve candidates in the sample thought the risks involved in external recruitment were so great that they decided not to attempt it, even in urban counties with their decentralized control structures. The position of the remaining five was well summarized by the statement of a successful candidate for a gubernatorial nomination:

> If a chairman was foolish enough to publicly back a candidate [for statewide office] even before he knows who his delegates are and you feel you have strength in his county, you would work through a friend there to get your supporters filed. But you never try to unseat any local stalwarts. The chairman won't like it, but it's the rule of the primary—kick, scratch, and bite. Few chairmen are going to be committed that early, though.

The infrequency of recruitment by external forces is reflected in the delegates' reports; only five of the eighty respondents said that a candidate for state office had asked them to run for a delegate seat.

Another factor limiting control by entrenched county leaders is the high rate of turnover among county chairmen. The factionalism that characterizes competition for urban delegate seats is also reflected in the rapid turnover of urban chairmen. In the four convention years from 1956 to 1962, urban counties averaged three turnovers in chairmen. In the rural counties, where less delegate competition is apparent, each county averaged slightly less than two turnovers. The rapid circulation of these elites makes it difficult, particularly in urban counties, for any individual to consolidate control. And, according to the interview evidence, virtually all changes in chairmanship involved changes in clique or factional control. Thus, even where a chairman controls the selection of delegates and seeks to minimize competition, his potential control extends over only a portion of the delegation and is unlikely to be perpetuated beyond one or two conventions.[16]

The types of norms individuals attach to their service as convention delegates may also serve to limit control by county chairmen or other external forces. Delegates were asked, "Why, in your own words, did you run for convention delegate?" Responses to this open-ended item were coded into four categories. Results indicate that 69 percent of the sample viewed their delegate service as a civic or party responsibility; most of these expressed their felt obligation to choose a competent man, a good representative of the party, and an election winner at the convention; others stressed the learning experience of the convention —how it could make them better qualified party workers in the fall election and in succeeding years; still others voiced a commitment to "making democracy work." An additional 13 percent wanted to run for a delegate seat so that they could support a specific candidate for nomination. Of the respondents 11 percent offered no reason for seeking the seat except that their county leaders requested it, and the final 8 percent viewed delegate service as an opportunity to advance their own political fortunes—as a trial balloon for their own future candidacies for some local office. What proportion of these delegates are amenable to control by leaders is open to conjecture. But given the norms most of them attach to their service, only a handful of them appear disposed primarily to follow the requests of party leaders. Control, most likely, must come in the form of advice and persuasion.

The evidence from the primary stage hardly describes a monolithic control structure. Recruitment and selection of delegates depends principally on the interest of party activists in seeking the seat and the interest of party identifiers in choosing their preferences among competitors. To be sure, party leaders attempt to recruit delegates and to control outcomes within their respective counties; in terms of foreclosing voter choice, they appear to be more successful in rural areas than in urban ones. Outside controllers are resisted. One can argue also that the social and political backgrounds of most delegates are not the kind generally associated with receptivity to control; more important, only a handful of delegates view their service chiefly as a response to the requests of leaders. Although tight control over delegate choice would not be predicted from the primary-stage evidence, nevertheless, much can happen between the primary election and the convention, as well as on the convention floor itself. Evidence of control prior to and during the convention must be examined.

## Control at the Convention Stage

Convention decisions represent the culmination of a process many months and years aborning. Candidates for major nominations often spend a decade in pursuit of their goal, moving upward from local, regional, and minor state offices. Their actual campaigns for a specific major office begin one to three years in advance of the appropriate convention. Seldom are they viewed as newcomers by party activists.

Given such widespread candidate visibility within the party, it is not surprising that delegates view the convention primarily as a ratifying procedure for decisions they have made much earlier. Nearly 80 percent of the delegate sample reported arriving at the convention with their minds made up on whom they would support for the top spots on the ticket; in fact, 75 percent of them were certain of their decisions several weeks—and, for some, months—prior to the convention. There seems to be little difference between urban and rural delegates in this respect. Generally, delegates from the strong Democratic and swing counties make their decisions earlier than delegates from weak Democratic counties. For nominations to minor offices, however, delegates report a considerably later date of decision; only half of them decide whom to support long before the convention, while the remaining half defer this decision until the final week or perhaps even until they enter the voting machine on the convention floor. Among reasons for the later decision date on minor offices are the lower visibility of candidates at this level; shorter campaigns; and the constraints of geographical, interest group, and party factional ticket-balance. A satisfactory ticket cannot be assembled by party leaders and delegates until a front-runner at the head of the ticket emerges. Usually this candidate is known during the final week leading up to the convention. Perhaps this is why chairmen and delegates attribute little influence on major office choice to the county and congressional district caucuses (held on the evening before the convention vote) or endorsements which emerge from them; for the more fluid remainder of the ticket, however, delegates often look to party leaders or other delegates for guidance at the caucus. As a long-time party leader summarized it:

> . . . [The impact of the caucus on most delegates' preferences is] very little, very little indeed. It's decided before then for major office but for minor office it may be important. Sometimes delegates don't see the guy who's running for minor office until the afternoon before, and they like to talk it over with friends from the other end of the state they haven't seen since last convention. So do we. But, for Governor and Senator, well, their mind was made up long ago.

Thus, if control over the principal convention decisions is to be located, one must generally look at behavior in the period between the primary and the convention.

This is the period during which candidates and their entourages mount the crucial campaign to reinforce the committed, persuade the uncommitted, and convert the hostile delegates. The locus of their appeals can provide insights about the convention control structure. Candidates direct their appeals to all levels of the party hierarchy. In initiating their candidacies, they will talk to congressional district chairmen and state leaders who have established reputations over time

for their influence in party circles. Such visits rarely gain commitments; they seem, rather, to precipitate curiosity and provoke preliminary discussion of the candidacy within leadership circles. Unless a
candidate receives a flat refusal from his home county or district chairman in the very early stages of his campaign, he will expand it to levels
lower in the party hierarchy—county chairmen, mayors, local influentials throughout the state, and previous and potential delegates.
Soundings from these lower levels of the hierarchy are acknowledged
by candidates, county chairmen, and state leaders as the most important determinants of district- and state-level leadership support.

Nevertheless, the level of the party hierarchy to which appeals are
pitched depends on the office sought. All candidates for major office—
U. S. Senator, Governor, and Lieutenant Governor—considered it important to talk to all levels. To bypass the county chairmen is considered an act of political stupidity; even if a chairman is known to favor
a rival, a candidate should at least pay a courtesy call. Regardless of
their attitude toward the candidate, chairmen considered it their obligation to guide the candidate around the country making introduc-
tions, if necessary, to local influentials and delegates; to invite him to a
party meeting to display his wares; and to provide him with a list of
previous convention delegates and committeemen. The rationale for
free access to delegates is well-stated by this chairman: "I think it's very
important for the enthusiasm of our county organization to bring every
candidate in here and give them all an equal chance. How else you
gonna know who to support in Indianapolis or get your people interested in a campaign in the fall?"

Candidates for major office disagreed whether it was more practical
to concentrate appeals on county chairmen or on the delegates. Although all candidates argued for widespread appeals to both, four candidates favored appeals mainly to delegates; two, to chairmen; and
one, to both mayors and delegates from urban areas. The position of
the majority is stated by this successful candidate: "For Governor, you
see both county chairmen and delegates. Mainly you work at the delegate level because this is where the control lies." Slightly over half of
the county chairmen, however, argued for the chairman receiving the
most attention. Said one: "I suppose it's better if they contact me; I
don't want to make myself sound big or something, but I do know the
(county) organization better than they do." Yet the demurrers ran
strong: "Since . . . [the 1958 convention], everything's changed. A man
has to make a career of meeting the delegates. . . . All the leaders can
do now is to sit tight until we find out how delegates are going and
then come out strong for that man."

Candidates for minor offices rely more heavily—in fact, almost entirely—on the leadership level of the party hierarchy. That they attract less money for their campaigns and receive less mention in the news media explain this reliance, although the principal reason for this strategy is their own location on the ticket. They tend to be pawns of the struggle at the top, often bartered about as trading-material, blockers, or ticket-balancers. Given the harsh realities of nominations to minor office, some aspirants withhold official declaration of their candidacies until the final week of the convention. As one candidate observed about her campaign: "You talk to leaders like the state chairman . . . and some county and district chairmen, but you don't do much more than write letters to delegates. Delegates don't really control things at this end of the ticket."

TABLE II

DELEGATES' DEPENDENCE ON COUNTY
CHAIRMAN'S ADVICE BY LEVEL OF NOMINATION

| RELIANCE ON CHAIRMAN'S ADVICE | LEVEL OF NOMINATION | |
| --- | --- | --- |
| | Major | Minor |
| Usually | 26% | 34% |
| Sometimes | 29 | 30 |
| Rarely | 45 | 36 |
| Total (N = 80) | 100% | 100% |

Delegates themselves corroborate the statements of the candidates. They were asked how often and at what level of office they relied on their county chairman's advice about which candidates to support. The results show that the persuasive efforts of chairmen are successful with some delegates, but advice on minor offices is considerably more important than advice on major nominations. The results are presented in Table II.

If county chairmen do give advice on nominations and if candidates do aim their appeals both at the chairmen and directly at the delegates, it becomes difficult to pinpoint the extent of control over convention decisions through the chairmen's persuasive efforts. Nevertheless, one way to define the limits of this control is to uncover the components of each delegate's decisions. To what individuals or groups does he feel he is responding? A series of questions was asked delegates in which they were to evaluate their dependence on their chairman's advice, the importance of the chairman's advice as opposed to personal contact with the candidate, and what obligation they felt to support the candidate favored by a majority of their county's delegation. Responses to both fixed-alternative and open-ended aspects of these questions were utilized to construct three types of decision-making orientations: (1) the county chairman advises the delegate which candidates he ought to support and the delegate views the chairman's advice as the most important element in his decision; (2) the delegate may open his ear to the appeals of the candidates, his chairman, and fellow-delegates, but he views his decision as a judgment arrived at independent of these external pressures; and (3) the delegate sees himself as part of a group—a collective nominating task-force involving himself, his chairman, and his fellow delegates—that arrives at more or less morally binding decisions on which candidates to support, following collective deliberation. The results are presented in Table III according to urban-rural class and party strength.

TABLE III

DECISION-MAKING ORIENTATIONS OF CONVENTION DELEGATES

| ORIENTATION | CLASS | | PARTY STRENGTH | | | |
| | Urban | Rural | Strong | Swing | Weak | Totals |
| --- | --- | --- | --- | --- | --- | --- |
| Chairman-<br>Determined | 35% | 32% | 48% | 29% | 15% | 34% |
| Self-Determined | 33 | 26 | 25 | 36 | 35 | 30 |
| Group-<br>Determined | 33 | 42 | 28 | 36 | 50 | 36 |
| Total | 101% | 100% | 101% | 101% | 100% | 100% |
| | (49) | (31) | (40) | (14) | (26) | (80) |

The lower limit on the persuasive powers of chairmen would appear to include somewhat over 30 percent of all convention delegates. If chairmen can manipulate the consensus of group-oriented delegates, the upper limit of their power would represent about 70 percent of the delegates. Urban and rural delegations differ little in their orientations except that pressures toward group conformity are more strongly felt by rural delegates who, as was pointed out earlier, were more likely to have been selected by county leaders. The influence of the county chairman is clearly most pervasive in strongly Democratic counties and least pervasive in the weak ones; yet, the group-orientation in the latter is shared by half of the delegates. Whether the group-orientation is a disguise for chairman control is open to question; nearly half of the chairmen admitted and most of the candidates believed that on nominations for major offices chairmen were swept along by the preferences of the majority of their delegations rather than vice versa. In fact, given this evidence, one may question whether even the 34 percent who rely primarily on their chairman's advice do not reflect control by the dispersed majority of the delegation rather than by the single chairman.[17]

Certain avenues of control by county chairmen during the period leading up to the convention must still be discussed. One concerns county delegation endorsements of candidates prior to the convention. Slightly over half of the county delegations in the sample endorsed candidates for major offices prior to the convention; one-third of them also endorsed candidates for other offices, but generally only when they were home-county or home-district candidates. The endorsement decision might be viewed as an informal sanction used by chairmen to enforce conformity. On the contrary, it is simply a statement that the overwhelming majority of a delegation favors a candidate and would like other counties to recognize this. Chairmen seldom pressed for an endorsement decision unless near-unanimity already existed. The importance of harmony; the desires of chairmen to maintain their office; and, closely related, the willingness to tolerate dissent when it is widespread inhibited chairmen from trying to force control.

Another avenue of control is to alter the composition of delegations selected by party identifiers in the primary election. Here presumably, the chairman can collect the proxy votes of delegates who refuse to go along with his intentions and replace them with controlled delegates. The practice is rumored to be widespread in convention nominating systems. Except for the single county where the alphabetical filing abuse was practiced, proxies represented more than 5 to 10 percent of a county delegation only in the most urban counties. In these latter counties it reached as high as 20 to 25 percent of the delegation. The most common reasons for the use of proxies, according to delegates and chairmen, were illness and inability to lay off work or to avoid business obligations for the two-day convention. In some urban counties where proxies were more prevalent, certain patronage workers were not permitted to attend the convention and party leaders reassigned their proxies; where the patronage whip was not available or chairmen refused to utilize it, however, delegates were free to award their proxy to whomever they chose. The point is evident: In the Indiana system, in which no individual can vote more than one proxy (assuming that officials properly police the convention), chairmen seldom control a significantly larger segment of their delegations through proxy votes than they controlled at the primary stage. Generally, they wrest proxies only from those whom they requested to seek the seat initially. Thus, little change in the effective control structure occurs.

A final avenue of control is the threat of using discipline on delegates who refuse to comply with the chairman's wishes. Both chairmen and delegates were asked whether there was any way a delegate could be disciplined under these circumstances. Two chairmen, both from rural counties, said that future favors could be withheld and that the recalcitrant delegate would not be asked to run again; all other chairmen, however, contended that the use of voting machines at the convention removed any possibility of effective coercion. In fact, several argued further that discipline was not only impossible but also a foolish practice for a chairman to attempt; said one: "You probably could refuse to recognize [a delegate who openly opposed you] later on patronage, office, or appointments to committees. But when somebody opposes you, it's for a reason and you usually have to do some favor to win them back to your side. You haven't time to punish your enemies, and it's bad policy if you want to win elections, so you usually forget about it." The possibility of discipline was perceived by only a handful of elected delegates; 15 percent of the sampled delegates said that a chairman could discipline them but, interestingly enough, less than half of these had actually attended the convention; of the remainder, most held patronage jobs and feared the loss of them. Many of the 85 percent who claimed that chairmen could not or would not discipline them pointed out that leaders were dependent on delegates, not vice versa. The importance of putting together an election-winning organization presumably subordinated personal antagonisms; as one delegate argued: "It would be very difficult to [discipline delegates], and we are not this uncivilized to let things start in that direction—we don't have a machine, but we have a team."

If both the structure of the Indiana convention and the norms shared by the overwhelming majority of the delegates and chairmen preclude the use of coercive devices, control, insofar as it reaches any sizable segment of the delegates, must rest on persuasion. Clues about the upper and lower limits on the extent of persuasive control were found in the norms delegates applied to nominating decisions. The ultimate test of control is found in behavior. Control by county and congressional district chairmen can be no greater, and certainly considerably less, than the extent of delegate cohesion behind specific candidates.[18]

Measures of delegation cohesion for various types of counties and congressional districts are presented in Table IV. They are based on contested nominations for major offices and minor and judicial offices in the four conventions from 1956 to 1962; derived from voting machine tallies, they measure the average percent of the county or district delegation voting for the candidate favored by a plurality of them on any given roll call.[19]

As might be expected, cohesion within congressional district delegations, except where a single county constitutes the district, is slightly lower than cohesion within a county or among neighboring counties. Cohesion figures in metropolitan counties, where early convention critics claimed that party bosses exercised tightest control, are considerably lower on major nominations than comparable figures for less urbanized areas. In fact, if Lake, St. Joseph, and Vigo counties, all of which experienced remarkable cohesion, were excluded from the metropolitan data, the median cohesion figure would decline to 56.9 per-

TABLE IV

COHESION WITHIN DISTRICT AND COUNTY DELEGATIONS

| TYPE OF DELEGATION | RANGE OF COHESION (%) | | MEDIAN LEVEL OF COHESION (%) | |
|---|---|---|---|---|
| | Major Office | Minor Office | Major Office | Minor Office |
| Districts | 83.7–49.1 | 88.5–64.7 | 59.4 | 70.1 |
| (N = 154 major) [a] | | | | |
| (N = 132 minor) | | | | |
| Metropolitan counties [b] | 87.6–46.3 | 88.5–68.9 | 61.8 | 76.3 |
| (N = 96 major) | | | | |
| (N = 96 minor) | | | | |
| Moderately urban and | | | | |
| rural counties [c] | 77.3–49.1 | 81.2–63.1 | 65.4 | 70.7 |
| (N = 144 major) | | | | |
| (N = 144 minor) | | | | |

[a] N is calculated in each category by multiplying the number of districts, metropolitan counties, etc., by the number of roll calls on contested nominations at the appropriate office level for all four conventions.

[b] Metropolitan counties refer to all Indiana counties which contain the principal city of an SMSA. They include Allen, Delaware, Lake, Madison, Marion, St. Joseph, Vanderburgh, and Vigo .These counties represented 46% of the total convention vote.

[c] Moderately urban and rural counties refer to all non-SMSA counties included in the sample (see Table 1). Unfortunately, most of these counties did not have large enough delegations to vote on a single machine; smaller counties are grouped with one to four other counties from their respective districts. Thus the measure of cohesion for these counties is not strictly within a delegate but among similar delegations. Despite this fact, they still show higher cohesion than urban counties do on the major offices. Whether lack of cohesion in this set of figures can be attributed to the multi-county vote is debatable; interview evidence as well as roll calls for the moderately urban counties (when available on a single machine) indicate that the lack of cohesion is within a county not among them; there is no way to be certain whether this is true of rural counties as well. These figures represent another 27% of the total convention vote.

cent on major offices. Uniformly, cohesion is greater on minor offices than major offices.

In short, evidence regarding control at the primary stage and regarding norms and behavior from the pre-convention stage are clearly reflected in convention outcomes. Where we would expect slightly greater cohesion, on minor offices and within rural areas, we find it. The behavioral data, of course, do not establish certainty about the extent of control by chairmen. They do indicate that the ceiling on the maximum amount of control is considerably lower than convention critics have argued. When combined with the previous information on delegate, candidate, and chairman norms, they establish a pattern of highly diffused, decentralized, and pluralistic control over outcomes.

The flow of influence between county and district leaders on the one hand and rank-and-file delegates on the other is two-way.

One might still argue, nevertheless, that this chapter has focused on control at a level too low in the party hierarchy. Above it all, perhaps, a compact power elite composed of state-level party influentials, interest group leaders, or factional leaders manipulates county and district leaders or acts directly on delegates. Or, one might alternatively argue that certain district and county delegations form enduring alliances, which consistently control outcomes and permit them to share in the rewards at the expense of other delegations.

The second argument can be dispensed with handily. Table V presents a comprehensive measure of the support given by each district to the winners of contested races from 1956 to 1962. The deviations above 1.00 in the winner-support ratio indicate which delegations have coalesced and to what degree they have contributed support to the winner on the roll call vote where the outcome was determined.[20]

The table indicates that no single coalition of district delegations dominates all nominations (1) within each convention or (2) among all four conventions. As each roll call vote is taken, two or three districts which ranked high in the winning coalition on the previous contest are likely to be replaced by other districts. The coalitions are often fluid and changeable; allies on one contest are enemies on the next. Given these figures, it is difficult to find any single coalition of districts capable of dominating all offices convention after convention. Political fortunes wax and wane swiftly within each convention and over a period of years. Even the districts that show positive winner-support ratios for all convention years on both levels of office—the Sixth, Seventh, and Fourth—stumbled badly on some contests. No single coalition at the major office level remained intact from one convention to the next and no district delegation found itself above the break-even 1.00 point at all four conventions on the offices of U. S. Senator, Governor, and Lieutenant Governor.[21]

The preceding data can also be utilized to refute the first argument. Chairmen, candidates, and delegates were asked a series of questions about convention control by reputed state-level influentials, interest groups, and factions. A total of forty-six individuals or collective groups were mentioned as being influential in determining convention outcomes; these included two former national party chairmen, two national committeemen, two governors, two state party chairmen, a U. S. Senator and two Congressmen, several state administrative officials and legislative leaders, prominent members of the state central committee, certain urban county leaders and mayors, a state labor organization, and a state teachers organization. Their principal resource for conven-

TABLE V

CONTROL OVER NOMINATIONS IN CONVENTIONS, 1956–1962
AS MEASURED BY THE WINNER-SUPPORT RATIO
WINNER-SUPPORT RATIO BY CONTEST

| Year | Office | 1 | 2 | 3 | 4 | 5 | District 6 | 7 | 8 | 9 | 10 | 11 |
|------|--------|---|---|---|---|---|-----|---|---|---|----|----|
| 1956 | Gov. | 1.51 | .87 | 1.39 | .62 | .91 | 1.64 | .53 | .91 | .58 | .96 | .84 |
| 1958 | Senator | .10 | 1.09 | .14 | 1.24 | 1.01 | 1.67 | 1.51 | 1.20 | 1.19 | 1.06 | 1.25 |
|  | Sec. | 1.43 | 1.41 | .77 | .84 | 1.28 | .60 | .38 | 1.34 | 1.34 | .74 | .78 |
|  | Treas. | 1.27 | 1.23 | .89 | .92 | .90 | 1.12 | 1.09 | 1.03 | .65 | .80 | 1.03 |
| 1960 | Gov. | 1.43 | .88 | 1.08 | 1.03 | .79 | .95 | 1.22 | 1.02 | .53 | .71 | 1.12 |
|  | Lt. Gov. | .18 | 1.16 | 1.21 | 1.23 | 1.36 | 1.21 | 1.11 | 1.28 | 1.06 | 1.09 | .41 |
|  | Sec. | 1.54 | 1.01 | 1.13 | .89 | .34 | 1.16 | 1.04 | 1.25 | .58 | .43 | 1.27 |
|  | Auditor | 1.73 | .99 | .27 | 1.28 | .97 | 1.59 | 1.11 | .84 | .50 | .88 | .96 |
|  | At.-Gen. | 1.21 | .85 | 1.13 | 1.14 | .52 | 1.01 | .86 | .33 | 1.11 | 1.12 | 1.64 |
|  | Ct.-Rep. | 1.63 | .64 | 1.13 | 1.22 | .61 | 1.29 | 1.26 | .54 | .82 | .54 | 1.21 |
|  | Sup. Ct. | 1.39 | .81 | 1.32 | 1.40 | .27 | 1.13 | 1.10 | .59 | .47 | 1.15 | 1.20 |
|  | App. Ct. | 1.19 | .81 | 1.10 | 1.03 | 1.05 | .91 | 1.07 | .59 | .87 | .99 | 1.08 |
|  | (2) | 1.39 | .47 | 1.23 | 1.01 | .55 | .84 | 1.01 | .87 | .96 | .94 | 1.22 |
| 1962 | Senator | 1.19 | 1.07 | 1.16 | 1.16 | .66 | 1.21 | 1.19 | 1.18 | 1.12 | .95 | .39 |
|  | App. Ct. | 1.04 | 1.05 | .95 | 1.03 | .86 | 1.03 | 1.04 | 1.06 | 1.03 | 1.00 | .96 |
|  | (2) | 1.11 | 1.16 | .96 | 1.05 | 1.05 | 1.13 | 1.14 | 1.17 | 1.14 | .91 | .45 |

AVERAGE WINNER-SUPPORT RATIO BY LEVEL OF OFFICE

| Level | 1 | 2 | 3 | 4 | 5 | District 6 | 7 | 8 | 9 | 10 | 11 |
|-------|---|---|---|---|---|-----|---|---|---|----|----|
| Major | .92 | 1.03 | .91 | 1.08 | .94 | 1.28 | 1.12 | 1.15 | .91 | .95 | .74 |
| Minor | 1.33 | .96 | 1.00 | 1.08 | .77 | 1.07 | 1.03 | .88 | .86 | .88 | 1.06 |
| All | 1.21 | .98 | .98 | 1.08 | .82 | 1.13 | 1.06 | .96 | .88 | .90 | .95 |
| Ave. Pct. of Total Delegates | 10.85 | 6.63 | 10.96 | 7.39 | 10.23 | 7.71 | 8.17 | 10.34 | 6.98 | 8.41 | 12.22 |

tion control was described as a bloc of delegates who looked to them for guidance; yet in no instance was any bloc reputed to constitute over 15 percent of the total convention delegation. The inability of these reputed influentials to form an enduring coalition was the principal reason offered by respondents for the lack of elite control; Table V, at the behavioral level, bore witness to this. The only factional alliance to persist over several conventions has been able to control nominations for a single office—state treasurer. Even an incumbent Democratic Governor, with the massive party, policy-making, and patronage powers he holds in Indiana, was unable to control outcomes at the top of the ticket in 1962 and 1964; reliable evidence about the activities of his associates indicates that he was forced to back down on his initial choice because of the ground-swell delegate support for a rival aspirant in each year. Thus, although certain influential individuals and groups operate above the county and district level, they fail to constitute an elite in terms of convention control.

Both at the primary stage and at the convention stage, control over outcomes is widely dispersed. Regardless of their level in the party hierarchy, in the Indiana Democratic conventions leaders act like participants in any responsive democratic system: They attempt to get what they can and learn to tolerate what they must. On major offices, leaders can get little; they must follow the ever-changing coalition of delegates as the delegates respond to the qualities of aspirants for nomination. On lesser nominations they can get much more; delegates perhaps reflect the voter fatigue of most Americans when faced by long ballots; as the office means less to them they are more responsive to the manipulative devices of leaders. In the latter respect, nominations for minor offices serve a party-building and election-winning function; the wishes of entrenched organizational leaders, within the bounds of ticket-balance, predominate. At the top, the delegates exert effective control; lower on the ticket, leaders control outcomes.[22]

## Efficacy and Alienation Among Convention Participants

If any political system is to survive, it must satisfy participants' demands for legitimacy and effectiveness. It must fulfill their prescriptions of what is right and proper, as well as their expectations for whatever is to be had from the system. Systems which meet these criteria are generally characterized by participants who have a relatively high sense of political efficacy; they desire to remain involved. Systems failing to meet these criteria are often characterized by citizen alienation; people expect little from the system and desire to participate even less.

The norm of democracy pervades much of American authority relationships. Particularly in the explicitly political order its implementation is expected. One might consider it reasonable, then, for questions about the legitimacy and effectiveness of the convention system to be couched in the idiom of democracy.

Delegates and chairmen were asked a series of fixed-alternative and open-ended questions about elite control of the convention and about the relative merits of the convention and the direct primary as democratic nominating techniques. Despite the fact that respondents had freshest in their minds the 1962 convention when an incumbent Democratic Governor occupied a position of prominence in the party, approximately 55 percent of the eighty delegates sampled claimed that no power elite controlled nominations. Of the remaining 45 percent who perceived elite control, 60 percent mentioned state party and governmental officials; 45 percent, mostly from urban and strongly Democratic counties, listed county officials; and 25 percent, all from urban counties, included interest groups. (Multiple mentions were possible.) The important question, however, concerns not the perception of an elite, but what this perception means in terms of delegates' evaluations of the convention system as a democratic nominating device.

Given a structural alternative to the convention, and given the fact that most delegates are party activists who are not likely to manifest their alienation by complete withdrawal from politics, one might expect that those delegates who perceive elite control and consider it undemocratic would approach an alternate structure, the direct primary,

TABLE VI

NOMINATING SYSTEM EVALUATIONS AMONG DELEGATES

|  | CONVENTION SYSTEM More Democratic | DIRECT PRIMARY More Democratic | Totals | |
|---|---|---|---|---|
| Do Not Perceive Elite Control | 27 | 13 | 40 | $X^2 = 5.08$ |
| Perceive Elite Control | 14 | 20 | 34 | $C = .25$ |
| Totals | 41 | 33 | 74 | $p = <.03$ |

as an avenue for democratizing the nominating process. On the other hand, those who do not think the convention is controlled by elites are likely to view it as an appropriate democratic technique and feel little affinity for an alternate structure. This expectation is borne out by Table VI.

The acceptable level of significance and the moderate coefficient of contingency indicate that many, but not all, who perceive elite control would consider the direct primary more democratic, while a relatively larger number of those who view the convention as devoid of elite control consider it more democratic than the primary. The legitimacy of the system, then, depends much on how the system is perceived to be operating. If the convention is viewed as an open system, the direct primary is not valued as a more democratic alternative. Slightly over half of those who perceived elite control and considered the primary more democratic raised questions about the nominating decision being delegated away from all voters; a delegate convention was simply a violation of popular sovereignty regardless of how it was run; convention participants collectively constituted an unwarranted power elite. These delegates were unable to justify their own participation in the convention; perhaps advocacy of the direct primary as a more democratic alternative relieved their anxiety.

A less complicated explanation for this withdrawal of affective support from the convention system is available. Some participants do not get what they want out of it. The convention is rationalized into illegitimacy because it is not an effective instrument for satisfying their expectations. In this view, if delegates or delegations go to the convention in hopes of nominating their choice and consistently lose, they may consider an alternate structure more democratic, that is, it would give them a greater opportunity to win. An old adage is appropriate: "If you can't beat them at the game, change the rules." The evidence

### TABLE VII

COMPARISON OF DELEGATES' AND CHAIRMEN'S NOMINATING SYSTEM PREFERENCES
AND THEIR CONVENTION SUCCESS

| COUNTY | % COHESION IN SUPPORT OF WINNERS | CHAIRMAN'S PREFERENCE | DELEGATES' PREFERENCE |
|---|---|---|---|
| Lake | 85.4 | Convention—s | Convention—s |
| Knox | 75.0 | Convention—s | Convention—s |
| Vermillion | 73.1 | Pre-Primary Convention | Primary—w |
| Hendricks | 72.6 | Convention—s | Convention—s |
| Noble | 72.5 | Convention—s | Convention—w |
| Harrison | 69.9 | Convention—s | Convention—s |
| Martin | 65.5 | Primary—s | Primary—s |
| Starke | 62.7 | Convention—s | Convention—s |
| Henry | 62.5 | Primary—s | Primary—s |
| Elkhart | 60.9 | Primary—w | Primary—w |
| Vanderburgh | 60.5 | — | Convention—w |
| Marion | 60.0 | Convention—w | Convention—w |
| Dearborn | 58.7 | Convention—s | Primary—s |
| Jennings | 56.2 | Primary—s | Primary—s |
| Howard | 53.1 | Primary—s | Primary—s |

to support this explanation is presented in Table VII. If a county chairman or the overwhelming majority of his delegates with no reservations advocated maintaining the present convention system as a democratic nominating device, each was classified as "convention-strong"; if a chairman preferred the convention but recognized certain shortcomings, or if only a narrow majority of delegates favored it, each was classified as "convention-weak." The same classification scheme was applied to advocates of the direct primary. Another arrangement, the pre-primary convention, was suggested by one chairman. The counties are listed by their solidarity behind the winners at the convention.[23]

The table not only underscores a considerable internal agreement between county chairmen and their delegations on the appropriate type of nominating system—the only major deviation is found in Dearborn County—but also tends to substantiate the hunch that delega-

tions who fare well at the convention generally develop an appreciation for it while delegations whose aspirations are unmet tend to seek
a change.[24] Deviations from the overall patterns are readily explained:
The Vanderburgh County response is totally inadequate—one delegate
and no chairmen—to provide valid data; Marion County, receiving
numerous lesser nominations and still the largest and one of the most
courted delegations at the convention, has fared sufficiently well to be
mildly in favor of maintaining the present system; finally, the Vermillion County proposal of a pre-primary convention has, in most instances, been known to lodge even more power in the hands of party
leaders since it is usually accompanied by less regulations than the Indiana system has. The evidence, in summary, would appear to support
the notion that alienation stems from one's inability to achieve success
within existing political structures. A power elite is in some instances
perceived to exist simply because one is on the losing side. But whether
or not consistent defeat is charged off to elite control, the losing delegates and chairmen—unless they are from potentially powerful metropolitan counties—will view another nominating system as the one
which will reinstate the "proper" relationship between citizen, party,
and candidate. For those who receive the tangible rewards and psychic
gratifications of backing convention winners, the existing structure is
sufficiently democratic.

Efficacy, in the form of continued participation and a high estimate
of the legitimacy of the system, persists among those who view the convention as open and effective. Alienation, in the form of a low estimate
of the legitimacy of the system and a preference for an alternate structure, is instilled in those who view the convention as closed and ineffective.

## A Note on Research Strategies for Political System Comparisons

This chapter has attempted to apply data on norms and behavior
to prescriptive and descriptive questions about a specific political
structure. Attention was focused on top-level, intermediate-level, and
low-level political elites. It does not go far enough in at least two respects: (1) The paper does not discuss norms of responsiveness governing the interplay between party leaders and delegates, on the one
hand, and voters and Indiana citizens in general, on the other, and
(2) The larger study from which this paper was derived did not include survey data on the norms and behaviors of party-voters and Indiana citizens who, of course, are affected by convention decisions. At the
rank-and-file citizen level, in particular, evidence about participation,

efficacy, and alienation would help explain the political culture associated with, affected by, and precipitating the Indiana political structures. It is hoped that the discipline of political science will address itself to a new type of comparative study of state political systems where the norms and behaviors of various types of participants are linked together with structural arrangements.

In the past, the discipline has tended to approach political system variation through one of two orientations: Either (1) we have focused on formal political structures and examined their effects on popular participation and control, or (2) we have examined the informal norms, mores, folkways of a system to see how these relate to participation and control. More recently, it has become popular to call this latter enterprise the study of political culture. What we now need is a synthesis of the two orientations.

But not only have we focused on two different objects of study with these orientations, we have also employed different techniques to measure and permit generalizations about these objects. The move toward greater precision in measurement can contribute to the desired synthesis of orientations. Examples of political system variation studies provide an elaboration of this argument. Four structural studies and four political cultural studies will be utilized.

The works of early convention critics cited at the beginning of this chapter illustrate the lowest level of precision in measurement of the structural studies. Assertions were made about the effects of structure on behavior with little effort to examine empirical data, except perhaps in an impressionistic way. Prescriptions for structural change are made prematurely, probably because no careful study has been made of the relationship between norms and structures. Structures are believed to determine attitudes and behavior.

A second technique for dealing with structures is frequently found in the works of V. O. Key and others inspired by him.[25] Utilizing keen insights, these political scientists seek to combine, in a more or less loose empirical way, quantitative data about the degree and nature of participation with qualitative data about political structures. Thus, standard political parties textbooks of the post-Key era will array sets of percentage distributions or simple correlational measures for the fifty states over against such things as ballot type or nominating forms. The data generally do show associations, but often the question of spuriousness must be raised.

A third technique for dealing with structure can be found in the recent work of Matthews and Prothro.[26] Measurement of association between structure and behavior is achieved through the rigid control of quantitative and qualitative variables. Factors which may contribute to spuriousness are partialled out. But on occasion, the authors admit that such things as "attitude formation dating to the turn of the century" appear to be hidden in the harder quantitative data. In other words, they direct future attention to the study of norms that persist through time.

A fourth technique applied within the structural orientation is found in a section of the Survey Research Center's classic, *The American Voter*.[27] In a chapter dealing with political system variation, the authors combine qualitative data about political structures with survey data about motivation and participation. Important relationships between norms and structures are derived through appropriate statistical measures. Ironically, the authors do not complete the explanatory circle by moving from norms to behaviors to structures, or vice versa. The use of aggregate voting data to corroborate survey data could contribute to the strength of the explanation.

All of the formal structural approaches are based on the implicit assumption that structure counts. Yet the latter two studies point out that structure tells only part of the story; in the one case, norm data are needed, while in the other data about behavior are desirable.

The explicitly or implicitly political cultural studies have argued that important clues about the effective operation of a political system and the factors which differentiate it from others are more likely to be found in the informal political norms and, to some degree, nonpolitical attitudes and practices of its citizens than in the formal political structures. Alexis de Tocqueville provides one of the earliest types of studies utilizing this orientation.[28] The technique is that of idiographic social analysis. By thoroughly immersing oneself in a culture or political environment, the researcher can understand what is unique about the interplay between attitudes and beliefs, behavior, and the structures of a specific system; he can explain why given structural forms work in a certain system. But this approach rests much on the insight of the researcher; the genius of the system is often the genius of the person who studied it. The approach is difficult to operationalize for public cross-systemic comparisons, resting as it does essentially on the private insight of one man. Yet, the insight of sound idiographic analysis can contribute to later inter-subjective studies; in this respect, substantively *The Civic Culture* differs little from *Democracy in America*.

A second political cultural technique stems also from the stimulus of V. O. Key.[29] It uses aggregate data as a means of inferring the effects political culture has on participation within given structures. For example, in dealing with the Indiana system, Key and Munger employ voting data which describe traditional partisan attachments as a benchmark for generating propositions about the legitimacy of parties as social institutions. From this initial norm of legitimate party attachments, the authors examine long-term secular trends and short-term factors which bring about changes in party loyalty and participation within the political system. The move is from behavioral data to inferences about structures and norms back to behavioral data. But this design is hampered by the same weakness that limited the third structural orientation: namely, the lack of more-or-less hard data about attitudes and beliefs which could permit greater certainty than that generated by the authors' inferential reasoning.

A third design for handling political culture rests almost strictly on survey research techniques. It is best illustrated by Almond and Verba.[30] Generally it involves (1) the postulation of a theory about political cultures, climates, or environments, and often this is a democratic theory, (2) the generating of propositions from it, and (3) the submission of these propositions to empirical test through data acquired by survey research. While little objection can be directed at this procedure, the findings which result are based solely on norm data that may or may not be translated into behavior. In the Almond-Verba study for example, one is struck by the absence of aggregate data relating norms to behavior or, for that matter, with the lack of hard data about structures. Both behavior and structures are treated in an impressionistic way.

A seminal design which may overcome some shortcomings of the other studies described here is implicit in the Stackton study reported by the political sociologists, Rossi and Cutwright.[31] It combines formal structural characteristics with sample survey data about norms and behavior and aggregate data about behavior—all in an effort to explain the political system operative in Gary, Indiana. The authors begin with descriptions of the social and economic setting of the community, its historical development, and the formal structure of its precinct-level political organization. Then, a series of ecological correlations between socioeconomic characteristics and voting behavior data, with the precinct as the unit, is calculated. With these as a basing point, elite survey data are utilized to uncover the norms of precinct-level leaders and chairmen, as well as descriptions of their behavior which are often heavily normative in content. Various indices and correlational measures permit tests of propositions regarding differences in observed behavior. Thus, precinct variations within the larger political system can be explained. The design is at all times cognizant of the need for corroborating findings through data on norms, behavior, and structures; considerable precision in measurement is achieved. It could well serve as a starting point for studies of political system variation at many levels of participation and for many types of systems.

It is hoped that this chapter has demonstrated the utility of turning away from strictly formal structural studies of state political systems. Ironically, in "a nation of states," as one author calls it, members of the discipline have failed to collaborate on cross-state comparisons which combine data on norms, behaviors, and structures. We have also been slow to apply the designs which have generated knowledge in other areas of political science. Comparative studies of community power have been successfully executed, and cross-national studies of political cultures are proving to be useful undertakings. Promising signs are appearing. The establishment of national and regional data archives, data-retrieval agencies, and state-wide survey research organizations will provide the necessary tools. Exhaustive cross-state studies of both elite and rank-and-file political norms and political behaviors ought soon to be forthcoming.

# TECHNICAL APPENDICES

---

*A. Statistical Methods Used in the Studies*

*B. Legislative Candidate Study Questionnaire*

# Appendix A

## *Statistical Methods Used in the Studies*

### CHARLES NELSON

BRIEFLY STATED, the basic purpose of statistics is to make raw data more meaningful. It gives us no new information; it only helps us make more sense out of the information we already have. It does so in basically three ways, each of which corresponds to one of the three main branches of statistics. In descriptive statistics, we measure as simply as possible certain properties of the data we have gathered.[1] In inductive statistics we use data we have to make inferences about related data which we do not have. In heuristic statistics,[2] we use data on familiar variables [3] to suggest the existence of new variables, not conceived of before the statistical analysis, and ways of measuring them.

In Appendix A we shall deal with the first two types only, since none of the statistical techniques used in this book can properly be called heuristic. Our treatment of descriptive and inductive statistics will by and large be both nontechnical and restricted to those techniques actually used or referred to in the body of the book. We shall not, however, take up in this appendix those measures which are adequately explained by the authors using them.

### Descriptive Statistics

Descriptive statistics is perhaps the simplest of the three branches; it is certainly the one most used by ordinary people in their daily routines. When we want to measure a proportion we generally use a statistic called a percentage. If we have a set of numbers and want to know not how large each number is but how large they are as a group, we calculate their average or mean. These are the most familiar descriptive statistics and are used throughout the book; but there are other, less familiar techniques. We have two distinct ways of measuring the approximate center of a set of numbers: (1) the mode,[4] that is, the number which occurs the most, or is repeated most often (there may be, then, more than one mode for a single set of numbers) ; and (2) the median,[5] the number at the point where as many of the numbers in the set are larger than itself as are smaller.

The standard deviation [6] is somewhat more complex. It measures dispersion, that is, the degree to which data differ among themselves, or how spread out they are. For example, the sets 3, 4, 5 and 2, 4, 6 both have a mean of 4, but the second set has a larger dispersion than the first and therefore a larger standard deviation. Though not the simplest measure of dispersion,[7] the standard deviation is certainly the most widely used,[8] and is defined by the following four steps: [9] (1) compute the mean of the data; (2) square the difference between each piece of data and the mean; (3) find the average value of these squared differences; and (4) take the square root of this average.

Various sets of numbers have different means and standard deviations. But there are times when it is convenient to express different sets of numbers in a standard form, in which the means and standard deviations of all sets are equal.[10] To transform data in this way we simply subtract the mean from each datum and divide the difference by the standard deviation. The result is a new set of data, with as many numbers as the untransformed set but always with a mean of zero and a standard deviation of unity.

The final type of descriptive statistic which we shall consider is a class of measures known as correlation coefficients. Correlation is just what the word itself says—co-relation, or the relationship between the changes in one variable and the changes in another. To say that two variables are highly correlated implies that as one variable changes, the other does too,[11] and that when one does not change, neither does the other. Low correlations imply that there seems to be no relationship between changes in the two variables. To put it another way, a high correlation means that, given one variable, you can make a good prediction of the other; a low correlation means one will not help you guess the other.

There are many different measures, or coefficients, of correlation; which one is appropriate to the data at hand depends on which of the three basic kinds of data you are correlating: [12] (1) Nominal data are a simple unordered classification (e.g., Republicans—Democrats or yes—no—abstain) of items or events (e.g., state legislators or votes on a number of bills) according to some characteristic (e.g., political party or type of vote cast). (2) Ordinal data are a ranking or ordering (first, second, third, fourth, . . .) of items or events (e.g., state legislators or votes on a number of bills) according to some characteristic (e.g., seniority or the importance of the bill). (3) And interval data (ordinary numbers) are a placement of items or events (e.g., state legislators or votes on a number of bills) along a scale (e.g., the cardinal numbers or the real number system) [13]—called an equal interval scale because all positions are equally distant from the positions adjacent to them [14]—according to some characteristic (e.g., age or number voting on each bill).

When two nominal variables [15] are to be correlated, the measure most widely used, both in this book [16] and in social science literature as a whole, is the chi-square. Briefly what the chi-square measures is the extent to which the data differ from what we would expect if we assumed the variables to be unrelated. Let us take as an example the chi-square test of Janda's eighth proposition.[17] In this sample there are 45 delegates and 47 trustees, 43 candidates without legislative experience and 49 with legislative experience. If there were no relationship between the delegate-trustee and inexperienced-experienced classifications, we would expect the ratio of delegates to trustees to be the same among inexperienced candidates or among experienced candidates as among all candidates, regardless of legislative experience: This ratio would be 45/47. Or, to say the same thing in a different way, we would expect the ratio of inexperienced candidates to experienced candidates to be the same among delegates or among trustees as among all candidates, whatever their attitudes toward their constituencies: In this case the expected ratio would be 43/49. In short, given our sample and assuming no relationship between the two classifications, we would expect the 2 x 2 table for Proposition 8 (rounded off to the nearest whole number) to look about like this:

|  | INEXPERIENCED CANDIDATES | EXPERIENCED CANDIDATES |
| --- | --- | --- |
| Delegates | 21 | 24 |
| Trustees | 22 | 23 |

But the actual table does not look like this: Five too many of the inexperienced candidates are delegates; five too many of the experienced candidates are trustees. The chi-square measures the deviation of the real table from this no-relationship ideal table: [18] The greater the chi-square, the greater the deviation.

The minimum value of the chi-square is zero, indicating the absence of any relationship (or that the real table is the ideal table). But the maximum value, implying a perfect relationship,[19] is a positive number equal to or greater than 2, the exact value of which depends on the sample size. This means simply that two chi-square coefficients are not comparable unless they refer to equal samples (and, for different reasons, to tables of the same size). Even when these conditions are fulfilled, a separate calculation must be made to obtain this maximum value.

The phi coefficient is a measure of correlation between nominal variables which meets this difficulty.[20] It resembles and is based on the chi-square, but differs from it in two respects: (1) It is independent of sample size, and (2) for 2 x 2 (or 2 x n or n x 2) tables, its maximum value is simply unity. This means that when you want to compare the correlations of a number of 2 x 2 tables, the phi coefficient, which varies between 0 (no relationship) and 1 (perfect relationship), may be used while the straight chi-square, which varies between 0 and some function of the sample size, may not.

Another measure of correlation between two nominal variables which, like the phi coefficient, is based on the chi-square is the coefficient of contingency.[21] Unlike the phi coefficient, however, the coefficient of contingency, even for 2 x 2 tables, does not have a simple maximum value (.7071 or, more exactly, $1/\sqrt{2}$). But the coefficient of contingency resembles phi in its minimum, no-relationship value of zero and independence from sample size.

Correlation between two ordinal variables is measured by two different coefficients in this book. Since the more common of these measures, the Spearman rho, is described elsewhere [22] it will not be taken up in this appendix.

The second coefficient is the Kendall tau-c.[23] Like the Spearman rho, it varies from −1 (perfect relationship, with a high rank for one variable implying an equally low rank for the other, and vice versa) to +1 (perfect relationship, with a high or low rank for one variable implying respectively an equally high or low rank for the other). A zero value of tau-c, like the zero value of rho, implies the absence of any relationship between the two sets of rankings. The main advantage of the tau-c over the rho is the former's relative ease of computation when, as in the case of Leege's Table VII, the ranks of one or both of the variables generally contain several cases each.[24] Another advantage of the Kendall tau-c is the ease of its adaption to the multiple and partial correlation of ordinal variables.

Analysis of variance is a technique for measuring the correlation between nominal and interval variables.[25] Its complexity puts an explanation of it beyond the scope of this appendix, but it is based on the fact that if the average value of the interval variable is the same for each of the categories of the nominal variable, the value of a measure called the F-ratio is about 1. The greater the F-ratio is than 1, the greater the apparent relationship between the variables; F-ratios near or below 1 imply the absence of such a relationship. Thus, in Conway's Table IV, the question is being asked: Is there a relationship between Republicans' voting support for the Republican party platform[26] and the percentage of votes they received in the last election?[27] The F-ratio (2.5858) measures the extent of this relationship. In general, however, F-ratios, like chi-square coefficients, are not comparable from one set of data to another. Thus, for instance, one cannot say that because the F-ratio for Table IV (2.5858) is greater than the F-ratio for Table VII (1.9768), the correlation between party platform support in legislative voting and the victory margin in the last election is greater for House Republicans than for Senate Democrats.

When we want a measure of correlation between two interval variables, we usually turn to the Pearsonian r or product-moment correlation.[28] The formula for this correlation coefficient is so complex that it will not be explained here.[29] Suffice it to say that the Pearsonian r takes on values between −1 and +1, and measures the degree to which changes in one variable are accompanied by proportional changes in another. Negative values for r indicate that the variables tend to change in opposite directions, while positive values indicate change in the same direction; values at or near zero show that there is little relationship between changes in the two variables. In the unlikely event that two variables had a correlation of exactly −1 or +1 we could predict perfectly the values for one of them if we were given the values of the other.[30]

Partial and multiple correlation coefficients are refinements of the basic Pearsonian r and, like it, vary between −1 and +1, with zero indicating the absence of a relationship.[31] The formulae for calculating them are very involved and such computations these days are generally done by machine; the relationships which they measure, however, are not hard to grasp. The partial correlation between two variables is simply the correlation between them when one or more other variables are held constant. The partial correlation technique enables us to measure that part of the relationship between two variables which is not attributable to the presence of certain other variables.[32] The multiple correlation is not a correlation of one variable with another; it is a correlation of one variable with a set of two or more others.[33] It measures the degree to which changes in the one variable are consistently accompanied by proportional changes in any of the others. This means that if a variable is highly correlated with a set of variables, you can make a good prediction of the single variable, given the values of the set.[34] Prediction, however, cannot be made in the opposite direction, that is, from the single variable to the set. In both the regular Pearsonian r and the partial correlation, prediction is equally good in either direction. The multiple correlation coefficient also differs from the Pearsonian r and the partial correlation coefficient by never taking negative values: Values at or slightly above zero indicate the absence of a relationship, a value of unity implies a perfect relationship, with all other degrees of relationship measured by values between these two extremes.

## Inductive Statistics

A correlation is itself only a description of the data we have collected. As political scientists, however, we are concerned not just with describing a particular political system (e.g., Indiana's in recent years) but also with making broader statements about more general phenomena (e.g., Indiana politics over the last century, all American state politics, or politics in general). It is of course logically impossible to "prove" anything about the whole from knowledge of a part; the leap from the specific to the general can never be made with absolute confidence. Nonetheless, some inductions are sounder and more persuasive than others, and inductive statistics is simply an attempt to make plausible inductions from specific data.

Though basically descriptive in nature, correlation coefficients find their most important use in inductive statistics. This begins with the assumption that the sample for which data are available are representative of a larger population.[35] We then use the correlation of variables in the sample to estimate the correlation of these same variables in the population as a whole. But we cannot assume that the sample correlation is simply equal to the correlation in the larger population, for the sample may have been distorted by the luck of the draw. Let us use an example we have used before, the chi-square test of Janda's eighth proposition (p. 135). The data in the 2 x 2 table refer to the 92 candidates, but let us consider them as a sample from the larger population, say 920,000, of all American legislative candidates of the twentieth century. If there were no relationship between experience and attitudes toward constituents and if the ratios of delegates to trustees and inexperienced to experienced candidates were the same for the larger population as for the 92-man sample (i.e., 45/47 and 43/49 respectively), we would then expect the 2 x 2 table for the larger population to look something like this: [36]

|          | INEXPERIENCED CANDIDATES | EXPERIENCED CANDIDATES |
|----------|--------------------------|------------------------|
| Delegates | 210,326                 | 239,674                |
| Trustees  | 219,674                 | 250,326                |

If the larger population were so distributed, we would expect the typical 92-candidate sample to be distributed as shown on page 231, above, and thus to have a correlation of zero. However, by sheer random variation we would expect some 92-man samples to differ from this typical sample and to have a correlation substantially different from zero. What we want to know, then, is the probability that the actual sample would differ enough from the typical sample to produce a correlation as high as the one we have,[37] if the larger population were distributed in a no-relationship fashion. For the correlations used in this book, such a probability can be, and usually is, calculated; we call it the value of the level of significance.[38]

As it becomes less likely that a no-relationship population could have produced a sample different enough from the typical sample to have as high a correlation as it does (i.e., as the value of the level of significance decreases), it becomes increasingly difficult to accept the idea that the larger population is in fact distributed in a no-relationship way; it becomes a good deal easier to explain the correlation in the actual sample by saying that the larger population has a correlation something like the sample's than by claiming that a fluke produced the highly correlated sample from an uncorrelated population. A correlation is called significant when the value of the level of significance reaches such a low level that the former explanation is substantially more satisfying than the latter;[39] thus a significant correlation lets us reject the no-relationship hypothesis for the larger population, while a non-significant correlation does not.

The exact value for the level of significance at which one should reject the no-relationship hypothesis is somewhat arbitrary, but the most widely used are .05 and .01. Acceptance of the .05 value means that, before you reject the hypothesis that the population is uncorrelated, you insist that the correlation of your sample have a level of significance value of .05 or less: that is, that the chances be one in twenty or less that your sample would have such a high correlation if it were randomly drawn from an uncorrelated population. To accept the .01 value is to require that the chances of getting such a high correlation in a random sample from an uncorrelated population be equal to or less than only one in a hundred. The danger of requiring too high a level of significance (i.e., too low a value of the level of significance) is that you will accept (or fail to reject) the hypothesis that the population is uncorrelated, when in fact it is substantially correlated.[40] The danger of setting the level of significance too low (i.e., by requiring too high a value of the level of significance, one that is too easily reached, for rejection of the no-relationship hypothesis) is simply that you will reject the no-relationship hypothesis for the population on the basis of a sample correlation which is due only to the luck of the draw and not to any relationship in the population as a whole.[41]

The usual purpose of correlational analysis is to shed some light on possible cause-effect relationships among the variables being correlated. However one may not simply conclude, if in a given sample two variables are significantly correlated with one another, that one is the cause of the other. There are many other possible explanations of correlation—for example: (1) Both variables might be effects of a third; (2) the first might cause a third, which then might cause the second; (3) the first might be necessary to the visibility of the second, not to its existence; and finally (4) the correlation between the two might be theoretically spurious.[42] This should be enough to show that, though a low correlation is good evidence against the existence of a cause-effect relationship between two variables, a high correlation is not necessarily good evidence for such a relationship. And it is basically true that correlations, like other statistical techniques and like facts in general, are by themselves more useful in disproving than in supporting or inventing hypotheses. In the last two jobs, facts, even when expressed statistically, are no more than tools in the hands of an intellectual craftsman, who may use them well or badly. Statistics only helps to keep these tools sharp and clean.

# Appendix B

## *Legislative Candidate Study Questionnaire*

Indiana University
Data Library on State Politics

*Legislative Candidate Study*
Summer, 1960

RESPONDENT INFORMATION:

(name)

(address)

(city)                    (phone)

INTERVIEW SCHEDULE FORMS:
    Green—for individuals with no
      prior legislative service
    Yellow—for individuals with
      previous service

INTERVIEWER INFORMATION:

(name)

(date of interview)        (time)

(place)

(comments)

TO BE COMPLETED BEFORE INTERVIEW:

Respondent Identification:
    Chamber of previous    None  0
    Service:    House  1
      Senate  2

    Identification number:
    Previous legislative experience:

    None  0
    Incumbent  1
    Holdover  2
    Previous Service  3
    Enter year of last session:
    Total no. of sessions served:

    Candidate for the:    House  1
      Senate  2

    District number:

    No. of counties:

    No. of members:

    Respondent's party  Democrat  1
    affiliation:  Republican  2

The questions I am about to ask are designed to furnish information for four separate studies of the 1961 Indiana General Assembly. These studies are being made by Indiana University graduate students as part of their program of study at the university. The answers you give me will be used for the purposes of scholarly research on American state politics and *only* for those purposes.

First, a few questions about your background:

1. Where were you born?

   1.
- In district    1
- In adjoining county    2
- In other Indiana county    3
- In other state    4
- In foreign country    5

2. And in what year?

   2. Enter last two digits of year:

3. How many years have you been living in this legislative district?

   3.
- All his life    1
- Since grade school age    2
- Since high school age    3
- Not above:
  - more than 30 years   4
  - 20–29 "   5
  - 15–19 "   6
  - 10–14 "   7
  - 5–9 "   8
  - less than 5 years   9

4. Now would you tell me a little about your education—what schooling have you had?

   4.
- Did not go to high school    1
- Went to high sch.—not graduate    2
- High school grad.—no further    3
- College—but not a graduate    4
- College graduate with degree    5

5a. What is your own principal occupation?

   5a.
- Lawyer    1
- Farmer    2
- Insurance and real estate    3
- Merchants, small business, etc.    4
- Laborers: union, tradesmen    5
- Salesmen & w. collar workers    6
- Newspapermen: editors, radio    7
- Other professions: Ph.D., M.D.    8
- Not otherwise classified    9

5b. Has this been your main occupation all your working life?

   5b.
- Yes    1
- No    2

(IF "NO" TO ABOVE QUESTION)

5c. What other major occupations have you    5c.                    NA    0
    had?
        Job:_____
        Job:_____
        Job:_____

6a. Is there any particular subject or field of    6a.              DK/NA  0
    legislation in which you might think your-                      Yes    1
    self to be particularly expert—I mean                          No     2
    when it comes to dealing with proposed
    legislation in that field?

(IF "YES" TO ABOVE QUESTION)

6b. What is that?                                  6b.              DK/NA  0

6c. Why is that?                                   6c.              DK/NA  0

Let's switch our focus to the political nature of your district:

7.  In general, within your legislative district  7.               DK/NA  0
    is there much competition in your party's          No competition      1
    primary?                                            Little             2
                                                        Moderate           3
                                                        A lot              4
                                                        Very competitive   5

7a. Did you have opposition in the primary         7a.              DK/NA  0
    this year?                                                      Yes    1
                                                                    No     2

(IF "YES" TO ABOVE)

7b. How much were you worried about it?            7b.              DK/NA  0
                                                        Not worried at all 1
                                                        Only a little      2
                                                        Moderately         3
                                                        A lot              4
                                                        Extremely so       5

7c. Why was that?                                  7c.              DK/NA  0

(IF NOT MENTIONED ABOVE—PROBE)

7d. Did organized labor endorse any candi-         7d.              DK/NA  0
    date? Whom did it endorse?                          Yes: NA to whom    1
                                                                    No     2
                                                        Endorsed respon.   3
                                                        Endorsed opponent  4

(ASK ONLY IF HAD PRIMARY OPPOSITION AND NOT
MENTIONED ABOVE)

7e. Were issues very important in the pri-         7e.              DK/NA  0
    mary in your district this year?                               Yes    1
                                                                    No     2

(IF "YES" TO ABOVE)
7f.  What ones?                                          7f.                        DK/NA  0

(ASK ONLY IF HE COMES FROM A JOINT-COUNTY
DISTRICT)
8    Do the party organizations in the counties         8.                         DK/NA  0
     of your district have an agreement con-                                        Yes    1
     cerning the distribution of nominations                                        No     2
     between the counties?

(IF "YES" TO ABOVE)
8a.  How does it operate?                                8a.                        DK/NA  0

Let's talk a little now about the general election:
9a.  How about the relative strength of the             9a.                        DK/NA  0
     parties in your district—over the years                 Safe Democratic              1
     has the district been safe Republican or                Mostly Democratic            2
     Democratic, fairly close, or what?                      Competitive                  3
                                                             Mostly Republican            4
                                                             Safe Republican              5

9b.  Do you think this is changing any?                  9b.                        DK/NA  0
                                                                                    Yes    1
                                                                                    No     2

(IF "YES" TO ABOVE)
9c.  How is that?                                        9c.                        DK/NA  0

(ASK ONLY IF JOINT-COUNTY DISTRICT)
10a. Do the individual counties in your district        10a.                       DK/NA  0
     vote pretty much alike, or do they favor                Pretty much alike            1
     different parties?                                       Vote differently             2

(IF "VOTE DIFFERENTLY" TO ABOVE)
10b. Could you classify these counties in terms         10b.      I    II   III   IV
     of Democrat or Republican tendencies               Sf. D.   1    1    1    1
     in voting?                                          M.D.     2    2    2    2
         County I:   _____                         Comp.    3    3    3    3
         County II:  _____                         M. R.    4    4    4    4
         County III: _____                         Sf. R.   5    5    5    5
         County IV:  _____                         DK/NA    0    0    0    0

11.  One last question about elections. In your         11.                        DK/NA  0
     district, which is usually the more im-                 Primary                      1
     portant election: the primary or the                    General                      2
     general?                                                Both the same                3

Now I'd like to ask you some general questions about factors which people have said
are important in political success. First, let's talk about organized political parties.

(NOTE: ASK ONLY IF A SINGLE-COUNTY DISTRICT)

12. How strong is the political party organization in your legislative district?

| 12. | | DK/NA | 0 |
|---|---|---|---|
| | Very weak | | 1 |
| | Pretty weak | | 2 |
| | About average | | 3 |
| | Pretty strong | | 4 |
| | Very strong | | 5 |

12a. How important is the organization in determining who will run for the legislature at the general election?

| 12a. | | DK/NA | 0 |
|---|---|---|---|
| | Totally unimport. | | 1 |
| | Unimportant | | 2 |
| | Important | | 3 |
| | Very important | | 4 |

12b. How likely is the candidate to win the nomination if the party organization were to oppose him?

| 12b. | | DK/NA | 0 |
|---|---|---|---|
| | He'd surely win | | 1 |
| | Probably win | | 2 |
| | Makes no diff. | | 3 |
| | Probably not win | | 4 |
| | He'd never win | | 5 |

12c. How important is the party in determining the outcome of the general election for the legislature in your district?

| 12c. | | DK/NA | 0 |
|---|---|---|---|
| | Totally unimport. | | 1 |
| | Unimportant | | 2 |
| | Somewhat import. | | 3 |
| | Quite important | | 4 |
| | Most important | | 5 |

(ASK ONLY IF A JOINT-COUNTY DISTRICT)

13a. Is there a party organization set up for your legislative district as such?

| 13a. | | DK/NA | 0 |
|---|---|---|---|
| | Yes | | 1 |
| | No | | 2 |

(ASK IF "YES" TO ABOVE)

13b. How important is this organization in determining who will run for the legislature at the general election?

| 13b. | | DK/NA | 0 |
|---|---|---|---|
| | Totally unimport. | | 1 |
| | Unimportant | | 2 |
| | Important | | 4 |
| | Very important | | 5 |

13c. How likely is the candidate to win the nomination if this organization were to oppose him?

| 13c. | | DK/NA | 0 |
|---|---|---|---|
| | He'd surely win | | 1 |
| | Probably win | | 2 |
| | Makes no diff. | | 3 |
| | Probably not win | | 4 |
| | He'd never win | | 5 |

13d. How important is this organization in determining the outcome of the general election for the legislature?

| 13d. | | DK/NA | 0 |
|---|---|---|---|
| | Totally unimport. | | 1 |
| | Unimportant | | 2 |
| | Somewhat import. | | 3 |
| | Quite important | | 4 |
| | Most important | | 5 |

(ASK IF ANSWER IS "NO" TO Q. 13a)

13e. Do the party organizations of the different counties in your district have anything to say about who is to run for the legislature at the general election?

13e.            DK/NA 0
                 Yes 1
                 No 2

(IF "YES" TO ABOVE)

13f. How important are these party organizations in determining who will run for the legislature at the general election?

13f.            DK/NA 0
     Totally unimport. 1
     Unimportant 2
     Important 4
     Very important 5

13g. How likely is the candidate to win the nomination if these party organizations were to oppose him?

13g.            DK/NA 0
     He'd surely win 1
     Probably win 2
     Makes no diff. 3
     Probably not win 4
     He'd never win 5

13h. How important are these organizations in determining the outcome of the general election for the legislature in your district?

13h.            DK/NA 0
     Totally unimport. 1
     Unimportant 2
     Somewhat import. 3
     Quite important 4
     Most important **5**

(ASK IF "NO" TO Q. 13c)

13i. What roles do the different county party organizations play concerning the legislative seat from this district—which organization is most important?

13i.            DK/NA 0

14. Aside from the party itself, what local organizations would you say are important in determining the outcome of an election in your district?

14.            DK/NA 0
            None 1

(GROUPS)      14a. Why are they important?

14a.            DK/NA 0

_____    _____

_____    _____

_____    _____

Now to talk some about the electorate in your district.

15. What particular groups of voters do you think contribute heavily to the outcome of an election here?

15.            DK/NA 0

(ASK IF ANY GROUPS ARE MENTIONED ABOVE)

15a. Of these groups, which do you think is most important?

15a.            DK/NA 0

16. In your district, how much is the vote affected by traditional party loyalties—people voting for a legislative candidate because he belongs to one party or for his
opponent because he belongs to the other?

| | | |
|---|---|---|
| 16. | DK/NA | 0 |
| | Not at all | 1 |
| | Little | 2 |
| | Some | 3 |
| | Much | 4 |
| | Very much | 5 |

16a. How much do you think the vote is affected by a man's record and his experience and personal qualities?

| | | |
|---|---|---|
| 16a. | DK/NA | 0 |
| | Not at all | 1 |
| | Little | 2 |
| | Some | 3 |
| | Much | 4 |
| | Very much | 5 |

(ASK ONLY IF A MULTI-MEMBER DISTRICT)

16b. As your district sends more than one man
to the House (Senate), the voters must
choose their legislators from more than
two candidates. How many voters do you
think consider the names of all the candidates when voting for the state legislative
offices?

| | | |
|---|---|---|
| 16b. | DK/NA | 0 |
| | Almost none do | 1 |
| | A few do | 2 |
| | Some do | 3 |
| | Many do | 4 |
| | Almost all do | 5 |

You've told me about elections in general in your district. Now I'd like to learn something of your present plans for the coming November election.

20. Do you intend to campaign for your election then?

| | | |
|---|---|---|
| 20. | DK/NA | 0 |
| | Yes | 1 |
| | No | 2 |

(ASK IF "NO" TO ABOVE)

20a. How come?

| | | |
|---|---|---|
| 20a. | DK/NA | 0 |

(ASK IF "YES" TO Q. 20)

20b. What are the main things you will try to
get across in your campaign?

| | | |
|---|---|---|
| 20b. | DK/NA | 0 |

(ASK IF NOT MENTIONED ABOVE)

20c. Will you emphasize any particular state
or local issues? What are they?

| | | |
|---|---|---|
| 20c. | DK/NA | 0 |

(ASK IF NOT MENTIONED ABOVE)

20d. Will you emphasize any particular aspects of your own record? What will these
be?

| | | |
|---|---|---|
| 20d. | DK/NA | 0 |

(ASK ONLY IF A SINGLE-MEMBER DISTRICT)

21. Could you tell me what you think your
opponent will emphasize in his campaign?

| | | |
|---|---|---|
| 21. | DK/NA | 0 |
| | He won't campaign | 1 |

(ASK ONLY IF RESPONDENT THINKS OPP. WON'T
CAMPAIGN)

21a. Why won't he campaign?

| | | |
|---|---|---|
| 21a. | DK/NA | 0 |

(ASK ONLY IF A MULTI-MEMBER DISTRICT)

22. Could you tell me what you think the candidates of the opposing party will emphasize in their campaign?

22.                DK/NA 0

Now I'm interested in learning some things about your legislative district.

23. Do you think that the average voters in your district have any specific preferences concerning the more important bills you vote on in the legislature?

23.                DK/NA 0
Almost none do  1
A few do  2
Some do  3
Most do  4
Almost all do  5

24a. Do you think that you generally know how the rank-and-file voters in your district feel about issues that concern them?

24a.                DK/NA 0
Hardly ever  1
Seldom  2
Sometimes  3
Quite often  4
Almost always  5

24b. Are there any specific groups of voters whose preferences you think you know particularly well. What groups are these?

24b.                DK/NA 0
No  2

25. How do you find out what people in your district feel about the issues which come before the legislature?

25.                DK/NA 0
Mail  1
Newspapers  2
Party  3
Personal contacts  4

26. While we're talking about issues, I'd like to ask you something about the work of this coming session of the legislature. As you see it, what would you say are the most important issues the legislature will be called upon to decide?

26.                DK/NA 0

    1._____
    2._____
    3._____
    4._____
    5._____

(ASK ONLY IF AN ANSWER IS GIVEN ABOVE)

26a. Of these issues, could you tell me in which you are personally most interested?

26a.                DK/NA 0

Back to the nature of your district again. Of course, districts differ a good deal in terms of their economic, racial, ethnic, occupational, religious, and social characteristics.

27. From this point of view, what are the important features of your district?

27.                DK/NA 0

(ASK THE ONES NOT MENTIONED ABOVE)

27a. How about the nationality and racial composition of the district? — 27a. — DK/NA 0

27b. How about the religious composition of the district? — 27b. — DK/NA 0

27c. How about the main economic activity of the district? — 27c. — DK/NA 0

27d. Is there much union political activity? — 27d. — DK/NA 0

27e. Is there much political interest on the part of business or industry? — 27e. — DK/NA 0

Now I'm interested in what you feel the people of your district know about the candidates they vote for.

28a. In general, how much would you say the average voter knows about what you do in the legislature?

| 28a. | | DK/NA | 0 |
| | Almost nothing | | 1 |
| | Very little | | 2 |
| | Some | | 3 |
| | Quite a bit | | 4 |
| | Almost everything | | 5 |

28b. How much do you think the average voter knows about your stands on issues like those we've talked about?

| 28b. | | DK/NA | 0 |
| | Almost nothing | | 1 |
| | Very little | | 2 |
| | Some | | 3 |
| | Quite a bit | | 4 |
| | Almost everything | | 5 |

28c. Are there any particular issues which, when they come before the legislature, draw your constituents' attention to what you do more than usual? (ASK IF "YES") What are these?

| 28c. | DK/NA | 0 |
| | No | 1 |

29. How do your constituents become informed about what you do in the legislature? — 29. — DK/NA 0

(ASK IF NOT MENTIONED ABOVE)

29a. What newspapers provide your constituents with coverage of the legislature's activities?

| 29a. | | DK/NA | 0 |
| | None | | 1 |
| | Local papers | | 2 |
| | Indianapolis | | 3 |
| | Both | | 4 |

That pretty well covers your political life. Now let's change our focus a little.

30. How much do you think the people of your district know about you as a person?

30.  DK/NA 0
- Almost nothing — 1
- Very little — 2
- Some — 3
- Quite a bit — 4
- Almost everything — 5

30a. What yould you say is the most important thing the people of your district know about you?

30a.  DK/NA 0

(IF NOT MENTIONED ABOVE)

31a. How much difference do you think your church preference makes to the people of your district?

31a.  DK/NA 0
- No difference — 1
- Very little — 2
- Some — 3
- Quite a bit — 4
- Most important — 5

31b. Could you tell me what your church preference is?

(INTERVIEWER: WRITE IN DENOMINATION IF NOT EASILY CLASSIFIED IN ADJOINING LIST)

31b.  DK/NA 0
- Catholic — 1
- Methodist — 2
- Christian Church — 3
- Baptist — 4
- Presbyterian — 5
- Lutheran — 6
- Anabaptist, U.B. — 7
- Episcopalian — 8

(ASK ONLY IF A SINGLE-MEMBER DISTRICT)

32. Turning now to some questions concerning your opponent, how much do the people of your district know about your opponent's stands on issues?

32.  DK/NA 0
- Almost nothing — 1
- Very little — 2
- Some — 3
- Quite a bit — 4
- Almost everything — 5

32a. How much do the people of your district know about your opponent as a person?

32a.  DK/NA 0
- Almost nothing — 1
- Very little — 2
- Some — 3
- Quite a bit — 4
- Almost everything — 5

32b. What would you say is the most important thing they know about your opponent?

32b.  DK/NA 0

Now I'd like to learn something about your dual roles as a legislator and a community citizen.

33. How many of your constituents can identify you— (MENTION FULL NAME HERE)—
as a member of the Indiana legislature?

| 33. | | DK/NA | 0 |
| | Almost none | | 1 |
| | Very few | | 2 |
| | Some | | 3 |
| | Many | | 4 |
| | Almost all | | 5 |

33a. Of those who know that you are a member of the legislature, would you say that,
in general, they hold views of legislators
which are favorable or unfavorable?

| 33a. | | DK/NA | 0 |
| | Highly unfavorable | | 1 |
| | Unfavorable | | 2 |
| | Mixed | | 3 |
| | Favorable | | 4 |
| | Highly favorable | | 5 |

34a. How much difference does it make to you
personally—that is, aside from getting re-
elected—to have your constituents in general approve of the way you vote in the
legislature?

| 34a. | | DK/NA | 0 |
| | No difference | | 1 |
| | Little difference | | 2 |
| | Some | | 3 |
| | Much | | 4 |
| | Most important | | 5 |

34b. Again aside from getting re-elected, what
groups of people would you like to have
approve of your performance as a legislator?

| 34b. | DK/NA | 0 |

35a. After voting on a measure, a legislator
sometimes finds out that he would have
voted exactly the opposite if he had
known more about the nature of the bill.
Has this ever happened to you?

| 35a. | DK/NA | 0 |
| | Yes | 1 |
| | No | 2 |

(ASK IF "YES" TO ABOVE)

35b. In general, does the knowledge that you
voted the wrong way on some bills bother
you at all later on?

| 35b. | | DK/NA | 0 |
| | Not at all | | 1 |
| | A little | | 2 |
| | Some | | 3 |
| | Quite a bit | | 4 |
| | Very much | | 5 |

36. Now, here are some statements that various legislators and other people have made concerning government and politics in general and the work of a legislator. Would you please read each one and then check how much you agree or disagree with it? Please check the following:

| | agree | tend to agree | unde- cided | tend to disagree | disagree |
|---|---|---|---|---|---|
| a. The best interests of the people would be better served if legislators were elected without party labels. | ( ) | ( ) | ( ) | ( ) | ( ) |
| b. Business enterprise can continue to give us our high standard of living only if it remains free from government regulation. | ( ) | ( ) | ( ) | ( ) | ( ) |
| c. Even though the legislator is firmly convinced that his constituents are not properly evaluating the issues, it is his job to disregard his *own* views and vote the way they want. | ( ) | ( ) | ( ) | ( ) | ( ) |
| d. Under our form of government, every individual should take an interest in government directly, not through a political party. | ( ) | ( ) | ( ) | ( ) | ( ) |
| e. A legislator has his main obligation to the people of Indiana, and he must be careful not to mistake the particular interests of his constituency for the interests of the state as a whole. | ( ) | ( ) | ( ) | ( ) | ( ) |
| f. The government has the responsibility to see to it that all people, poor or rich, have adequate housing, education, medical care, and protection against unemployment. | ( ) | ( ) | ( ) | ( ) | ( ) |
| g. A legislator can decide how to vote on most issues by asking himself if the proposed law is morally right. | ( ) | ( ) | ( ) | ( ) | ( ) |
| h. The two parties should take clear-cut stands on more of the important state issues in order to encourage party responsibility. | ( ) | ( ) | ( ) | ( ) | ( ) |
| i. Because his constituents seldom know all the various aspects of important issues, the legislator serves his constituency best if he is left alone to make careful decisions by himself. | ( ) | ( ) | ( ) | ( ) | ( ) |
| j. Organized labor has far too much influence in the Indiana legislature. | ( ) | ( ) | ( ) | ( ) | ( ) |
| k. If a bill is important for his party's record, a member should vote with his party even if it costs him some support in his district. | ( ) | ( ) | ( ) | ( ) | ( ) |
| l. First and foremost, the legislator's job is to represent his constituents, even before the interests of the state. | ( ) | ( ) | ( ) | ( ) | ( ) |

37a. You hear a lot these days about the power          37a.                          DK/NA 0
of interest groups and lobbies in state
politics. What would you say are the most
powerful organizations of this kind here
in Indiana?

  1._____  2._____
  3._____  4._____
  5._____  6._____

37b. Now, what would you say makes these               37b.                          DK/NA 0
groups so powerful—what are the main
reasons for their influence?

(GROUPS)        (REASONS FOR INFLUENCE)
  1. _____
     _____
  2. _____
     _____
  3. _____
     _____
  4. _____
     _____
  5. _____
  6. _____
     _____

(GROUPS IN GENERAL)
   _____
   _____

37c. How well do you think that spokesmen for          37c.                    DK/NA   0
these organizations reflect the views of               Almost none             1
those members who reside in your district              A few                   2
—that is, how many members would you                   Some                    3
say they speak for?                                    Most                    4
                                                       Almost all              5

37d. Are there any interest groups or lobbies          37d.                    DK/NA   0
that are particularly strong in your own               None    1
district? (Which are these?)

38. Below is a list of some organizations which have been interested in public policy.
Could you give me your estimate of how effective these organizations are in influencing public policy and especially of how effective they are in making their
case before the legislature?

|  | very effective | somewhat effective | unde-cided | relatively ineffective | completely ineffective |
|---|---|---|---|---|---|
| a. American Fed. of State, County, and Municipal Employees, South Bend | ( ) | ( ) | ( ) | ( ) | ( ) |
| b. Indiana League of Women Voters | ( ) | ( ) | ( ) | ( ) | ( ) |
| c. American Legion | ( ) | ( ) | ( ) | ( ) | ( ) |
| d. Indiana State Teachers Association | ( ) | ( ) | ( ) | ( ) | ( ) |
| e. Hammond Chamber of Commerce | ( ) | ( ) | ( ) | ( ) | ( ) |
| f. Indiana AFL-CIO | ( ) | ( ) | ( ) | ( ) | ( ) |
| g. Indiana Farm Bureau | ( ) | ( ) | ( ) | ( ) | ( ) |
| h. Indiana State Chamber of Commerce | ( ) | ( ) | ( ) | ( ) | ( ) |
| i. Federation of Indiana Chiropractors | ( ) | ( ) | ( ) | ( ) | ( ) |
| j. Indiana Municipal League | ( ) | ( ) | ( ) | ( ) | ( ) |

39. Below are listed some of the more or less well-known interest groups in Indiana. Could you check the extent of your agreement with their policies and activities on public issues?

|  | agree | tend to agree | unde-cided | tend to disagree | disagree |
|---|---|---|---|---|---|
| a. Indiana Farm Bureau | ( ) | ( ) | ( ) | ( ) | ( ) |
| b. Indiana Conference of Teamsters | ( ) | ( ) | ( ) | ( ) | ( ) |
| c. Indiana Manufacturers Association | ( ) | ( ) | ( ) | ( ) | ( ) |
| d. Indiana State Chamber of Commerce | ( ) | ( ) | ( ) | ( ) | ( ) |
| e. Indiana AFL-CIO | ( ) | ( ) | ( ) | ( ) | ( ) |
| f. Indiana State Teachers Association | ( ) | ( ) | ( ) | ( ) | ( ) |
| g. Taxpayers Federation, Inc. | ( ) | ( ) | ( ) | ( ) | ( ) |
| h. Indiana State Medical Association | ( ) | ( ) | ( ) | ( ) | ( ) |

40. Before the primary election, you had to make a decision to run for public office. Did any groups urge you to run for the legislature? (Which ones?)

40.               DK/NA 0
                 No    2

41. At the election stage, are interest groups important because of their financial resources or because of the number of votes they can deliver?

41.              DK/NA 0
   Finances most imp.    1
   Finances more imp.    2
   Both equally imp.    3
   Votes more impt.    4
   Votes most impt.    5

We would like to have your views on pre-legislative decision-making—that is, decisions which are made before the legislature meets. These decisions may range from ideas on what issues will be brought up before the legislature to agreements on bills to be introduced.

| | | | |
|---|---|---|---|
| 42a. What would be your guess as to the importance of this pre-legislative activity? | 42a. | DK/NA | 0 |
| | | Totally unimport. | 1 |
| | | Unimportant | 2 |
| | | Some importance | 3 |
| | | Important | 4 |
| | | Very important | 5 |

(UNLESS "TOTALLY UNIMPORTANT" TO ABOVE)

| | | | |
|---|---|---|---|
| 42b. What people are most influential in this pre-legislative thinking, talking, and deciding? | 42b. | DK/NA | 0 |

(ASK IF NOT MENTIONED ABOVE)

| | | | |
|---|---|---|---|
| 42c. What would you estimate the role of interest groups to be in this pre-legislative activity? | 42c. | DK/NA | 0 |
| | | Totally unimportant | 1 |
| | | Unimportant | 2 |
| | | Some importance | 3 |
| | | Important | 4 |
| | | Very important | 5 |

(UNLESS "TOTALLY UNIMPORTANT" ABOVE)

| | | | |
|---|---|---|---|
| 42d. To your knowledge of Indiana politics, do interest groups which frequently oppose each other on legislation get together before the session meets to iron out differences? | 42d. | DK/NA | 0 |
| | | Yes | 1 |
| | | No | 2 |

| | | | |
|---|---|---|---|
| 42e. Again to your knowledge, do they get together while the legislature is in session to iron out differences? | 42e. | DK/NA | 0 |
| | | Yes | 1 |
| | | No | 2 |

Now let's turn to your opinions on the operations of interest groups in the legislative process.

| | | | |
|---|---|---|---|
| 43a. In general, how much consideration do you give to the information furnished by an interest group in your voting decision in the legislature? | 43a. | DK/NA | 0 |
| | | Practically none | 1 |
| | | A little | 2 |
| | | Some | 3 |
| | | Quite a bit | 4 |
| | | Very much | 5 |

| | | | |
|---|---|---|---|
| 43b. How important a part do interest groups play in telling you what you want to know about your constituency? | 43b. | DK/NA | 0 |
| | | Totally unimportant | 1 |
| | | Unimportant | 2 |
| | | Some importance | 3 |
| | | Important | 4 |
| | | Very important | 5 |

44. (HAND RESPONDENT PAGE)
Please check the following:

| | agree | tend to agree | unde- cided | tend to disagree | disagree |
|---|---|---|---|---|---|
| a. Interest groups in general make un-reasonable demands on public officials. | ( ) | ( ) | ( ) | ( ) | ( ) |
| b. Under our form of government, every individual should take an interest in government directly, not through interest group organizations. | ( ) | ( ) | ( ) | ( ) | ( ) |
| c. Interest groups aid the democratic process by communicating to the legislator what the people want. | ( ) | ( ) | ( ) | ( ) | ( ) |
| d. Allowing interest groups to operate in the legislature is a desirable way of allowing the people to get at the legislature. | ( ) | ( ) | ( ) | ( ) | ( ) |
| e. The job of the legislator is to work out compromises among conflicting interest. | ( ) | ( ) | ( ) | ( ) | ( ) |
| f. It would be desirable for opposing interest groups to get together and iron out their differences on proposed legislation rather than throw the issue open in the legislature. | ( ) | ( ) | ( ) | ( ) | ( ) |
| g. So many groups want so many different things that it is often difficult to know what stand to take. | ( ) | ( ) | ( ) | ( ) | ( ) |
| h. A legislator can decide how to vote on most issues by asking himself if the proposed law is fair to groups which will be affected by the law. | ( ) | ( ) | ( ) | ( ) | ( ) |
| i. Even if a legislator suspects that the leadership of an interest group is not representative of the membership it is generally too difficult to find out how well the leadership represents the membership. | ( ) | ( ) | ( ) | ( ) | ( ) |
| j. The operations of interest groups provides an inexpensive means of giving the legislature information. | ( ) | ( ) | ( ) | ( ) | ( ) |
| k. It is difficult for a legislator to distinguish between what interest groups want and what is in the best interest of the state of Indiana. | ( ) | ( ) | ( ) | ( ) | ( ) |
| l. It is necessary for legislators to explain their vote to interest group leaders. | ( ) | ( ) | ( ) | ( ) | ( ) |

45.  In general, do you think that public attention is helpful or harmful to the work of interest groups in the legislature?

45.
| | |
|---|---|
| | DK/NA 0 |
| Helpful | 1 |
| Makes no diff. | 2 |
| Harmful | 3 |

I'd like to learn something about the effectiveness of lobbyists in the legislature.

46.  What personal qualities and factors in his          46.                          DK/NA  0
     background make for an effective lobby-
     ist in the legislature?

47.  Interest group leaders and lobbyists seek           47.                          DK/NA  0
     our legislators, but how frequently do                    Almost never                 1
     legislators seek out lobbyists and interest               Seldom                       2
     group leaders in order to obtain support                  Sometimes                    3
     for their own bills?                                      Often                        4
                                                               Very often                   5

48.  It has been said that interest groups some-         48.                          DK/NA  0
     times try to exert political influence by                 Yes                          1
     threatening to provide the legislator with               No                           2
     an opposition candidate in the primary.
     Have you ever known cases in which op-
     position was provided in this manner?

(IF "YES" TO ABOVE)

48a. How effective would you say this means              48a.                         DK/NA  0
     of influence is?                                          Totally ineffect.            1
                                                               Mostly ineffect.             2
                                                               Somewhat effect.             3
                                                               Often effective              4
                                                               Very effective               5

48b. Do you know of any organizations that               48b.                         DK/NA  0
     made a financial contribution to a state                 No                           2
     legislative candidate in your district dur-
     ing the 1960 primary? (What organiza-
     tions made such contributions?)

49.  How much can an interest group help the             49.                          DK/NA  0
     legislator by trying to interpret his bills               Very harmful                 1
     and activities to the public?                            Somewhat harmful             2
                                                               No help                      3
                                                               Somewhat helpful             4
                                                               Very helpful                 5

50.  Which type of group do you think is more            50.                          DK/NA  0
     effective in the legislature—specialized                 Specialized groups           1
     groups which focus their attention on only               Broad-interest gr.           2
     one or two bills *or* groups with wider in-              Both the same                3
     terests in broad areas of legislation?

51a. What kind of impact would the appear-               51a.                         DK/NA  0
     ance of a large group of sympathizers at a               Almost none                  1
     committee hearing have on the commit-                    A little                     2
     tee's action?                                            Some                         3
                                                               A lot                        4
                                                               Very much                    5

| | | | |
|---|---|---|---|
| 51b. | How much importance do you attach to a flood of telegrams and letters, urging you to vote a particular way on a bill? | 51b. | DK/NA 0 |
| | | No importance | 1 |
| | | Little | 2 |
| | | Some | 3 |
| | | A lot | 4 |
| | | A great deal | 5 |

52. On which people in the legislative process are interest groups likely to direct their activity?

52. DK/NA 0

(ASK IF NOT MENTIONED ABOVE)

| | | | |
|---|---|---|---|
| 52a. | Do these groups ever concentrate on party leaders— | 52a. | DK/NA 0 |
| | | Yes | 1 |
| | | No | 2 |

| | | | |
|---|---|---|---|
| 52b. | —on committee chairmen, or on— | 52b. | DK/NA 0 |
| | | Yes | 1 |
| | | No | 2 |

| | | | |
|---|---|---|---|
| 52c. | —Senate and House leadership? | 52c. | DK/NA 0 |
| | | Yes | 1 |
| | | No | 2 |

That finishes the questions on interest groups in general. I now have just a few questions to ask you on a specific subject-matter area, labor legislation.

| | | | |
|---|---|---|---|
| 53. | First of all, how much would you say that you are interested in this particular issue area? | 53. | DK/NA 0 |
| | | Not at all | 1 |
| | | A little | 2 |
| | | Some | 3 |
| | | A lot | 4 |
| | | Very much | 5 |

| | | | |
|---|---|---|---|
| 54. | How effective is organized labor in the state in promoting its interests in this particular area? | 54. | DK/NA 0 |
| | | Totally ineffect. | 1 |
| | | Mostly ineffect. | 2 |
| | | Moderately effect. | 3 |
| | | Mostly effective | 4 |
| | | Very effective | 5 |

55. (HAND THE RESPONDENT THE FOLLOWING PAGE TO FILL OUT)

| | | | |
|---|---|---|---|
| 56a. | Let's be a bit more specific about the matter of "Right-to-Work." How much does this matter concern you? | 56a. | DK/NA 0 |
| | | No concern | 1 |
| | | Very little | 2 |
| | | Some | 3 |
| | | Quite a bit | 4 |
| | | Very much | 5 |

| | | | |
|---|---|---|---|
| 56b. | Do you think the legislature will have to grapple with this issue in the coming session? | 56b. | DK/NA 0 |
| | | Yes | 1 |
| | | No | 2 |

(IF "YES" TO ABOVE)

56c.  Can you tell me what solution you would          56c.                              DK/NA  0
      personally favor for this general problem?

How do you think the following groups in your district feel about the "Right-to-Work"
issue?

56d.  How about most businessmen?                      56d.                              DK/NA  0

56e.  How about most union workingmen?                 56e.                              DK/NA  0

56f.  How about non-union workingmen?                  56f.                              DK/NA  0

57.   You often hear some legislators say that,        57.                               DK/NA  0
      on certain issues or subjects, there are one
      or two organizations whose advice *ought*
      to be taken, whether or not they are par-
      ticularly important organizations other-
      wise. I wonder, what organizations do
      you feel should be listened to on labor
      legislation?

58a.  Now, I have just one more question to            58a.                              DK/NA  0
      ask with regard to labor organizations.                                            Yes    1
      Have you ever been a member of a labor                                             No     2
      union?

(IF "YES" TO ABOVE)

58b.  Would you tell me which union?                   58b.                              DK/NA  0

58c.  Did you ever hold an office in the union?        58c.                              DK/NA  0
                                                                                         Yes    1
                                                                                         No     2

(ASK IF "YES" TO ABOVE)

58d.  What office or offices did you hold?             58d.                              DK/NA  0

(INTERVIEWER: SKIP TO QUESTION 61 IF SHORT OF
TIME)

Somewhat earlier I asked you how competitive you thought your district was.

59a.  When you label a district as being "com-         59a.                              DK/NA  0
      petitive" what things do you consider in
      making the judgment?

(ASK IF NOT MENTIONED ABOVE)

59b.  How about the relative difference in votes       59b.                              DK/NA  0
      cast for each party?

59c.  Do you weigh the results of the most re-         59c.                              DK/NA  0
      cent election more than past ones? How
      much so?

59d.  Do you include the voters' tendency to
      split their tickets as a factor in competi-
      tiveness?                                        59d.                              DK/NA  0

Students of government have frequently tried to determine party competitiveness by analyzing election returns in terms of percentages, split-ticket voting, and so on. However, there is some disagreement as to the value of this kind of study.

| 60. | Do you ever study the election returns in your district? | 60. | | DK/NA | 0 |
| | | | Yes | 1 |
| | | | No | 2 |

(ASK IF "YES" TO ABOVE)

| 60a. | When trying to determine voting patterns, how far back do you study these returns? | 60a. | DK/NA | 0 |

| 60b. | Do you look only at county totals, or do you examine the returns at smaller levels? | 60b. | DK/NA | 0 |

| 60c. | Do you pay any special attention to the size of turnout in interpreting returns? (How is that?) | 60c. | DK/NA | 0 |

| 60d. | What effect do Presidential and non-Presidential elections have on voting in your district? | 60d. | DK/NA | 0 |

| 60e. | Is there anything else about analyzing election returns that you think we should consider? | 60e. | DK/NA | 0 |
| | | | No | 2 |

I have only a few more questions left to ask you, and these deal with your evaluation of your legislative service.

| 61. | Speaking now purely of the legislative session as a personal experience—that is, considering the people you have met and the friends you have made—how would you rate your experience in the legislature? | 61. | DK/NA | 0 |
| | | Very unpleasant | 1 |
| | | Unsatisfactory | 2 |
| | | Both good and bad | 3 |
| | | Satisfactory | 4 |
| | | Most enjoyable | 5 |

| 62. | As far as you know now, if you win in the general election, do you think you will continue your political career by running for office again? | 62. | DK/NA | 0 |
| | | Yes | 1 |
| | | No | 2 |

(IF "YES" TO ABOVE)

| 62a. | Do you think you would like to stay in the legislature, or would you want to run for another office? | 62a. | DK/NA | 0 |
| | | Stay in | 1 |
| | | Run for other | 2 |

| 63. | From a purely financial standpoint, do you think the salary and mileage you get from the state is adequate compensation for the time you spend on legislative business? | 63. | DK/NA | 0 |
| | | Yes | 1 |
| | | No | 2 |

64. Would you say that service in the Assembly helps, hinders, or makes no difference in your earning power in your business or occupation?

64.                       DK/NA 0
    Helps                1
    Hinders            2
    Makes no diff.     3

65. And finally, would you please indicate into which of these five income groups your total annual income falls? (HAND RESPONDENT PAGE)

65.                       DK/NA 0
    Less than $5,000      1
    $5,000–$10,000     2
    $10,000–$15,000     3
    $15,000–$20,000     4
    Over $20,000       5

Is there anything else which you think is especially important that I've forgotten to ask you? ——Well then, thank you very much for your cooperation.

THIS PAGE TO BE COMPLETED BY INTERVIEWER

66a. Were other persons present or within earshot during the interview?

    Yes, throughout         ( )
    Yes, at times           ( )
    No                    ( )

66b. Interviewer's estimate of frankness/sincerity of respondent's replies.

    Very frank            ( )
    Frank                ( )
    Not very frank       ( )
    Very evasive         ( )

66c. Interviewer's estimate of general cooperativeness of respondent throughout interview.

    Very coop.            ( )
    Cooperative         ( )
    Not very coop.      ( )
    Very uncoop.        ( )

66d. Interviewer's general impressions of respondent, especially concerning (1) his personal characteristics, (2) his general political attitudes, orientation to politics, (3) his conceptions of party, pressure groups, constituents, and administration, and (4) his conception of himself as a legislator.

# Bibliography

Adrian, Charles R. *Governing Our Fifty States and Their Communities* (New York: McGraw-Hill, 1963).

Alderfer, Harold. *American Local Government and Administration* (New York: Macmillan, 1956).

Almond, Gabriel and Verba, Sidney. *The Civic Culture* (Princeton: Princeton University Press, 1963).

Babcock, Robert S. *State and Local Government and Politics,* 2d ed. (New York: Random House, 1962).

Bain, Henry M. and Hecock, Donald S. *Ballot Position and Voter's Choice* (Detroit: Wayne State University Press, 1957).

Barnhart, John and Carmony, D. F. *Indiana: From Frontier to Industrial Commonwealth* (New York: Lewis Historical Publishing Company, 1954).

Beckett, Paul and Sunderland, Celeste. "Washington State's Lawmakers: Some Personnel Factors in the Washington Legislature," *Western Political Quarterly,* X (March, 1957), pp. 180–202.

Berry, Burton Y. "The Influence of Political Platforms on Legislation in Indiana, 1901–1921," *American Political Science Review,* XVII (February, 1923), p. 57.

Blalock, Hubert M. *Causal Inferences in Non-experimental Research* (Chapel Hill: University of North Carolina Press, 1964).

Blalock, Hubert M. *Social Statistics* (New York: McGraw-Hill, 1960).

Bone, Hugh A. *American Politics and the Party System* (New York: McGraw-Hill, 1965).

Brooks, Robert C. *Political Parties and Electoral Problems* (New York: Harper and Brothers, 1923).

Campbell, Angus et al. *The American Voter* (New York: John Wiley and Sons, 1960).

Coleman, James S. *Introduction to Mathematical Sociology* (New York: The Free Press of Glencoe, 1964).

Crane, Wilder. "A Caveat on Roll Call Studies of Party Voting," *Midwest Journal of Politics,* IV (August, 1960), pp. 237–249.

Dallinger, Frederick W. *Nominations for Elective Office in the United States* (New York: Longmans, Green, and Company, 1897).

David, Paul T.; Goldman, Ralph M.; and Bain, Richard C. *The Politics of National Party Conventions* (Washington: The Brookings Institution, 1960).

DeGrazia, Alfred. *Essay on Apportionment and Representative Government* (Washington: American Enterprise Institute for Public Policy Research, 1963).

DeGrazia, Alfred. *Public and Republic* (New York: Alfred A. Knopf, 1951).

DeTocqueville, Alexis. *Democracy in America*, 2 vols. (New York: Vintage Books, 1954).

Derge, David R. "The Lawyer as Decision-Maker in the American State Legislature," *Journal of Politics,* XXI (August, 1959), pp. 408–433.

Derge, David R. "The Lawyer in the Indiana General Assembly," *Midwest Journal of Political Science,* VI (February, 1962), pp. 19–53.

Derge, David R. "Metropolitan and Outstate Alignments in Illinois and Missouri Legislative Delegations," *American Political Science Review,* LII (December, 1958), pp. 1051–1065.

Dye, Thomas R. "A Comparison of Constituency Influences in the Upper and Lower Chambers of a State Legislature," *Western Political Quarterly,* XIV (June, 1961), pp. 473–490.

Epstein, Leon. *Politics in Wisconsin* (Madison: University of Wisconsin, 1958).

Eulau, Heinz. "The Ecological Basis of Party Systems: The Case of Ohio," *Midwest Journal of Political Science,* I (August, 1957), pp. 125–135.

Eulau, Heinz. "Party as a Reference Group in the Process of Legislative Consent" (mimeographed), American Political Science Association meeting, St. Louis, September, 1961.

Eulau, Heinz et al. "The Role of the Representative: Some Empirical Observations on the Theory of Edmund Burke," *American Political Science Review,* LIII (September, 1959), pp. 742–756.

Ezekiel, Mordecai and Fox, Karl A. *Methods of Correlation and Regression Analysis,* 3rd ed. (New York: John Wiley and Sons, 1959).

Flinn, Thomas A. "Party Responsibility in the States: Some Causal Factors," *American Political Science Review,* LVIII (March, 1964), pp. 60–71.

Francis, Wayne. "Influence and Interaction in a State Legislative Body," *American Political Science Review,* LVI (December, 1962), pp. 953–960.

Francis, Wayne L. "Interaction and Influence in the Indiana General Assembly" (Ph.D. dissertation, Department of Government, Indiana University, 1961).

Francis, Wayne. "The Role Concept in Legislatures: A Probability Model and a Note on Cognitive Structure," *Journal of Politics,* XXVII (August, 1965), pp. 567–585.

Friedman, Robert S. "The Urban-Rural Conflict Revisited," *Western Political Quarterly,* XIV (June, 1961), pp. 481–495.

Friedman, Robert S. and Stokes, Sybil L. "The Role of Constitution-Maker as Representative," *Midwest Journal of Political Science,* IX (May, 1965), pp. 148–166.

Green, Bert F. *Digital Computers in Research* (New York: McGraw-Hill, 1963).

Grumm, John. "A Factor Analysis of Legislative Behavior," *Midwest Journal of Political Science,* VII (November, 1963) , pp. 336–356.

Grumm, John. "The Means of Measuring Conflict and Cohesion in the Legislature," *Southwestern Social Science Quarterly,* XLIV (March, 1964) , pp. 377–388.

Guetzkow, Harold et al. *Simulation in International Relations* (Englewood Cliffs, N. J.: Prentice-Hall, 1963) .

Guetzkow, Harold (editor), *Simulation in Social Science* (Englewood Cliffs, N. J.: Prentice-Hall, 1962) .

Guild, Frederick H. "The Operation of the Direct Primary in Indiana" in J. T. Salter, ed., "The Direct Primary," *Annals,* CVI (March, 1923) , pp. 172–180.

Harris, Louis and associates. "A Survey of Issues and Candidates in the 1958 Indiana Elections (Last of Two Surveys) ," October, 1958 (unpublished) , p. 21, cited by John H. Fenton, *Midwest Politics* (New York: Holt, Rinehart and Winston, 1966) , p. 189.

Hollingshead, August B. and Redlich, Frederick C. *Social Class and Mental Illness: A Community Study* (New York: John Wiley and Sons, 1958) .

Hunter, Floyd. *Community Power Structure* (Chapel Hill: University of North Carolina Press, 1953) .

Huntington, Samuel P. "A Revised Theory of Party Politics," *American Political Science Review,* XLIV (September, 1950) , pp. 669–677.

Hyman, Herbert H. and Sheatsley, Paul B. " 'The Authoritarian Personality' —A Methodological Critique," in Richard Christie and Marie Jahoda (eds.) , *Studies in the Scope and Method of 'The Authoritarian Personality'* (Glencoe: The Free Press, 1954) , pp. 50–122.

Hyneman, Charles S. "Legislative Experience of Illinois Lawmakers," *University of Chicago Law Review,* III (December, 1935) , pp. 104–118.

Hyneman, Charles S. "Tenure and Turnover of the Indiana General Assembly," *American Political Science Review,* XXXII (February, 1938) , pp. 51–66, and (April, 1938) , pp. 311–331.

Hyneman, Charles S. "Tenure and Turnover of Legislative Personnel," *Annals,* CVC (January, 1938) , pp. 21–31.

Hyneman, Charles S. "Who Makes Our Laws?" *Political Science Quarterly,* LV (December, 1940) , pp. 556–581.

Hyneman and Ricketts, Edmond. "Tenure and Turnover of the Iowa Legislature," *Iowa Law Review,* XXIV (May, 1939) , pp. 673–696.

Indiana, House of Representatives. *Standing Rules and Orders for the Government of the House of Representatives for the Regular Session* 1965 (94th General Assembly, 1965) .

Indiana. *Report of the Debates and Proceedings of the Convention for the Revision of the Constitution of the State of Indiana,* 1850, Vol. II.

*Indiana Votes: U. S. House of Representatives, General Assembly, 1922–1958* (Bloomington: Indiana University Bureau of Government Research, 1962) .

Jacob, Herbert. "Initial Recruitment of Elected Officials in the U. S.—A Model," *Journal of Politics,* XXIV (November, 1962) , pp. 703–716.

Janda, Kenneth. *Data Processing: Applications to Political Research* (Evanston: Northwestern University Press, 1965), Ch. 5 and Appendices C-1 and C-2.

Janda, Kenneth. "Democratic Theory and Legislative Behavior: A Study of Legislator-Constituency Relationships" (Ph.D. dissertation, Indiana University, 1961).

Janda, Kenneth. "Representational Behavior," in *International Encyclopedia of the Social Sciences* (New York: Crowell, Collier and Macmillan, forthcoming).

Janda et al. *Legislative Politics in Indiana: A Preliminary Report to the 1961 General Assembly* (Bloomington: Indiana University Bureau of Government Research, 1961).

Jewell, Malcolm E. "Party Voting in American State Legislatures," *American Political Science Review,* XLIX (September, 1955), pp. 773–791.

Jewell, Malcolm E. *The State Legislature: Politics and Practice* (New York: Random House, 1962).

Jones, Charles O. "Representation in Congress: The Case of the House Agriculture Committee," *American Political Science Review,* LV (June, 1961), pp. 358–367.

Keefe, William J. "Comparative Study of the Role of Political Parties in the State Legislatures," in H. Eulau, S. Eldersveld and M. Janowitz (eds.), *Political Behavior* (Glencoe: The Free Press, 1956), pp. 308–316.

Keefe, William J. "Parties, Partisanship, and Public Policy in the Pennsylvania Legislature," *American Political Science Review,* XLVIII (June, 1954), pp. 450–464.

Key, V. O. *American State Politics* (New York: Alfred A. Knopf, 1956).

Key, V. O. *Politics, Parties, and Pressure Groups* (New York: Crowell, 1958).

Key, V. O., and Munger, Frank. "Social Determinism and Electoral Decision: The Case of Indiana," in Eugene Burdick and Arthur J. Brodbeck, eds., *American Voting Behavior* (Glencoe: Free Press, 1959), pp. 281–299.

Leege, David C. "The Place of the Party Nominating Convention in a Representative Democracy: A Study of Power in the Indiana Democratic Party's State Nominating Conventions, 1956–1962," (Ph.D. dissertation, Indiana University, 1965).

Lipset, Seymour. *Political Man* (Garden City, New York: Doubleday, 1960).

Lockard, W. Duane. "Legislature Politics in Connecticut," *American Political Science Review,* XLVIII (March, 1954), pp. 166–173.

Lockard, Duane. *The Politics of State and Local Government* (New York: Macmillan, 1963).

Lockard, Duane. "The State Legislator," *State Legislatures in American Politics,* ed. Alexander Heard (Englewood Cliffs: Prentice-Hall, 1966), pp. 103–105.

MacRae, Duncan. "The Relation Between Roll Call Votes and Constituencies in the Massachusetts House of Representatives," *American Political Science Review,* XLVI (December, 1952), pp. 1046–1055.

Matthews, Donald R. and Prothro, James W. "Social and Economic Factors and Negro Vote Registration in the South," *American Political Science Review,* LVII (March, 1963), pp. 24–44.

Matthews, Donald R. "Political Factors and the Negro Vote Registration in the South," *American Political Science Review,* LVII (June, 1963), pp. 355–367.

Matthews, Donald R. *U. S. Senators and Their World* (Chapel Hill: University of North Carolina Press, 1960).

McMurray, Carl D. and Parsons, Malcolm B. "Public Attitudes Toward the Representational Roles of Legislators and Judges," *Midwest Journal of Political Science,* IX (May, 1965), pp. 167–185.

Meller, Norman. " 'Legislative Behavior Research' Revisited: A Review of Five Years' Publications," *Western Political Quarterly,* XVIII (December, 1965), pp. 776–793.

Merriam, Charles E. and Overacker, Louise. *Primary Elections* (Chicago: University of Chicago Press, 1928), pp. 257–267.

Meyer, Ernst C. *Nominating Systems* (Madison: published by author, 1902).

Miller, Warren A. and Stokes, Donald E. "Constituency Influence in Congress," *American Political Science Review,* LVII (March, 1963), pp. 45–56.

Munger, Frank J. "Two-Party Politics in the State of Indiana" (Ph.D. dissertation, Harvard University, 1955).

Ostrogorski, M. *Democracy and the Party System in the United States* (New York: Macmillan, 1910).

Patterson, Samuel C. "The Role of the Lobbyist: The Case of Oklahoma," *Journal of Politics,* XXV (February, 1963), pp. 72–92.

Pesonen, Pertti. "Close and Safe State Elections in Massachusetts," *Midwest Journal of Political Science,* VII (February, 1963), pp. 54–70.

*The Political Philosophy of Robert M. LaFollette as Revealed in His Speeches and Writings* (Madison, 1920), pp. 29–31.

Pool, Ithiel de Sola et al. *Candidates, Issues, and Strategies: A Computer Simulation of the 1960 and 1964 Elections* (Cambridge: M.I.T. Press, 1965).

Pool, Ithiel de Sola et al. "A Postscript on the 1964 Election," *American Behavioral Scientist* (May, 1965), pp. 39–44.

Rice, Stuart. *Quantitative Methods in Politics* (New York: Alfred A. Knopf, 1928), pp. 208–211.

Rossi, Peter and Cutwright, Phillips. "The Impact of Party Organization in an Industrial Setting," in Morris Janowitz, ed., *Community Political Systems* (Glencoe: Free Press, 1961), pp. 81–116.

Schattschneider, E. E. *Party Government* (New York: Farrar and Rinehart, 1942).

Schlesinger, Joseph. *How They Became Governor* (East Lansing: Government Bureau Research, Michigan State University, 1957).

Schlesinger, Joseph. "A Two Dimensional Scheme for Classifying the States According to Degree of Inter-Party Competition," *American Political Science Review,* XLIX (December, 1955), pp. 1120–1128.

Schumpeter, Joseph A. *Capitalism, Socialism, and Democracy* (New York: Harper and Brothers, 1942).

Scott, William A. and Wertheimer, Michael. *Introduction to Psychological Research* (New York: John Wiley and Sons, 1962), pp. 344–347.

Seligman, Lester. "Political Recruitment and Party Structure: A Case Study," *American Political Science Review,* LV (March, 1961) , pp. 77–87.

Siegel, Sidney. *Non-Parametric Statistics* (New York: McGraw-Hill, 1956) , p. 107.

Simon, Herbert A. *Models of Man: Social and Rational* (New York: John Wiley, 1957) .

Sorauf, Frank J. *Party and Representation* (New York: Atherton Press, 1963) .

Standing, William and Robinson, James A. "Inter-Party Competition and Primary Contesting: The Case of Indiana," *American Political Science Review,* LII (December, 1958) , pp. 1066–1077.

Teune, Henry. "Indiana Legislative Candidates' Attitudes Toward Interest Groups" (Ph.D. dissertation, Department of Government, Indiana University, 1961) , pp. 173–174.

Truman, David. *The Governmental Process* (New York: Alfred A. Knopf, 1951) .

Turner, Julius. *Party and Constituency: Pressures on Congress,* The Johns Hopkins University Studies in Historical and Political Science, Series LXIX, No. 1 (Baltimore: The Johns Hopkins Press, 1951) .

Wahlke, John C. "Organization and Procedure," *State Legislatures in American Politics,* ed. Alexander Heard (Englewood Cliffs: Prentice-Hall, 1966) , p. 140.

Wahlke, John et al. *The Legislative System* (New York: John Wiley, 1962) .

Watts, Thomas M. "Indiana Primary Elections: The Selection of Candidates and the Distribution of Power" (Ph.D. dissertation, Indiana University, 1963) .

Weizenbaum, J. *Symmetric List Processor.* Computer Laboratory, General Electric, Sunnyvale, California.

Wilder, Philip S., Jr. and O'Lessker, Karl. *Introduction to Indiana Government and Politics* (Indianapolis: Indiana Sesquicentennial Commission, 1967) .

Whyte, William H. *The Organization Man* (New York: Simon and Schuster, 1956) .

Wright, Charles R. and Hyman, Herbert. "Voluntary Association Memberships of American Adults," *American Sociological Review,* XXIII (June, 1958) , pp. 284–294.

Zeller, Belle, ed. *American State Legislatures* (New York: Thomas Y. Crowell, 1954) , pp. 194–197.

# Notes

## 1. *McCall:* The Indiana Legislature and Politics

NOTE: This chapter draws heavily on data collected by Charles S. Hyneman and tabulated by him. The author owes him much.

1. Charles R. Adrian, *Governing Our Fifty States and Their Communities* (New York: McGraw-Hill, 1963), p. 57.

2. John C. Wahlke, "Organization and Procedure," *State Legislatures in American Politics,* ed. Alexander Heard (Englewood Cliffs, N. J.: Prentice-Hall, 1966), p. 140.

3. Belle Zeller, ed., *American State Legislatures* (New York: Thomas Y. Crowell, 1954), pp. 194–197.

4. A study of the 1963 session indicated, for example, that the longer and the more frequent the Republican caucuses in the Senate, the less unity the party displayed on roll calls. Mary Margaret Conway, "Party and Constituency in the 1963 Indiana General Assembly: A Case Study of Party Responsibility" (Ph.D. dissertation, Department of Government, Indiana University, 196), pp. 116–118.

5. Indiana, House of Representatives, *Standing Rules and Orders for the Government of the House of Representatives for the Regular Session 1965* (94th General Assembly, 1965), p. 21.

6. Wayne L. Francis, "Interaction and Influence in the Indiana General Assembly" (Ph.D. dissertation, Department of Government, Indiana University, 196), pp. 116–118.

7. Burton Y. Berry, "The Influence of Political Platforms on Legislation in Indiana, 1901–1921," *American Political Science Review,* XVII (February, 1923), 57.

8. Conway, "Party and Constituency," p. 58.

9. Ibid., pp. 105–116.

10. Henry Teune, "Indiana Legislative Candidates' Attitudes Toward Interest Groups" (Ph.D. dissertation, Department of Government, Indiana University, 1961), pp. 173–174.

11. Kenneth Janda, Henry Teune, Melvin Kahn, and Wayne Francis,

*Legislative Politics in Indiana: A Preliminary Report to the 1961 General Assembly* (Bloomington: Indiana University Bureau of Government Research, 1961) , pp. 18–19.

12. Teune, "Indiana Legislative Candidates' Attitudes," pp. 86–88.

13. Indiana, *Report of the Debates and Proceedings of the Convention for the Revision of the Constitution of the State of Indiana* (1850) , II, 1046.

14. Louis Harris and Associates, "A Survey of Issues and Candidates in the 1958 Indiana Elections (Last of Two Surveys) ," October, 1958, p. 21 (unpublished), cited by John H. Fenton, *Midwest Politics* (New York: Holt, Rinehart and Winston, 1966) , p. 189.

15. Duane Lockard, "The State Legislator," *State Legislatures in American Politics,* ed. Alexander Heard (Englewood Cliffs, N. J.: Prentice-Hall, 1966) , pp. 103–105.

16. John C. Wahlke, Heinz Eulau, William Buchanan, and Leroy C. Ferguson, *The Legislative System* (New York: John Wiley, 1962) , p. 206.

17. Francis, "Interaction and Influence," pp. 49–57.

18. Ibid., pp. 66–70.

19. Kenneth Frank Janda, "Democratic Theory and Legislative Behavior: A Study of Legislator-Constituency Relationships" (Ph.D. dissertation, Department of Government, Indiana University, 1961) , pp. 218–220.

20. Francis, "Interaction and Influence," pp. 97–98.

21. Charles S. Hyneman, "Tenure and Turnover of the Indiana General Assembly," *American Political Science Review,* XXXII (February, 1938) , 53.

22. Wahlke et al., *The Legislative System,* p. 120.

23. David R. Derge, "The Lawyer in the Indiana General Assembly," *Midwest Journal of Political Science,* VI (February, 1962) , 24–47.


## 2. *Janda et al.:* Legislative Politics in Indiana

NOTE: This chapter was originally prepared as a report to the 1961 General Assembly in return for the fine cooperation given the authors in the summer of 1960, when they interviewed legislative candidates in a joint project designed to provide information for their separate Ph.D. dissertations.

1. In 1965, Democrats controlled the Indiana House and Senate and the governorship. During the 1965 session of the General Assembly both houses of the legislature were reapportioned, presumably to the advantage of the Democrats. In the 1967 session, however, Republicans controlled the House, and it is possible for them to regain control of the Senate. Notwithstanding the reapportionment, the authors' statements about party competition in Indiana are as pertinent today as they were in 1961.

2. In scoring the responses to these statements, we assigned values from +2 to −2 according to whether or not the person agreed or disagreed with the statement. The "tend to" categories were weighted +1 and −1 respectively, and "undecided" responses received a score of 0. In order to prepare compa-

rable scores for groups of legislators, all the individual scores for a particular statement were summed and divided by the highest possible value for any given statement. Consider a group which contained 25 individuals. If all individuals were to agree with a statement, it would receive a score of +50. If, however, not all individuals agreed and the resulting score was, say, only +25, then the score to the groups would be 25 divided by 50 or +.50. This procedure has the effect of averaging out the agree-disagree responses to give a single measure. As is the case with all averages, this figure does not say how much individuals deviate from the group figure.

3. For those with statistical training, we utilized the Spearman rank-order correlation coefficient calculated by this formula:

$$R = 1 - \frac{6\Sigma d^2}{N(N^2 - 1)}$$

4. It was felt that any localized interest group, such as the Chamber of Commerce of city X, would tend to be rated ineffective. Therefore, one local group was included to draw out the ineffective responses, but we wished to avoid mentioning localities and thus did not report the name of the city.

### 3. *Francis:* Influence and Interaction in a Legislative Body

1. The Democrats held 26 seats and the Republicans 24. The Democratic majority was the first in the Indiana Senate since 1939.

2. $x^2 = 15.7$, df = 1, p < .001.

3. $x^2 = 16.34$, df = 1, p < .001.

4. The interaction scale is an adaptation from a scale presented by Theodore Caplow and Robert Forman, "Neighborhood Interaction in a Homogeneous Community," *American Sociological Review,* 40 (June, 1950) , 358. An elaborate description of its reliability and usefulness can be found in a work by Theodore Caplow, Sheldon Stryker, and Samuel E. Wallace, *The Urban Microcosm: Neighborhood Structure in a Changing Metropolis* (manuscript in preparation) . Establishing the reliability of the neighborhood interaction scale, of course, only indirectly supports the use of a similar scale in a legislative situation. In the adaptation of the scale it was feared that the seasonal nature of legislative activity would raise the interaction ratings during the latter part of the interviewing period. Consequently, three weeks were allowed to elapse before beginning the interviews, in the hope that the social patterns would stabilize by that time. The evidence indicates that this was the case. The first ten interviews were compared with the last ten and no rise occurred in the average scale value for the ratings made by the latter ten. By necessity, no interviews were conducted during the last week of the session; however, for each group of ten interviews the party distribution and experienced-inexperienced distribution reasonably approximated the distributions in the entire Senate and for all those interviewed.

5. $x^2 = 17.8$, df $= 1$, $p < .001$.

6. Ties occurring at the lowest boundary of categories were broken randomly. For more precise purposes the index would not require equal groups of ten or any other number, but for the sake of clarity it is helpful to think of a .7 index value as an overlap of seven Senators out of ten for two separate sets of data.

7. Carl I. Hovland, Irving L. Janis, and Harold H. Kelly, *Communication and Persuasion* (New Haven, Conn.: Yale University Press, 1953). The authors emphasize the importance of personality in determining influence patterns.

8. This classification is based upon an accumulative quartile ranking. Let $Q_1$ be the highest ranking and $Q_4$ the lowest for both bill success and formal position success. A legislator's accumulative ranking can then range from the sum of 2 to the sum of 8. The line between high and low was drawn at that class boundary which most closely approaches the median (between the sums of 4 and 5).

9. $r\phi = \sqrt{x^2/N}$ The phi coefficient has more meaning when it is considered in conjunction with chi-square $(x^2)$. When N is constant $r\phi$ varies directly with $x^2$; therefore, certain values of $r\phi$ reflect significant values of $x^2$. When $N = 50$, the probability of a distribution occurring by chance less than five times out of a hundred reflects a phi coefficient of at least .277. Thus when $p < .05$, $r\phi > .277$; when $p < .02$, $r\phi > .329$; when $p < .01$, $r\phi > .365$; when $p < .001$, $r\phi > .466$.

10. $x^2 = 2.00$, df $= 1$, $p > .05$.

11. See, for example, Hubert M. Blalock, Jr., *Causal Inferences in Nonexperimental Research* (Chapel Hill, N. C.: University of North Carolina Press, 1964).

12. John C. Wahlke, Heinz Eulau, William Buchanan, and Leroy Ferguson, *The Legislative System* (New York: John Wiley, 1962). See also Samuel C. Patterson, "The Role of the Lobbyist: The Case of Oklahoma," *Journal of Politics*, XXV (February, 1963), 72–92.

13. Wayne L. Francis, "The Role Concept in Legislatures: A Probability Model and a Note on Cognative Structure," *Journal of Politics*, XXVII (August, 1965), 567–585.

## 4. *Conway:* Party Responsibility: Fact or Fiction in an American State Legislature

1. Thomas A. Flinn, "Party Responsibility in the States: Some Causal Factors," *American Political Science Review*, XVIII (March, 1964), 60.

2. The opportunity to observe the political processes on which this chapter is based was provided by a Legislative Internship during 1962–63 in the office of Richard O. Ristine, Lieutenant Governor of Indiana, and was sponsored by the Ford Foundation, Indiana University, and the Indiana Legislative Advisory Commission. Financial support for data analysis was provided by the Computer Science Center of the University of Maryland.

3. E.g., see W. Duane Lockard, "Legislative Politics in Connecticut," *American Political Science Review*, XLVIII (March, 1954), 166–167, and Frank J. Sorauf, *Party and Representation* (New York: Atherton Press, 1963), pp. 121, 133–146, 147–154.

4. The two Senate leaders were nominated for the offices mentioned. The Speaker of the House denied the rumors of his ambitions for office and actually did not campaign for the nomination.

5. The two most prominent factions opposing the leadership were the one led by former U.S. Senator William Jenner, which united elements of the more conservative wing of the Indiana Republican party, and another led by former Governor Ralph Gates and his son, Fourth Congressional District Republican Chairman Robert Gates, the latter an aspirant to the gubernatorial nomination.

6. The Republican state chairman, annoyed because he was unable to influence the policy preferences of legislative leaders especially on major tax law changes including the institution of a state sales tax, threatened to resign. After the legislative adjournment he did resign as the Republican Party's state chairman.

7. The examination of conflict and cohesion on roll calls pertaining only to platform legislation sets this analysis apart from previous studies, which have selected roll calls on the basis of other criteria. See, for example, Malcolm E. Jewell, "Party Voting in American State Legislatures," *American Political Science Review*, XLV (September, 1955), 773–791; William J. Keefe, "Parties, Partisanship, and Public Policy in the Pennsylvania Legislature," *American Political Science Review*, XLVIII (June, 1954), 450–464; Wilder Crane, Jr., "A Caveat on Roll Call Studies of Party Voting," *Midwest Journal of Politics*, IV (August, 1960), 237–249.

All issues regarded as major by the majority party's elected leaders in the legislature and by the news media representatives who covered the session were included on the platform list with two major exceptions: the state's biennial budget and major changes in the state's tax structure. These were excluded because no official party stand was taken on them in the platform.

8. The methods used for calculating the indices of cohesion and likeness were those defined by Stuart Rice and used by Julius Turner in his study of party and constituency influences in congressional voting. See Stuart Rice, *Quantitative Methods in Politics* (New York: Alfred A. Knopf, 1928), pp. 208–211, and Julius Turner, *Party and Constituency: Pressures on Congress*, The Johns Hopkins University Studies in Historical and Political Science, Series LXIX, No. 1 (Baltimore: The Johns Hopkins Press, 1951), pp. 26 and 36.

9. Malcolm Jewell, *The State Legislature: Politics and Practice* (New York: Random House, 1962), pp. 58–59.

10. Ibid.

11. Heinz Eulau, "Party as a Reference Group in the Process of Legislative Consent" (mimeographed), American Political Science Association meeting, St. Louis, September, 1961.

12. William J. Keefe, "Comparative Study of the Role of Political Parties

in the State Legislatures," in H. Eulau, M. Janowitz, and Samuel Eldersveld, eds., *Political Behavior* (Glencoe: The Free Press, 1956), p. 315, note 27.

13. David Truman, *The Governmental Process* (New York: Alfred A. Knopf, 1951), p. 392.

14. Wayne Francis, "Influence and Interaction in a State Legislative Body," *American Political Science Review*, LVI (December, 1962), 913–960.

15. John J. Grumm, "A Factor Analysis of Legislative Behavior," *Midwest Journal of Political Science*, VII (November, 1963), 348; Thomas A. Dye, "A Comparison of Constituency Influences in the Upper and Lower Chamber of a State Legislature," *Western Political Quarterly*, XIV (June, 1961), 473–490.

16. Grumm, "A Factor Analysis," p. 347.

17. Mordecai Ezekiel and Karl A. Fox, *Methods of Correlation and Regression Analysis*, 3rd ed. (New York: John Wiley, 1959), p. 193.

18. Charles S. Hyneman, "Tenure and Turnover of the Indiana General Assembly," *American Political Science Review*, XXXII (February, 1938), 51–67 and 311–331.

19. Sorauf, *Party and Representation*, Chapter IV.

20. Formula 6.4, Sidney Siegel, *Non-Parametric Statistics* (New York: McGraw-Hill, 1956), p. 107.

21. Jewell, *State Legislature*, pp. 119–127.

22. John C. Wahlke, Heinz Eulau, William Buchanan, and Leroy Ferguson, *The Legislative System* (New York: John Wiley, 1962), pp. 344–345.

23. Jewell, *State Legislature*, p. 57.

24. Sorauf, *Party and Representation*, p. 103; Wahlke et al., *Legislative System*, p. 98; Lester Seligman, "Political Recruitment and Party Structure: A Case Study," *American Political Science Review*, LV (March, 1961), 84.


## 5. *Carey:* A Comparison of Rural and Urban State Legislators in Iowa and Indiana

1. Among them: David R. Derge, "Metropolitan and Outstate Alignments in Illinois and Missouri Legislative Delegations," LII *American Political Science Review* (December, 1958); 1051–1065; Robert S. Friedman, "The Urban-Rural Conflict Revisited," *Western Political Quarterly*, XIV (June, 1961); 481–495; John G. Grumm, "The Means of Measuring Conflict and Cohesion in the Legislature," *Southwestern Social Science Quarterly*, XLIV (March, 1964), 377–388; Thomas A. Flinn, "Party Responsibility in the States: Some Causal Factors," *American Political Science Review*, LVIII (March, 1964), 60–71; and Alfred De Grazia, *Essay on Apportionment and Representative Government* (Washington: American Enterprise Institute, 1963).

2. It should be noted that significant population differences exist between the most urban districts of Iowa and Indiana which prevent precise comparison between the two states. In Iowa the seven largest cities vary from 177,965 (Des Moines) to 45,429 (Council Bluffs). There is no city in Iowa besides

Des Moines with a population in excess of 100,000. The size of the five largest population centers in Indiana (1950 Census) varies from 427,123 (Indianapolis) to 128,636 (Evansville). In both states the percentage of the population of the most urban districts within the limits of the largest cities varies from 65% to 80%.

3. An analysis of the Missouri and Illinois lower chambers also shows that lawyers enter at an earlier age than non-lawyers. Also lawyers in these states terminate their legislative careers at an earlier date.

4. Until 1949 Iowa legislators were paid $1,000 a session. From 1949 to 1957 the compensation was $2,000 per session. Since 1957 the pay has been $30 per session day; there is no constitutional limitation on the length of sessions in Iowa. In Indiana, where there is a 61-day limit to sessions, the pay for legislators until 1943 was $10 per day. From 1943 to 1951 this was increased to $1,200 per year. From 1955 to the present the compensation has been $3,600 per biennium.

5. For a more extensive analysis of primary competition for state legislative offices see V. O. Key, *American State Politics: An Introduction* (New York: Alfred A. Knopf, 1956), Chapter 6; Leon Epstein, *Politics in Wisconsin* (Madison: University of Wisconsin Press, 1958), Chapter 7; and William Standing and James Robinson, "Inter-party Competition and Primary Contesting: The Case of Indiana," *American Political Science Review,* LII (December, 1958), 1066–1077. To the extent that the proportion of incumbents defeated in the primary is an indication of primary competition, the proposition that primary competition is greater within the party which has the best prospects of victory in the general election is further supported by these data.

6. The seniority system is not used in either state, but, in general, a legislator does not hold a committee chairmanship his first term. Most legislators of the majority party do hold a chairmanship their second term.

7. I am indebted to Dr. Robert Pitchell, former Associate Director of the Bureau of Government Research, Indiana University, for his advice concerning the most important committees of the Indiana legislature and for allowing me to utilize a study, prepared by him, of bills referred to standing committees in the Indiana General Assembly.

For the most important committees of Iowa, I have used the appraisal of Russell Ross, Professor of Political Science, State University of Iowa. Professor Ross's appraisal was only for the 1957 session of the Iowa legislature. However, appraisals obtained from 2 Senators and 3 Representatives of the Iowa General Assembly, all of whom have served more than four sessions, almost without exception list the same committees as Professor Ross. Because estimates of the most important committees vary slightly, I have attempted to use only those committees, in this analysis, about which there is general agreement.

I have taken only a 6-session period for the analysis of the chairman of these important committees because the importance of these committees can, and probably does, vary over extended periods of time. On the other hand, it is felt that this period of time will allow some determination to be made concerning the division of these chairmanships between rural and urban legislators.

8. David R. Derge, "The Lawyer as Decision-Maker in the American State Legislature," *Journal of Politics,* XXI (August, 1959), 408–433.

9. Seymour Martin Lipset, *Political Man* (New York: Doubleday, 1960), p. 265.

10. For other studies of state legislatures which employ much the same type analysis see: Charles S. Hyneman, "Legislative Experience of Illinois Law-makers," *University of Chicago Law Review,* III (December, 1935), 112; Hyneman, "Tenure and Turnover of the Indiana General Assembly," *American Political Science Review,* XXXII (February, 1958), 51 and 311; Hyneman and Edmond Ricketts, "Tenure and Turnover of the Iowa Legislature," *Iowa Law Review,* XXIV (May, 1939), 673; Hyneman, "Who Makes our Laws?" *Political Science Quarterly,* LV (December, 1940), 556; Hyneman, "Tenure and Turnover of Legislative Personnel," *Annals,* CVC (January, 1938), 21; and Paul Beckett and Celeste Sutherland, "Washington State's Lawmakers: Some Personnel Factors in the Washington Legislature," *Western Political Quarterly,* X (March, 1957), 198.

11. In this connection, William H. Whyte makes an interesting observation about the impact of political districting upon the general behavior of citizens: "The experience of Levittown, Pennsylvania, demonstrates the importance of political unification. It straddles four townships, and quite possibly always will. There was a chance early for Levittown being incorporated as a town in its own right, but the civic leadership was inept and the move failed. Since then there has been less community-wide spirit, and many who otherwise would have been active have withdrawn from participation. There is plenty of local activity in the 'sections,' but it does not stir banked passions." *The Organization Man* (New York: Simon and Schuster, 1956), p. 291.


## 6. *Teune:* Legislative Attitudes Toward Interest Groups

1. See R. Joseph Monsen, Jr., and Mark W. Cannon, *The Makers of Public Policy* (New York: McGraw-Hill, 1965).

2. Harmon Zeigler, *Interest Groups in American Society* (Englewood Cliffs, N. J.: Prentice-Hall), p. vi.

3. Two legislative candidates were interviewed but were later nominated for high state posts. These were excluded from the analysis and were defined as not in the universe of legislative candidates.

4. The dissertations of Wayne L. Francis, Kenneth F. Janda, Melvin A. Kahn, and the author were based in part on these interviews. Interviewing was conducted jointly and to some extent analyzed jointly. Professor David R. Derge supervised three of the dissertations. Professor Charles S. Hyneman supervised one and gave research money and advice for all. Professor York Willbern provided the financial and institutional support of the Bureau of Government Research.

5. These categories are a version of the familiar Likert categories of "strongly agree," "agree," etc.

6. Special thanks are due to this research team which since has published most of their findings in John Wahlke, Heinz Eulau, William Buchanan, and LeRoy Ferguson, *The Legislative System* (New York: John Wiley, 1963).

7. The index of order of agreement was computed for all pairs of the twelve interest group items. The procedure for this computation is given in William A. Scott and Michael Wertheimer, *Introduction to Psychological Research* (New York: John Wiley, 1959), pp. 344–347. Most of these order of agreement scores were low. In the sequence of the presentation of the items, the averages of the index of order of agreement ("h") for each item compared with every other item were: (1) .182; (2) .123; (3) .155; (4) .096; (5) .063; (6) .023; (7) .020; (8) .003; (9) .002; (10) .011; (11) —.027; and (12) —.151. If these items were purified so that only those that are highly intercorrelated were included in the final set of items on which respondents were distributed, then only the first five items presented above should be used for a scale and the rest excluded. These five items add to the average inter-item correlations; the other subtract from the averages of the best items. Item no. 12 in any event should be scored positively, for those who agreed with it tended to show themselves more favorable toward interest groups on all the other items. If only the first five items were included, the averages of the index of the order of agreement for each of the five items would be: (1) .37; (2) .35; (3) .29; (4) .22; and (5) .17. Adding any other items reduces the sizes of these indexes. These items, the first five, would be a good, short interest group scale.

8. Apart from striking Democratic-Republican differences on agreement with the policies of specific interest groups and with such ideological statements as, "The government has the responsibility to see to it that all people, poor or rich, have adequate housing, education, medical care, and protection against unemployment," most of the party differences on other variables, such as interest group attitudes, were obscured. A possible interpretation of this is that Republicans who get defeated are more similar to Democrats who win than they are to Republicans who win. The implications of these findings about party differences for the study of American politics have not been explored in the data from this questionnaire. Because candidates were interviewed, it is possible to compare winners and losers for both parties. For some of the party differences found in the study, see Janda, Teune, Kahn, and Francis, *Indiana Legislative Politics* (Bloomington: Bureau of Government Research, 1961), and Chapter 2 in this volume.

9. Although the same question was asked about business political activity, the responses were not distributed sufficiently for analysis.

10. Four items were used to measure partisanship, such as "The two parties should take a clear-cut stand on more of the important state issues to encourage party responsibility." The other three items were from Wahlke, Eulau, Buchanan, and Ferguson. If the high and low quartiles on the partisanship and interest group sets of items are compared, there is a significant relationship between groups that are high in partisanship, and

high in favorable attitudes toward interest groups ($X^2 = 8.8$, significant at the .01 level).

### 7. *Janda:* Some Theory and Data on Representational Roles and Legislative Behavior

NOTE: This chapter was prepared in the fall of 1965 and submitted for publication in January, 1966. Unfortunately, other commitments have prevented me from rewriting it to accommodate important studies on representational roles that have appeared since that time.

1. See Alfred de Grazia, *Public and Republic* (New York: Alfred A. Knopf, 1951), for a survey and analysis of normative doctrines concerning the theory of representation.

2. Heinz Eulau, John Wahlke, William Buchanan, and LeRoy Ferguson, "The Role of the Representative: Some Empirical Observations on the Theory of Edmund Burke," *American Political Science Review,* LIII (September, 1959), 742–756.

3. The major publication from the study is John Wahlke, Heinz Eulau, William Buchanan, and LeRoy Ferguson, *The Legislative System: Explorations in Legislative Behavior* (New York: John Wiley, 1962).

4. For the questions in the context of the entire interview schedule, see ibid., p. 494.

5. Charles O. Jones, "Representation in Congress: The Case of the House Agriculture Committee," *American Political Science Review,* LV (June, 1961), 358–367.

6. Wahlke et al., *The Legislative System,* Chapters 12 and 13.

7. Carl D. McMurray and Malcolm B. Parsons, "Public Attitudes Toward the Representational Roles of Legislators and Judges," *Midwest Journal of Political Science,* IX (May, 1965), 167–185.

8. Robert S. Friedman and Sybil L. Stokes, "The Role of Constitution-Maker as Representative," *Midwest Journal of Political Science,* IX (May, 1965), 148–166.

9. Norman Meller, " 'Legislative Behavior Research' Revisited: A Review of Five Years' Publications," *Western Political Quarterly,* XVIII (December, 1965), 776–793.

10. For a more extensive discussion of types of data needed in studying representative-constituency relationships, see Kenneth Janda, "Representational Behavior," in *International Encyclopedia of the Social Sciences,* 13 (New York: Macmillan and The Free Press, 1968), 474–479.

11. Warren A. Miller and Donald E. Stokes, "Constituency Influence in Congress," *American Political Science Review,* LVII (March, 1963), 45–56.

12. Herbert H. Hyman and Paul B. Sheatsley, " 'The Authoritarian Personality'—A Methodological Critique," in Richard Christie and Marie Jahoda, eds., *Studies in the Scope and Method of the Authoritarian Personality* (Glencoe: The Free Press, 1954), pp. 50–122.

13. Herbert A. Simon, *Models of Man: Social and Rational* (New York: John Wiley, 1957), p. 201.

14. For an explanation of the various senses of "ought" and their relationships to normative and empirical political theory, see Kenneth Janda, "Democratic Theory and Legislative Behavior: A Study of Legislator-Constituency Relationships" (Ph.D. dissertation, Indiana University, 1961).

15. Ibid., Chapter 8.

16. Henry Teune, Melvin Kahn, Wayne Francis, and Kenneth Janda, then graduate students in the Department of Government at Indiana University, undertook a project aimed at interviewing candidates for the 1961 Indiana General Assembly and holdover Senators from the 1959 session. Interviews were obtained from 238 individuals or 87% of the universe.

Most of the expenses of this project were ultimately borne by the Social Science Research Council, through a grant to Professor Charles S. Hyneman for the study of state politics. Additional support was given by the Bureau of Government Research, which aided substantially in financing the actual interviewing. The Research Committee of Indiana University also made available a small grant to Henry Teune and Kenneth Janda for the purposes of doctoral research, which allowed for completion of the interviewing. Partial results of the study are contained in Kenneth Janda, Henry Teune, Melvin Kahn, and Wayne Francis, *Legislative Politics in Indiana: A Preliminary Report to the 1961 General Assembly* (Indiana University: Bureau of Government Research, 1961). It is also Chapter 2 in this book.

17. Eulau et al., "Role of the Representative."

18. Ibid., p. 749.

19. Ibid.

20. The data were processed and chi-square values calculated by NUCROS, a cross-classification program originally written for the IBM 709 computer and revised for the Control Data 3400. For a write-up of the program and the FORTRAN IV listing, see Kenneth Janda, *Data Processing: Applications to Political Research* (Evanston: Northwestern University Press, 1965), Chapter 5 and Appendices C-1 and C-2. The program does not calculate Yates' correction for continuity in the case of four-fold tables. However, correction for continuity is important for calculating chi-square values in four-fold tables only when N is "small," which in practice seems to be regarded as less than 30. Given the fact that all the tables have N's considerably larger than 30, the correction for continuity was deemed unnecessary.

The conventional .05 level of significance was used to determine acceptance or rejection of the first six propositions, which were non-directional. The last ten propositions, however, stated the direction of relationship and were subjected to a one-tailed test.

21. Friedman and Stokes, "Role of Constitution Maker," p. 161.

22. Wahlke et al., *The Legislative System,* p. 292.

23. Friedman and Stokes, "Role of Constitution-Maker," and McMurray and Parsons, "Public Attitudes."

24. This objective of empirical research has been stressed by many statistics texts in discussing the importance of regression analysis over correlations. See,

for example, Hubert M. Blalock, *Social Statistics* (New York: McGraw-Hill, 1960), p. 273. For a more extensive discussion, however, see James S. Coleman, *Introduction to Mathematical Sociology* (New York: The Free Press of Glencoe, 1964), Chapter 1.

25. Miller and Stokes, "Constituency Influence," pp. 45 ff.

## 8. *Francis:* Simulating Legislative Processes

1. John Wahlke, Heinz Eulau, William Buchanan, and LeRoy Ferguson, *The Legislative System: Explorations in Legislative Behavior* (New York: John Wiley, 1962).

2. Ithiel de Sola Pool, et al., *Candidates Issues and Strategies: A Computer Simulation of the 1960 and 1964 Elections* (Cambridge, Mass.: M.I.T. Press, 1965). Also see this author's piece: "A Postscript on the 1964 Election," *American Behavioral Scientist* (May, 1965), pp. 39–44.

3. For a report see Kenneth Janda et al., *Legislative Politics in Indiana* (Indiana University: Bureau of Government Research, 1961); it is Chapter 2 in this book.

4. Wayne L. Francis, "Influence and Interaction in a State Legislative Body," *American Political Science Review,* LVI (December, 1962), 953–960; it is Chapter 3 in this book.

5. Information exists on punch cards and in *Indiana Votes: U. S. House of Representatives, General Assembly, 1922–1958.* Indiana University: Bureau of Government Research, 1962.

6. For example, see Harold Guetzkow et al., *Simulation in International Relations* (Englewood Cliffs, N. J.: Prentice-Hall, 1963). For an introduction to several aspects of simulation and modelling see Harold Guetzkow, ed., *Simulation in Social Science* (Englewood Cliffs, N. J.: Prentice Hall, 1962).

7. IPL-V is well suited to psychological processes. LISP is closer to common mathematical notation and is used frequently in problems of artificial intelligence. COMIT was developed for linguistic material. See Bert F. Green, *Digital Computers in Research* (New York: McGraw-Hill, 1963), pp. 96–99, for a discussion of these languages and relevant citations. SLIP is a relatively new language that is imbedded in FORTRAN. See J. Weizenbaum, *Symmetric List Processor* (General Electric: Computer Laboratory, Sunnyvale, California).

8. The survey was conducted by the author. It includes the responses of 839 legislators. The full study will appear under the title *A Comparative Analysis of Legislative Issues in the Fifty States.*

## 9. *Ori:* The Politicized Nature of the County Prosecutor's Office, Fact or Fancy?—The Case in Indiana

1. Alderfer, *American Local Government and Administration* (New York: Macmillan, 1956), p. 493.

2. Babcock, *State and Local Government and Politics*, 2nd ed. (New York: Random House, 1962), p. 168.

3. Indiana has 92 counties with 84 judicial circuits, numbered 1–85. There is no judicial circuit 77. Data on county prosecutors are drawn from 66 prosecuting attorneys responding to my questionnaire, who constitute 79% of the total. Professor David R. Derge of Indiana University provided me with the data cited on 133 members of the 1959 General Assembly from his files. Eighty-nine percent of all the state legislators of the 1959 session are represented in Professor Derge's findings.

4. See David R. Derge, "The Lawyer in the Indiana General Assembly," *Midwest Journal of Political Science,* VI (February, 1962), 19, 36 (Table 7). These data are for the period from 1925 to 1959.

5. Basic data on Indiana political leaders, i.e., Indiana Governors, U. S. Senators and Representatives from Indiana, used in this table are compiled from the following sources: *Biographical Directory of the American Congress; Congressional Directory; Current Biography; Dictionary of American Biography; Who's Who and What's What in Indiana Politics; Who's Who in America; Who Was Who in America.*

6. Derge, "Lawyer in Indiana General Assembly," p. 30, note 4.

7. Information on county prosecutors is taken from the Martindale-Hubbell *Law Directory,* the 87th and 91st editions. The other data presented in this table are drawn from Derge, "Lawyer in Indiana General Assembly," p. 30, note 4 (Table V).

8. Derge, "Lawyer in Indiana General Assembly," p. 31, note 4.

9. Ibid., 31–34. See also Derge, "The Lawyer as Decision-Maker in the American State Legislature," *Journal of Politics,* XXI (August, 1959), 412–15; and Charles S. Hyneman, "Who Makes Our Laws?" *Political Science Quarterly* LV (December, 1940), 573.

10. Derge, "Lawyer in Indiana General Assembly," p. 23, note 4 (Table I).

11. In a study of Indiana state legislators, it was reported that "about three-fourths of the present legislators (1959) stated that they were content to continue their political careers by remaining in the Indiana General Assembly," and that "the other quarter thought they might try their hands at running for other offices, with at least three individuals having Congressional aspirations." Janda, Teune, Kahn and Francis, *Legislative Politics in Indiana* (Indiana University: Bureau of Government Research, 1961), p. 20; it is also chapter 2 in this book.

12. Schlesinger, *How They Became Governor* (East Lansing: Government Bureau Research, Michigan State University, 1957), p. 11.

13. Ibid.

14. This writer followed the classification used by Schlesinger (ibid., p. 10) in his study of governors.

15. It is reasonable to assume that the percentage of law-enforcement offices, including that of the prosecuting attorneyship, was much greater for the period between 1870 and 1900 than the era after 1900, because only 8.5% of the Hoosier Governors since 1900 had held some kind of law-enforcement positions, while Schlesinger puts Indiana in the 20–29 percent category in

reference to law enforcement for the period of 1870 to 1950, ibid., pp. 14–15.

16. In this connection, it is interesting to note the findings of Donald R. Matthews in his study of U. S. Senators who served during the period 1947 to 1957. He reports, for example, that "almost exactly half of the senators began either as law-enforcement officers (28%) (prosecuting attorneys, judges, or marshals) or by serving in their state legislatures (29%)." Matthews, *U. S Senators and Their World* (Chapel Hill: University of North Carolina Press, 1960), p. 51. The Indiana case confirms this national pattern.

17. In the end office ranking, an almost exact reverse of the Indiana pattern, is observed by Matthews. Five significant end offices nationally, noted by Matthews, are: United States Representative, 28%; State Governor, 22%; Administrative Office, 17%; Law Enforcement, 15%; and State Legislature, 10%. Ibid., p. 55.

18. An index of finality as designed by Schlesinger is used here. According to this definition, "the index of finality is the percentage of those holding a particular office who held it as an end office." The index is to indicate "the place which an office has had in the governors' careers whether it has been transitional or an immediate stepping-stone to the governorship." Schlesinger, *How They Became Governor,* p. 12, note 13.

19. Ibid., p. 74, note 13.

20. The majority of Indiana Congressmen with prosecutor background came primarily from three regions. Expressed in terms of current Congressional seats, these areas are the Fifth, Seventh and Eighth districts. These regions in Indiana seem to be more fitted to fostering the prosecutors office as a means of political advancement, perhaps because in them "maintenance of order itself has been and is today, of primary political importance." Schlesinger, ibid, p. 83, note 13. My hypothesis is that, in these areas, the prosecuting attorneyship has been and perhaps is the only readily available public office for the politically minded lawyers, and political traditions and attitudes are such that they bring prosecuting attorneys to the foreground. Two of these regions are basically southern rural counties, and the other is located in central Indiana.

21. Ibid., pp. 81–82, note 13. This observation is cited in Duane Lockard, *Politics of State and Local Government* (New York: Macmillan, 1963), p. 459, in conjunction with his discussion of county prosecutors, with an apposite qualification in the footnote that Schlesinger's data give "no indication whether the prosecutors office itself has had a comparable increase in incidence in gubernatorial backgrounds."

22. The probable reason for these trends is that the era in which law enforcement was of prime significance in Indiana is passing. Prior to 1900, the prosecuting attorneyship was of considerable importance in the career-promotion pattern because Indiana retained its frontier characteristics. With increased industrialization, the importance of law enforcement declined. However, the position of law enforcement was sustained during the Progressive era and Aspirin Age which articulated the significance of law-enforcement offices. In the last two decades, the politically interested Hoosiers are perhaps finding other avenues to Congress. See Matthews, *U. S. Senators,* p. 51, note 21; and

John D. Barnhart and Donald F. Carmony, *Indiana: From Frontier to Industrial Commonwealth* (New York: Lewis Publishing Co., 1954), vol. 2.

## 10. *Watts:* Party Leadership and County Candidate Selection

1. Lester G. Seligman, "Political Recruitment and Party Structure: A Case Study," *American Political Science Review,* LV (March, 1961), 77.

2. Support for portions of this research was supplied by Indiana University and the Relm Foundation in the form of fellowships and research grants. I am particularly indebted to Professors Charles S. Hyneman and David R. Derge of Indiana University for their aid and suggestions at all stages of the project. For detailed presentation of data and analysis, see my Ph.D. dissertation, "Indiana Primary Elections: The Selection of Candidates and the Distribution of Power" (Indiana University, 1963).

The other counties in the study were: Allen, Bartholomew, Cass, Clark, Floyd, Grant, Henry, Knox, Kosciusko, Laporte, Monroe, Porter, Tippecanoe, Vanderburgh, Wayne.

3. There are obvious hazards in using this approach in isolation from the context within which this process operates. Further analysis considered candidacy, office holding, and leadership as forms of participation related to social status; and attempted to control for other aspects of a community's political structure, particularly the effect of varying strengths of party organizations.

4. For elaboration of this model see my "The Attribution Model and Political Recruitment," in William Crotty, ed., *Approaches to the Study of Party Organization,* (Boston: Allyn and Bacon, 1968), Ch. 8.

5. In Indiana, the formal organization is provided for in a detailed Election Code and is comprised of a hierarchy of committees ranging from precinct committees at the base to the State Central Committee at the top. Except for State Convention delegates, the only party official elected directly by the people is the precinct committeeman. The committeeman is elected by the votes of his party every two years in the primary election preceding the general election. He in turn appoints a vice-committeeman (of the opposite sex) and together with their counterparts in all other precincts in a county, they comprise the county committee. This committee meets for organization on the Saturday following the primary and selects a chairman, a vice-chairman (of the opposite sex), a secretary, and a treasurer.

The nonformal leaders in this study were located by securing nominations from informants and judges according to an adaptation of methods originally suggested by Floyd Hunter (*Community Power Structure,* Chapel Hill: University of North Carolina Press, 1953) and developed by other reputational researchers. The Republican list contained twenty-five names, the Democratic thirty-nine. Several pieces of evidence point to the existence of a smaller informal leadership group in each party in Howard as well as in other comparable Indiana counties. These groups are relatively cohesive and work closely with the formal party structure. Most of the nineteen interviewed belonged to this first-level group.

6. In any given election year the offices to be filled vary somewhat in different counties, but the following were included for this study; County clerk, auditor, sheriff, assessor, recorder, judge, county commissioner, and prosecutor. The regular term for these offices is four years, and, except for the last three, they do not have special educational or residential requirements. Aspirants for these offices face the voters in the spring of each year in which there is to be a general election in the fall. Indiana has a closed primary, requiring a record to be kept of whether a voter votes a Democratic or a Republican ballot.

7. Data on nonparty groups consisted primarily of the perceptions of candidates and leaders.

8. Status rankings were derived by use of a two-factor index of social position perfected by August B. Hollinshead and adapted from a three-factor index in his and Frederick C. Redlick's *Social Class and Mental Illness: A Community Study,* (New York: John Wiley, 1958) .

9. "Brokerage occupations" and their relations to public office are described in Herbert Jacob, "Initial Recruitment of Elected Officials in the U. S.—A Model," *Journal of Politics,* XXIV (November, 1962) , 709.

10. V. O. Key, Jr., *Politics, Parties, and Pressure Groups* (New York: Thomas Y. Crowell, 1958) , p. 416.

11. Ibid., p. 418.

12. V. O. Key, Jr., *American State Politics* (New York: Alfred A. Knopf, 1956) , pp. 175–177.

13. Charles S. Hyneman, "Tenure and Turnover of the Indiana General Assembly," *American Political Science Review,* XXXII (1938) , pp. 320–321.

14. William Standing and James A. Robinson, "Inter-party Competition and Primary Contesting: The Case of Indiana," *American Political Science Review,* LII (December, 1958) , 1066–1077.

15. Key, *Politics,* p. 418.

16. Ibid., p. 419.

17. Oregon has a closed direct primary, but unlike Indiana, under Oregon laws the official party organization must observe strict neutrality in the primary contests.

18. William J. Crotty, "The Party Organization and Its Activities," in Crotty, *Approaches,* esp. pp. 260–269.

19. "A Two Dimensional Scheme for Classifying the States According to Degree of Inter-Party Competition," *American Political Science Review,* XLIX (December, 1955) , 1120–1128.

20. Certain procedures must be followed if an endorsed list of favored candidates is circulated or published.

21. One incumbent publicly announced that no one should oppose incumbents.

22. That the number of organizations reported in Table II (28) varies slightly from those expected from analysis of counties reported in Table I (32) is due to missing data for these questions on some of the interviews. Because of small n's, the maximum number of counties and organizations were analyzed whenever data were available.

23. Other reference groups listed were family connections, church connections, labor affiliations, service club connections, nationality group identification and veteran organizations.

24. Each candidate was asked to name those who came to him about the nominations and those he himself sought out, before he actually filed his candidacy. These were to be persons having some importance beyond being part of his immediate family or of holding only a potential vote.

25. Admittedly, there may be some who are involved in party activity because of their outside group interests, but those persons classified as "political" either held some party office, had been candidates, or were long enough identified with party activity that their concerns were probably as much those of the party as those of their outside group. Therefore, some attorneys are grouped as political and some were seen as independently speaking for themselves and their profession. Or, if an active police chief was instrumental in recruiting a candidate for sheriff, he was viewed as a member of the law enforcement interest, whereas a former sheriff who was also a former county party chairman was considered political if he was reported as a contact with a potential assessor.

26. Only persons clearly identified as party-connected were included in this category. Those of opposite party who were more clearly identified with their occupation or other interest group were so classified.

27. Twelve of the thirteen who had been identified as first-level leaders were reported present at such meetings.

28. The question was phrased in this manner in order to: (1) identify leaders whose attachments were strong enough to have prompted extra effort by a leader in behalf of a candidate; (2) to avoid the necessity of asking the leader how he voted in each case; and (3) to permit him to express himself for a candidate of the other party. No doubt each leader interviewed by his vote made a choice in each contest.

29. See, for example, Lewis Bowman and G. R. Boynton, "Recruitment Patterns among Local Party Officials: A Model and Some Preliminary Findings in Selected Locales," *American Political Science Review*, LX (September, 1966) , 667–680.

## 11. *Leege:* Control in the Party Convention Nominating System: The Case of Indiana

1. E. E. Schattschneider, *Party Government* (New York: Farrar and Rinehart, 1943) , p. 64.

2. See M. Ostrogorski, *Democracy and the Party System in the United States* (New York: Macmillan, 1910) ; Frederick W. Dallinger, *Nominations for Elective Office in the United States* (New York: Longmans, Green, and Company, 1897) ; Ernst C. Meyer, *Nominating Systems* (Madison, Wis.: published by the author, 1902) ; *The Political Philosophy of Robert M. LaFollette as Revealed in His Speeches and Writings* (Madison, 1920) , pp. 29–31.

3. V. O. Key, Jr., *American State Politics* (New York: Alfred A. Knopf, 1956) , p. 97.

4. An earlier version of this chapter was presented at the annual meeting of the Midwest Conference of Political Scientists in Chicago, April 28–30, 1966. The data utilized in this chapter were gathered for a more extensive study of the power structure in a convention nominating system: David C. Leege, "The Place of the Party Nominating Convention in a Representative Democracy: A Study of Power in the Indiana Democratic Party's State Nominating Conventions, 1956–62" (Ph.D. dissertation, Indiana University, 1965) .

In addition to standard documentary sources, the author employed complementary interview schedules and a questionnaire to generate data from a purposive sample of 12 previous candidates and 15 county, district, and state chairmen, as well as a stratified random sample of 167 convention delegates. An attempt was made to produce a representative sample in the first two instances. Criteria applied to previous candidates included successful-unsuccessful candidacy, year of candidacy, level of office sought, and geographic location of residence. Counties on which chairmen and delegate data were gathered were selected according to: geographic location, urban-rural classification, party strength as measured by election-winning and minority-party competitiveness, pattern of voter turnout in county, and size of convention delegation. Eighty usable questionnaires were returned by the delegates; the mailout return bias slightly favored those delegates with greater convention experience. Two additional sources of data were utilized: (1) official records of candidate filings for delegate seats and (2) roll call tabulations from voting machines used at the state conventions.

Indiana's biennial party conventions are two-day affairs in Indianapolis during late June of each election year. Roughly 2,500 delegates have been elected in each party's early May primary by the party's registered voters. Delegate seats are apportioned at a ratio of 1 delegate seat per each 400 votes cast for the party's nominee for secretary of state in the last general election. Each county election board draws delegate-district boundaries. All elected delegates must pay a $10 assessment to the state central committee. Proxies are permissable but are regulated to avoid abuse.

By majority rule, the delegates select their party's nominees for all statewide offices. Depending on the staggered terms of office, delegates must select nominees for (1) major offices—U. S. Senator, Governor, and Lieutenant Governor; (2) minor offices—secretary of state, treasurer, auditor, attorney general, etc.; and (3) judicial offices—judges of supreme court and appellate court. Candidates for these nominations must pay to the state central committee a graduated filing fee ranging from $2,000 for U. S. Senator and Governor to $750 for minor offices if they wish to be placed on the convention ballot. Competition for most offices except judicial nominations is heavy until the final week prior to the convention. At that point, many candidates for minor offices drop out, or candidates for major offices seek lesser nominations because they have insufficient support for the top spots. At the minor office level from 1956 to 1962, only half of the nominations were actually contested on the convention floor. At the major office level, in no instance was an office uncontested; more commonly, 3 to 6 candidates went before the convention.

According to the 1947 Convention Reform Law, Indiana convention delegates vote by a unique secret ballot. County and congressional district delegations are assigned to voting machines on the perimeter of the convention floor, but the individual delegate may cast his vote as he pleases and his preference remains anonymous. The unit rule can no longer be enforced. This provision has removed delegates from a host of controls party leadership could exert on them in the past. Each delegation is still led by its county chairman—who has been elected by all the precinct committeemen and vice-committeemen in his county—and oftentimes he is the most influential political personality in the county. Since the totals on each machine are ascertainable, he will usually seek to unify his delegation behind a potential "winner." But even the cohesion and winner-support figures within smaller counties are difficult to determine, since their delegations may be assigned to a voting machine with one or more other county delegations. This fact raises some measurement problems later in the paper.

The author is indebted to his doctoral committee at Indiana University, particularly David R. Derge and Sheldon Stryker, for their assistance on the larger study.

5. For summaries of their arguments and evidence see: Charles E. Merriam and Louise Overacker, *Primary Elections* (Chicago: University of Chicago Press, 1928), pp. 257–267; Robert C. Brooks, *Political Parties and Electoral Problems* (New York: Harper and Brothers, 1933), pp. 257–259; Meyer, "Robert M. LaFollette," pp. 55–63.

6. Data for some of the following generalizations were graciously supplied the author by Karl O'Lessker from his study of social and political characteristics of 1960 convention delegates. The author's own data came from delegates to the 1962 convention.

7. Comparable data for Indiana adults are not available; the American adult data are presented in Charles R. Wright and Herbert Hyman, "Voluntary Association Memberships of American Adults," *American Sociological Review,* XXIII (June, 1958), 284–294.

8. Joseph A. Schumpeter, *Capitalism, Socialism, and Democracy* (New York: Harper and Brothers, 1942), p. 269.

9. Frederic H. Guild, "The Operation of the Direct Primary in Indiana," in J. T. Salter, ed, "The Direct Primary," *The Annals,* CVI (March, 1923), pp. 172–180. Guild's data are drawn from delegate races in 1920 and 1922.

10. Frank J. Munger, *Two-Party Politics in the State of Indiana* (Ph.D. dissertation, Harvard University, 1955), pp. 183–186.

11. See Ostrogorski, *Democracy and Party System;* Meyer, *Robert M. La-Follette,* pp. 23–24, 38–39.

12. Similar evidence on the conditions of competitiveness is offered in Heinz Eulau, "The Ecological Basis of Party Systems: The Case of Ohio," *Midwest Journal of Political Science,* I (August, 1957), 125–135; Samuel P. Huntington, "A Revised Theory of Party Politics," *American Political Science Review,* XLIV (September, 1950), 669–677.

13. This argument is reflected in the delegates' own statements about their recruitment. Delegates were asked whether their county chairman or one of his assistants had asked them to run for a convention delegate seat or whether they had decided on their own to run. Responses are broken down in the following table:

| | CHAIRMAN-RECRUITED | SELF-STARTER | TOTALS | |
|---|---|---|---|---|
| Urban | 15 | 34 | 49 | $X^2 = 4.64$ |
| Rural | 17 | 14 | 31 | $C = .22$ |
| Totals | 32 | 48 | 80 | $p = <.03$ |

The moderate coefficient of contingency and the acceptable level of significance indicate that rural delegates are somewhat more likely and urban delegates much less likely to have been recruited by their chairmen. At least at the recruitment stage, there is evidence of less control being exerted by the chairmen in urban counties.

14. Merriam and Overacker, *Primary Elections,* pp. 318–322.

15. For evidence from several Michigan electoral contests which relates ballot position to the prospects of victory, see Henry M. Bain and Donald S. Hecock, *Ballot Position and Voter's Choice* (Detroit: Wayne State University Press, 1957).

16. Delegate turnover tends to resemble chairman turnover except in rural counties. The percentage of a county delegation new at each convention is higher in urban and more competitive counties than in rural and less competitive counties—also the counties with greatest chairman turnover. In some rural counties where evidence of chairman control was strongest, delegate turnover was high due to the entrenched chairman's selection process. In these latter cases, there is reason to believe that the uninitiated delegate will look to his chairman for guidance at the convention. In the urban counties, however, the uninitiated delegate may well represent a different local faction than his chairman. In either case, over 60% of all convention delegates have experienced more than one convention.

17. In this respect it is interesting to note that many of the "group-determined" and "chairman-determined" delegates felt it important for the candidates to contact them; in other words, they were not likely to take their chairman's or their colleagues' word for it unless they themselves had developed similar impressions about or at least a receptivity to a candidate. Over all, twice as many delegates (53) thought personal contact with the candidate was more important than their chairman's advice (27).

18. This argument assumes that "spreading," i.e., assigning certain proportions of a delegation to vote for each of several candidates for the same nomination until the eventual winner becomes apparent, is no longer a widespread practice. Based on interview responses, "spreading" is more likely to be proof of real differences within a delegation and of the impossibility of cohesion behind a single candidate; from this standpoint, "spreading" is hardly evidence of a chairman's control.

Cohesion represents only the maximum possible chairman control. It may be illusory. Cohesion may have resulted more from independent arrival at the same conclusion by many delegates than from careful manipulation by a county chairman. In fact, if cohesion were not high behind a winner, one would seriously question whether the party could unite behind him for the general election.

19. Congressional district data are introduced at this point because they represent the "hardest" measure of cohesion. Since assignment to voting machines did not overlap by districts, these data are accurate. The same is true with metropolitan counties; there was no overlap between metropolitan and smaller counties in the voting machine data. The least reliable measures of cohesion are found in the moderately urban and rural counties where several counties might be assigned to a single machine.

The district data are also useful because, in two instances, a single metropolitan county constituted the district, and in four additional cases, a moderately large metropolitan county dominated the politics of a district. Thus, frequently congressional district cohesion will differ little from within-county cohesion.

20. The "winner-support ratio" is drawn from Paul T. David, Ralph M. Goldman, and Richard C. Bain, *The Politics of National Party Conventions* (Washington: The Brookings Institution, 1960), pp. 389–406.

It involves several factors important to convention outcomes: (1) the size of each delegation, (2) its cohesion, and (3) its ability to go with—and to that extent, determine—winners. It is calculated by (1) determining the percentage of the total convention voting strength held by each delegation, (2) determining the percentage of the total critical vote—i.e., on the ballot where the outcome is formally decided—contributed by each delegation, and (3) determining the ratio of the percentage contribution to winner to the percentage of voting strength; it is calculated by dividing the latter by the former.

In effect, the winner-support ratio is an adjusted measure of cohesion where cohesion counts—in determining the winner. David et al., note this: "Regardless of how the convention as a whole splits for and against the winner, any delegation that splits its vote in the same proportions will have a winner-support ratio of 1.00. Those giving a lower percentage to the convention winner will fall below 1.00, while those giving a higher percentage will rise above 1.00" (p. 391).

The versatility of the winner-support ratio is that it sufficiently acknowledges delegations which have contributed heavily to narrow victories. For example, if a candidate garners 85% of the total vote, a delegation displays no great evidence of control over the outcome by delivering 100% of its vote to that candidate; nearly every other delegation has done likewise; still, the delegation's winner-support ratio will be on the positive side. On the other hand, it a candidate wins by a narrow 51% margin and the delegation has delivered 100% of its votes, then it has significantly shared in the control over the nomination; the resulting winner-support ratio will give the delegation a premium value for this type of contribution to the winner. Of course, the larger a district delegation is, the easier it would become to put together a majority coalition with other delegations. The data indicate, however, that urban districts have been unable to generate such coalitions without considerable support from rural districts as well; when rural districts are excluded from these coalitions, the urban districts consistently lose. Large urban districts can be kept from dominating conventions by this judo principle.

21. One might argue that the data only discount perpetual control by district coalitions. Cannot certain counties form such coalitions? Although winner-support ratios on a county-by-county basis are not available except for metropolitan and some moderately urban counties, the fact that single counties constitute or dominate six of the districts, and the fact that these six districts do not form convention-winning coalitions from office to office or year to year, tends to indicate that county-level coalitions are unlikely places to look for convention control. When one moves further to the more rural counties, the total delegate vote becomes too low to constitute a majority of the convention. Urban and rural counties must coalesce to win, but no consistent evidence of such coalitions appears in the district or large county data.

22. This chapter does not deal with delegates' norms of responsiveness to party identifiers and Indiana general election voters. Nevertheless, there is good evidence that these norms predominate in decisions concerning the top of the ticket. See Leege, "Party Nominating Convention."

23. Ideally, individual rather than aggregate (group) data should be utilized in this table. However, given the secret ballot at the convention and the response bias likely to accompany a question about how the individual delegate voted, aggregate data on support of winners must suffice. This is an impasse most studies of voting behavior must recognize.

The cohesion figures are drawn from the same data utilized in Table 4 and are subject to the same reservations.

24. This statement can also be substantiated through a summary statistic if one is willing to make an assumption about the nature of the data in Table VII. If the "chairman's and delegates' preferences" are treated as ordinal data in four classes—convention strong, convention weak, primary weak, and primary strong (pre-primary convention is treated as primary weak because of its empirical effects), then Kendall's tau-c may be applied as a measure of rank-correlation between delegation cohesion behind winners and nominating system preference. For chairmen, tau-c $= .449$, significant beyond the .08 level; for delegates, tau-c $= .557$, significant beyond the .02 level. Since tau-c, like the phi coefficient, can reach unity only when all cells except the diagonal are empty, these correlation coefficients can be interpreted as quite high for a $14 \times 4$ and $15 \times 4$ table, respectively. The level of significance is also high, considering the small sample sizes involved. In short, the summary statistic, with its heuristic assumption about the data, supports a conclusion reached by inspection of the table.

25. Cf. V. O. Key, Jr., *Politics, Parties, and Pressure Groups* (New York: Crowell, 1958), pp. 622–643, 672–698; Duane Lockard, *The Politics of State and Local Government* (New York: Macmillan, 1963), pp. 189–197; Hugh A.

Bone, *American Politics and the Party System* (New York: McGraw-Hill, 1965), pp. 285–290.

26. See Donald R. Matthews and James W. Prothro, "Social and Economic Factors and Negro Voter Registration in the South," *American Political Science Review*, LVII (March, 1963), 24–44; and "Political Factors and Negro Vote Registration in the South," *American Political Science Review*, LVII (June, 1963), 355–367.

27. Angus Campbell et al., *The American Voter* (New York: John Wiley, 1960), pp. 266–289.

28. Alexis de Tocqueville, *Democracy in America*, 2 vols. (New York: Vintage Books, 1954).

29. V. O. Key, Jr., and Frank Munger, "Social Determinism and Electoral Decision: The Case of Indiana," in Eugene Burdick and Arthur J. Brodbeck, eds., *American Voting Behavior* (Glencoe: Free Press, 1959), pp. 281–299.

30. Gabriel A. Almond and Sidney Verba, *The Civic Culture* (Princeton: Princeton University Press, 1963).

31. Peter Rossi and Phillips Cutwright, "The Impact of Party Organization in an Industrial Setting," in Morris Janowitz, ed., *Community Political Systems* (Glencoe: Free Press, 1961), pp. 81–116.

## Appendix A. *Nelson:* Statistical Methods Used in the Studies

1. We often call such a measure a "statistic."
2. E.g., some uses of factor analysis and scale analysis.
3. Variables are characteristics (e.g., annual income); a piece of data measures, usually numerically, the presence of the characteristic in a given person, thing, or event (e.g., $15,000 is Senator Smith's annual income).
4. Cf. Leege, Chapter 11, pp. 202–204.
5. Cf. Carey, Chapter 5, pp. 84–85; and Leege, Chapter 11, pp. 202–204, 215–216.
6. Cf. Conway, Chapter 4, pp. 73–74.
7. A simpler measure might be the average distance between the individual numbers and the mean; the standard deviation, though defined differently, often has about the same numerical value as this measure.
8. The standard deviation, while not the easiest measure of dispersion to conceive of, is probably the easiest to calculate and is still close to the intuitive notion of what dispersion is.
9. Algebraically expressed as

$$\sqrt{\frac{\sum_{i=1}^{n} (x_i - \overline{X})^2}{n}},$$

where $x_i$ is the $i_{th}$ piece of data, $\overline{X}$ is the mean, and $n$ is the number of pieces of data available.

10. Cf. Teune, Chapter 6, pp. 104–105; and Appendix A, pp. 233–234.

11. And in a proportionate amount, if the data are ordinal or interval (see next paragraph). Also, changes may be in the same or opposite directions, as long as they are consistently one or the other.

12. To correlate two variables means to measure the correlation between them, not to bring them into correlation.

13. The cardinal numbers are the positive integers: 1, 2, 3, 4, . . . ; real numbers are all numbers, positive or negative, rational or irrational, which do not contain the square root of −1.

14. Thus 4 is as far from 3 and 5 as 12 is from 11 and 13, as 1358 is from 1357 and 1359, as − 129 is from − 130 and − 128, etc. The distance separating any real number from the next largest or the next smallest is, of course, infinitesimal, but nonetheless the same for all real numbers.

15. A nominal variable is a characteristic classified in an unordered way, i.e., measured by nominal data.

16. Cf. Francis, Chapter 3, pp. 47, 50, 57, 265, 266; Conway, Chapter 4, pp. 75–77; Teune, Chapter 6, pp. 109, 110–113, 114, 115, 272; Janda, Chapter 7, pp. 133–139, 273; Leege, Chapter 11, p. 220.

17. Chapter 7, p. 135.

18. The formula as follows:

$$\sum_{i=1}^{N} (f_{ai} - f_{ei})^2/f_{ei},$$

where N is the number of cells in the table (i.e., the number of rows times the number of columns), $f_{ai}$ is the actual number of cases in the $i^{th}$ cell, and $f_{ei}$ is the number of cases you would expect to find in the $i^{th}$ cell if there were no relationship between the variables.

19. For the example cited in the preceding paragraph, the perfect-relationship tables would be

|  | INEXPERIENCED CANDIDATES | EXPERIENCED CANDIDATES |
|---|---|---|
| Delegates | 43 | 0 |
| Trustees | 0 | 49 |

and

|  | | |
|---|---|---|
| Delegates | 0 | 49 |
| Trustees | 43 | 0 |

though the latter relationship would be "perfect" in the direction opposite from what was expected.

20. Cf. Francis, Chapter 3, pp. 55–56, 266. The formula for the phi coefficient is $\sqrt{x^2/n}$, where $x^2$ is the chi-square and n is the sample size.

21. Cf. Leege, Chapter 11, pp. 220, 282.

The formula for the coefficient of contingency is $\sqrt{x^2/(x^2+n)}$, where $x^2$ is the chi-square and n is the sample size.

22. Cf. Janda et al., Chapter 2, pp. 34–38, 265; and Francis, Chapter 3, p. 52.

23. Cf. Leege, Chapter 11, pp. 221–222, 284.

24. In Table VII, on p. 221, nominating system preferences are ranked as follows: (1) Convention-strong; (2) Convention-weak; (3) Primary-weak; and (4) Primary-strong. Thus the first of these rankings contains seven chairmen and five sets of county delegates; the second contains two chairmen and three sets of county delegates; the third, one chairman and two sets of county delegates; and the fourth, four chairmen and five sets of county delegates. For the other variable—percent cohesion in support of winners— each county has its own rank; there are no ties.

25. Cf. Conway, Chapter 4, pp. 72–74. Tables IV and VII are considered in this paragraph.

26. As measured by "the number of roll call votes on which the legislator voted to support the legislation selected by the Republican party legislative leadership to carry out the 1962 Indiana Republican Party platform" (p. 73). This is the interval variable.

27. Although percentages are interval data, for purposes of this analysis, the percentages of total vote are divided into three categories and are thereby transformed into nominal or classificatory data.

28. Cf. Conway, Chapter 4, pp. 70–72; Teune, Chapter 6, pp. 104–105; and Leege, Chapter 11, p. 206.

29. The formula for the Pearsonian r can be written many ways. For computation from raw data it is frequently written as follows:

$$\frac{n \sum_{i=1}^{n} (x_i y_i) - \sum_{i=1}^{n} x_i \sum_{i=1}^{n} y_i}{\sqrt{\left[ n \sum_{i=1}^{n} (x_i)^2 - \left( \sum_{i=1}^{n} x_i \right)^2 \right] \left[ n \sum_{i=1}^{n} (y_i)^2 - \left( \sum_{i=1}^{n} y_i \right)^2 \right]}}$$

where $x_1$ and $y_1$ are respectively the values of the x and y variables for the $i^{th}$ case, and n is the total number of cases. When the variables are written in standard form (p. 230, above), this formula simplifies to:

$$\frac{\sum_{i=1}^{n} (x'_i y'_i)}{n},$$

where $x'_1$ and $y'_1$ are the values of the x and y variables for the $i^{th}$ case written in standard form, and n is the total number of cases.

30. In fact, given the data for one variable (untransformed or in standard form), we could predict the other only in standard form. In order to be able to predict the untransformed values of one variable, we would need the mean of that variable and the untransformed values of the variable with which it was perfectly correlated.

31. Cf. Conway, Chapter 4, pp. 70–72; and Leege, Chapter 11, p. 206.

32. These other variables are said to be "partialled out" p. 224. For an

example of partial correlation, see Table III, p. 71, the correlation for Senate Republicans between voting support for the Republican platform and percentage of constituency living in their own homes is 0.332 regardless of the percentage employed in manufacturing, the percentage living in urban areas, and population increase or decrease.

33. For instance, in the four multiple correlations in Table III, on p. 71, one variable (Republican platform vote score, for each of four groups of state legislators) is correlated with four others (percentage employed in manufacturing, living in urban areas, etc.) .

34. The qualification of footnote 30 applies to perfect multiple correlations as well.

35. By "representative" we do not mean "identical" but only "alike in ways relevant to the behavior we are studying." Thus an Indiana sample of state legislators is not geographically representative of state legislators throughout the country, but we might assume geography to have little effect on, say, legislative voting behavior.

36. This is basically the same as the "no-relationship" ideal table on p. 231, above, but based on 920,000 instead of 92 candidates, and with each entry calculated more precisely.

37. In the case of Proposition 8, the value of chi-square is 4.31, though the typical sample would have a chi-square of about zero. (It would generally be a little more than zero because the numbers in the sample distribution would always have to be whole numbers) .

38. Thus, for Proposition 8, the probability is equal to or less than .025 that a larger population with a no-relationship distribution and a correlation of zero would have produced a sample with this large a value of chi-square (Janda, Chapter 7, p. 135) . The probability that a given $2 \times 2$ table could be a random sample from a larger population in which the variables are not interrelated may be calculated directly, without reference to the chi-square or to any other correlation coefficient, by the Fisher technique. (Cf. Conway, Chapter 4, pp. 75, 76.)

The value of the level of significance is often represented by "p" or by the word "significance." For some uses in this book of the notion of level of significance, see Francis, Chapter 3, pp. 47, 50, 57, 265, 266; Conway, Chapter 4, pp. 72–77; Teune, Chapter 6, pp. 105, 109, 114, 115, 271–272; Janda, Chapter 7, pp. 133–139; and Leege, Chapter 11, pp. 220, 282.

39. Note that the lower the value of the level of significance the more significant a correlation is (the higher is its level of significance) and the more plausible is the rejection of the no-relationship hypothesis for the larger population, providing, of course, that the sample may reasonably be assumed to be randomly selected.

40. Thus, if your level of significance criterion were .001, you would not reject the no-relationship hypothesis for the population when the correlation of your sample was significant at the .005 level, even though there would still be only one chance in two hundred that such a sample could have been randomly selected from an uncorrelated population.

41. Thus, if your level of significance criterion were .3, you would assume if

your sample had a correlation whose level of significance was .25 that the larger population was also correlated, when in fact the chances would still be one in four that random selection from a wholly uncorrelated population would produce a sample as highly correlated as the one you actually have.

42. Such a correlation is one which is significant statistically but nonsensical theoretically—for instance, a significant correlation between the height of women's skirts and the speed of trans-Atlantic airplane flights since World War II. Such correlations crop up occasionally simply because there is by definition one chance in a hundred that even the most bizarre pair of variables will be correlated at the .01 level of significance.

# Index